GW01486514

Winter Papers

Edited by KEVIN BARRY and OLIVIA SMITH

CURLEW
EDITIONS

CURLEW
EDITIONS

Published in 2020 by

Curlew Editions Ltd
Co Sligo
Ireland

Editors: Kevin Barry and Olivia Smith

Editorial Advisory Panel: Shane Curtin, Cristín Leach, Jessica Traynor.

Designed by John Foley at Bite! Associates, Cork.
Printed by Waterman Printers Ltd, Cork.

Printed on 120gsm Munken Pure by Arctic Paper.
The text of this book was set in Calluna and the folios were set in Geotica, both typefaces designed by Jos Buivenga, exljbris Font Foundry.

© copyright remains with authors and contributors 2020.

All rights reserved.

No part of this work may be reproduced or utilised in any form or by any means, electronic or mechanical, including photocopying, recording or by any information storage and retrieval system without prior permission of the publisher and authors.

ISBN: 978-0-9933029-5-4

www.winterpapers.com

Acknowledgements: Joan Barry, John Foley, Cormac Kinsella, Lisa Sheridan.

Curlew Editions gratefully acknowledges the financial support of
The Arts Council/An Chomhairle Ealaíon.

CONTENTS

CONTRIBUTORS 4

DON'T FUCK WITH THE FAIRIES Doireann Ní Ghríofa 7

IMBOLC Louise Kennedy 12

An interview with CONOR J. O'BRIEN by Siobhán Kane 19

DEATH AND THE FAMILY John Patrick McHugh 28

DADDY Oisín Fagan 37

I KNOW, BUT ONLY JUST Claire-Louise Bennett and Ruby Wallis 47

PAISANO Tim MacGabhann 58

CONNEMARA CHRONICLE Nidhī Zak/ Aria Eipe 67

LIFE FORCE FREQUENCIES Roisin Kiberd 71

NIAMH ALGAR and NICOLE FLATTERY in conversation 81

OFF YOUR CHEST Dave Tynan 89

Conversations with COOL C and ESTR by Shane Curtin 96

LET ME GO MAD IN MY OWN WAY Elaine Feeney 104

An interview with RADIE PEAT by Jim Carroll 109

A QUICKENING IN THE STILLNESS Susan Cahill 114

HONG KONG DIARY Oliver Farry 119

THE EYE OF A STORM Oonagh Montague 131

WORKS ON PAPER Dónal Geheran 135

DREAM OF A LOST FRIEND Dominic Stevens 142

A conversation with LOUISE LOWE and OWEN BOSS by Jessica Traynor ... 149

A FALSE CRAWL Una Mannion 161

An interview with JILL BEARDSWORTH and KEITH WALSH by Peter Murphy ... 167

CACOPHONY OF BONE Kerri ní Dochartaigh 174

THE MOON IS A HEALING BEING Chiamaka Enyi-Amadi 181

THE HEALING BREATH Martin Dyar 182

CONTRIBUTORS

NIAMH ALGAR is an actor from Mullingar. Her film and TV credits include The Virtues, Pure, Calm with Horses and the forthcoming HBO series Raised by Wolves. She has been nominated for three IFTAs in 2020.

CLAIRE-LOUISE BENNETT is the author of Pond and Fish Out Of Water (Juxta Press, 2020)

SUSAN CAHILL is a writer and former academic. She is currently writing her first novel.

JIM CARROLL is a writer, editor and journalist from Tipperary who lives in Dublin.

SHANE CURTIN is a teacher. He has had an involvement with the Irish hip hop scene for over twenty-five years.

MARTIN DYAR's poetry collection Maiden Names (Arlen House) was shortlisted for the Pigott Prize. He won the Patrick Kavanagh Poetry Award in 2009. He is the editor of the anthology Vital Signs: Poems about Illness and Healing, which will be published by Poetry Ireland in 2021.

NIDHĪ ZAK/ ARIA EIPE is poetry editor at Skein Press, and co-editor of The Ireland Chair of Poetry Special Commemorative Anthology (UCD Press, 2021). Her first book of poetry is forthcoming with Faber & Faber in Autumn 2021.

CHIAMAKA ENYI-AMADI is a writer, editor and performer. Her work is published in Poetry International, Poetry Ireland Review, RTE Poetry Programme, IMMA Magazine, Architecture Ireland and The Irish Times. She is co-editor of Writing Home (Dedalus Press, 2019).

OISÍN FAGAN is the author of the novel Nobber (JM Originals, 2019) and the story collection Hostages (Head of Zeus, 2018).

OLIVER FARRY is from Sligo and lives in Hong Kong where he works as a writer, journalist and translator. His writing has appeared in The Guardian, The New Statesman, The New Republic, The Irish Times, The Stinging Fly, gorse, and elsewhere.

ELAINE FEENEY teaches at the National University of Ireland, Galway. Feeney has published four collections of poetry and a drama WRoNGHEADED. Her novel, As You Were, is published by Harvill Secker/ Vintage. Feeney was chosen by The Observer as a best debut novelist for 2020.

NICOLE FLATTERY's work has appeared in the LRB, The Stinging Fly and The White Review, among others. Her story collection Show Them a Good Time was published by The Stinging Fly in Ireland and Bloomsbury in the UK in 2019. She is working on her debut novel.

DÓNAL GEHERAN is an artist based in Dublin. A recent graduate of NCAD, he primarily works with ink on paper.

SIOBHÁN KANE is an academic and arts journalist, and currently lectures at University College Dublin. She has run the collective Young Hearts Run Free since 2008 putting on arts events in unusual spaces raising money for the Simon Community.

LOUISE KENNEDY has been published in The Guardian, the Irish Times, The Stinging Fly, and on BBC Radio 4. Her debut short story collection The End of the Word is a Cul de Sac is due Spring 2021 from Bloomsbury.

ROISIN KIBERD has been published in the Dublin Review, The Stinging Fly, The White Review, the Guardian and others, and wrote a column on internet subcultures for Vice. Her book, The Disconnect, will be published by Serpent's Tail in 2021.

TIM MACGABHANN is the author of Call Him Mine and How to Be Nowhere. His fiction, non-fiction, and poetry also appear in gorse, The Stinging Fly, and the Dublin Review. He lives in Mexico City.

UNA MANNION was born in Philadelphia and lives in County Sligo. She has won numerous prizes for her poetry and fiction. Her debut novel A Crooked Tree will be published by Faber and Harper Collins in January 2021.

JOHN PATRICK MCHUGH is from Galway. His fiction has appeared in The Stinging Fly, Banshee, Winter Papers, The Tangerine, and Granta.

OONAGH MONTAGUE is a writer from Cork.

PETER MURPHY is a writer, spoken word performer and musician from Wexford. He has published two novels, John the Revelator and Shall We Gather at the River (Faber), and this year he and his band released their eponymous debut album Cursed Murphy Versus the Resistance.

KERRI NÍ DOCHARTAIGH lives in an old stone railway cottage in the middle of Ireland. She writes about nature, literature, and place. Her first book, Thin Places will be published by Canongate in January 2021.

DOIREANN NÍ GHRÍOFA's most recent book is A Ghost in the Throat, an exploration of the 18th-century poet Eibhlín Dubh Ní Chonaill.

HUGH O'CONOR is an actor, photographer, and writer/director.

BRÍD O'DONOVAN is a Cork-born, Dublin-based photographer who specialises in portraiture, fashion, and food photography.

DOMINIC STEVENS has lived in Dublin, Leitrim and Berlin. He has published two non-fiction books, Domestic, and Rural. He is working on his first novel, The Coloured Room.

JESSICA TRAYNOR's collections include The Quick and Liffey Swim (Dedalus Press). The Quick was a 2019 Irish Times poetry choice. She is the 2020 poet in residence at the Yeats Society, Sligo, and a Creative Fellow of UCD.

DAVE TYNAN is a writer and director from Dublin. He has twice been awarded the IFTA for Best Short Film and his first feature Dublin Oldschool had its premiere at the BFI London Film Festival. His fiction has been published in The Stinging Fly.

RUBY WALLIS is a visual artist who works with photography and the moving image. She teaches Studio Art at the Burren College of Art and exhibits and publishes her work internationally.

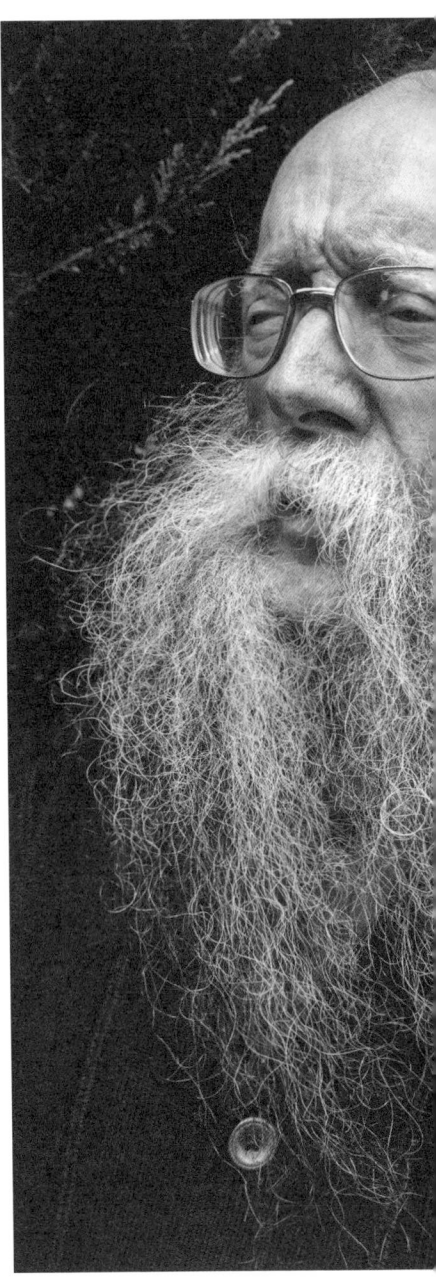

WINTER PAPERS 6

DON'T FUCK WITH THE FAIRIES
An encounter with Eddie Lenihan

Doireann Ní Ghríofa

Photographs by Ruby Wallis

In the village of Crusheen in County Clare, on a quiet cul-de-sac scattered with dented footballs, kids' bikes and wheelie bins, there is a doorway. There, a dog is barking ferociously, her little body tense with outrage at the brazen approach of a stranger. I am the stranger. The dog belongs to Eddie Lenihan. The moment that I bend to greet her, she grins, giving me her soft belly, and then I spot Eddie himself, smiling as he says her name: *Dolly*. He's just as I remember him, all long, wild locks and whiskers, although in person there is a sort of hypnotic gentleness to such hairy abundance. I was six or so when I first encountered his performances on Dempsey's Den, a storytelling I found vivid, frightening, and intensely thrilling. I can only assume that I praised him often, because birthdays began to bring more of his work my way; one year, I smiled giddily at his book Defiant Irish Women, and on another, I received a story-tape that conjured a pair of pigs grinding a man's flesh between their teeth. I listened to this tape so often that I knew the cadence of his voice by heart; perhaps that's why his presence feels so familiar now.

Inside, a clutch of logs glows beyond the glass of a dark-green stove. Eddie settles into his comfy chair and Dolly plonks herself at my feet with a happy sigh. My eye roams the room, pausing on a miniature 'fairy door' of the kind sold in toy shops and glued to skirting boards all over Ireland. This one, however, is the only one I've seen with the handwritten warning: DON'T PISS OFF THE FAIRIES.

It is Eddie's advocacy on behalf of the Sí – those dark beings traditionally associated with ringforts – that has most often drawn media interest his way. His objection to the planned path of a motorway at Latoon in 1999 prevented the obliteration of a hawthorn tree imperative to Sí journeys. The intervening decades have seen much media coverage of this victory, and yet the prevailing tone often turns to a baffled mockery about the existence of 'fairies'. There are those, however, who would never laugh at such a subject; I count myself among them. As an aphorism often attributed to Paul Éluard puts it: 'There is another world, but it is in this one.' Like an airborne virus, the Sí exist, irrespective of whether or not we deign to believe in them, and, like a virus, they are powerful and best avoided. Eddie understands the cognitive dissonance required to balance the cynicisms of contemporary Irish life with vestigial acceptance of the Sí. In his book Meeting the Other Crowd, he writes that 'most Irish people have some instinctive belief in the world of the fairies, even if sometimes it has to be excavated carefully from under a veneer of busy modernity.' His activism reminds us of how flimsy that veneer can be. Beyond the hectic days of advocacy and media interviews, however, lie the many ordinary days of his craft. Today, I am eager to learn of the slow accretion that constitutes a lifetime of devotion to the art of story and to human voice.

Voice, after all, is how it all begins. The voice will be that of an elderly person who sits by Eddie's side to tell him a story – this part of his craft is as simple and as charming as that. He listens carefully. So does his machine. Minidiscs are his tool of choice, although they are becoming increasingly difficult to obtain. In recording, he uses no prompts or cues, rather he cultivates an encounter where 'conversation skips from here to there to the other, and that's how it works. I just let the people talk for themselves.' In an era of rural isolation, such sustained attention and care is a gift, as is the fact that Eddie will return again and again, often becoming a trusted friend. In reminiscing about these story-tellers now, he frequently pauses to shake his head in sorrow, remembering a recent hospital visit, or a funeral. Let it be clear that this is a dying art. To offer companionship to its final practitioners is to accept the inevitability of grief. Time is taking their voices and their friendship from him, one by one. Something of these shared moments remains alive in his recordings, however – the sound of a smile, the murmur of a sigh, all the small silences a person might use to gather their thoughts – such peripheral moments pulse, still, in Eddie's recordings.

Once the session is complete, he thanks and is thanked, then packs up his equipment and carries the disc home to 'label it with the person's age, date, address, and put it up on the shelf.' If one aspect of this role demands the precision of a collector, another is necessarily protective, for he is sole custodian of this repository of voices. I had imagined a fancy personal library of some sort, shelved high with recordings, but Eddie guffaws when I suggest as much. In fact, his archive is so vast that it spills into every room of his home. Are there secrets on those tapes? 'Oh absolutely! There's two murders there that were never solved.' Eddie is the only person who will access these recordings. As he sees it, to allow admittance to anyone else would be to breach the ethics of trust he has forged with the storytellers. In recounting the many researchers who have sought to purchase the recordings, he grows irritated. 'I don't give copies to anyone. I will tell people about things [on the tapes] but I will never play them back for them.' He shakes his head, imagining how a teller might feel were they to discover such a transgression. 'Would they trust me to come into their home and record them again? No,' he slams his fist emphatically, 'No.' At my feet, Dolly snuffles in her sleep.

Months or years might pass before Eddie reaches for the recording once more. Such an impulse might be sparked by a sudden urge to revisit a topic, he explains, to incorporate it into one of his articles on local folklore, perhaps, or to adapt it for a performance. As I understand it, two fidelities find expression in his artistic practice: a devotion to listening (the quiet diligence of assembling an archive of folklore recordings), and a devotion to expression (encompassing both writing and public performance). The retrieval of the recording indicates the threshold of the second phase, one that is marked by a different register of intensity. Transcription 'is slow, slow, slow work. A slow job.' The specificity of his routine, however, is a comfort to him. First he draws down the tape, and then it's off to Fogarty's, where he calls a pint and settles into his usual nook, a snug nicknamed 'The Ship'. There, he readies pen and paper, slides on his headphones, presses play, and sets all his concentration on transcribing the voice that speaks back. Precision is vital in capturing the exact wording used by the original teller: 'the least I could do for those people is do them the honour of preserving the voices they spoke in.' It is this allegiance to the human voice that adds such charm to his books, one feels as though one is listening to a spoken story, rather than simply reading it. He nods. 'Voice reveals character,' he reminds me.

To Eddie, the vernacular is precious, and each little oddity of Hiberno-English a delight. He attributes this joy to his time studying in Galway with a master phonetician he still refers to as The Professor: 'I thought he was a bastard at the time, but he taught me the value of hard work.' It was this professor who set the original university assignment that set Eddie on his way, directing him to find an elderly person whose particularities of speech might be subjected to phonetic analysis. Eddie drove home to Brosna, where his father pointed him in the direction of a suitable subject. Hopping back on his motorbike – 'a Yamaha 200 ... lethal ... lethal' – he roared onwards, foxgloves and brambles trembling behind him. In knocking on that first door, he was placing himself in the path of a passion that would propel the rest of his days. How mysterious life can be, when on any ordinary afternoon, we might find ourselves face to face with precisely the individual who will change our lives. Eddie recounts that encounter with the mix of fervour and fondness with which all artists recall

DOIREANN NÍ GHRÍOFA

their baptisms. 'He was just the kind of person that I needed to meet then,' he smiles.

I wonder then, as I often have, what it is that compels us to proceed with a craft beyond the buzz of a first encounter, what sends us back to the canvas or to the blank page the second time, the fifth time, the hundredth time. What provoked Eddie to continue to seek out new doors, new storytellers, once the demands and deadlines set by his professor had passed? He answers quickly: 'the vision of a world being lost before our eyes and no one caring enough to preserve it.' Eddie found that he cared.

He still cares. He cares for those he has recorded, from whom he learned so much. Once he wrote that he wouldn't 'claim to be an apostle or prophet of anything – a disciple, rather, of great, though very often uneducated teachers.' He cares for the landscape too, and the ways in which the past makes itself felt in the present there, through ringforts, sacred sites, and the tracks of the long-abandoned West Clare railway. He cares for language, how it veers and swerves, and how nimbly it carries the stories he cherishes. The fact of his broad caring is inescapable in conversation, as he gesticulates and curses copiously through sudden divergences, his whiskers trembling as he leaps from the intricacies of recording technology to the homelessness crisis to pub manners to superhero films to the reasons the word 'shall' has been shunned by Irish people, and onwards, ever onwards, relentlessly. It is a joy to sit with a person in whom the twin fires of curiosity and indignation burn so brightly.

Every day, he wakes and sets to work again in new urgency, despite the seeming futility of his task. Modernity may be winning, but in Eddie Lenihan it faces a determined foe. Despite the hecklers, the snide remarks, and the vandals, he perseveres. The tree he saved from the motorway's path was subsequently attacked, and every one of its branches was hacked off. Why is it that people rage against the old ways – would it be facetious to attribute it to some sort of post-colonial disgust? He pauses a moment, and when he finally replies, his eyes spark in exasperation above his whiskers. 'It's that we hate ourselves. We're angry against ourselves.' I ask how he persists in the face of such contempt. 'I know behind it all that people do care.' He pauses, tilts his head, and clarifies, 'well … more people care than don't care.' He stands, then, to tend the fire. A cumbersome length of metal must be slotted in the stove door before it will open. He struggles for many moments to align the handle with the aperture, batting my hand aside when I offer help. Much later, on finding myself beyond this scene and beyond this time, transcribing his words from recording to computer, I feel compelled to listen back to this section repeatedly. I don't know why – little is audible beyond the repeated scrape and clunk of metal failing to connect with metal, and small sounds of exasperation. I listen. I listen again. Again, the grappling, again, the dark door, again, the tool, and the failing human effort to connect them. Eventually, this struggle ends in success. Eddie persists, and the fire blazes on, and on, and on.

Sitting back, he falls silent a moment, and I watch him, thinking of all he has achieved over his decades of dedication. Appetite for his work transcends age and borders, and he works hard to fulfil this interest, publishing book after book and performing on a busy circuit of schools, libraries, and festivals, both in Ireland and worldwide. When I ask whether he has a sense of his audience, he answers with confidence. 'I do. I know myself that my books will keep selling.' He enjoys both public and private elements of his practice, finding it immensely satisfying to perform to a full house, where audiences often 'request a certain type of story, or a theme, and I deliver the story to fit.' Some gigs proceed like that for three hours or more, with Eddie tailoring each tale to the audience's wishes, until eventually he leaves the stage exhausted, 'and I'll tell you something else, the stink of sweat off me!' Does he find, on such occasions, that people are drawn to particular genres of stories? 'I do. People like fairy stories. There's no doubt about it. Because there's an element of ... *Could it be true? Might it be true?* ... and there were always people who said it was. You see, there's dark countryside, and they're on their way home ...' Sometimes the very engine that drives belief is doubt itself; even the most fervent non-believer might shudder in a certain place, in a certain light, or in a certain gloom.

I wonder how the collective imagination adapts to the loss of inherited literature, whether it is simply supplanted by a different kind of shared narrative, drawn from TV or literature, say, or whether the stories once shared by our forebears still lurk somewhere within us. Perhaps some deep well of the psyche, finding itself depleted, begins to crave the familiarity of the old tales, told in the old way, left to seep again like water seeps down through stone. Just before Ireland's coronavirus lockdown was announced, Eddie appeared on a live podcast recording with Blindboy of the Rubberbandits. Months later, we speak on the phone, and he tells me that he's still reeling from the repercussions – such was the leap in his website sales that he ran clean out of envelopes. He is simultaneously delighted that his work is finding so many new readers, and weary. He longs to be focused on new writing now, a longing that clashes with the logistical energies required to ferry books to the post office. Every art form maintains a certain ambivalence between its public and private sides, and Eddie's is no different. There is so much he wants to write, and so little time. He lists his favoured projects on his fingertips. There's a book on military memories to finish, and a Civil War novel, as well as further writing on the Sí, a new volume for children, and many others. He has achieved so much already, and yet, he still longs for more. When I ask whether he feels any regrets, there is only one. He thinks of all his recordings and shakes his head – 'I came too late,' he says.

A lifetime devoted to any craft must change a person irreversibly. If Eddie was to find himself on a boreen as an old Yamaha 200 roared towards him, bearing a young man on the cusp of beginning his own craft, what wisdom might he impart to his young self? 'You never know what's ahead of you. All you can do is go through the day that's in it and do your best.' He pauses, then leans forwards again. 'The harder a thing is to do, the more you'll enjoy looking back at it.' In the art of looking back, Eddie Lenihan is a maestro.

IMBOLC

Louise Kennedy

Elaine hauled Grace out of her cot and slung her onto her hip. The other baby, the one in her belly, she was carrying low, and there wasn't much room. She went along the hall. Liam had put turf in the range before he left for the lambing shed and the kitchen was warm and quiet. She squashed Grace into her highchair and put on a pan of milk for their breakfast.

She stood at the sink and looked up at the hill farm. They still called it that, even though Liam's father had lost the rest of the farm, the good land further down the mountain, where he'd once kept a dairy herd. They just had sheep now. A few of them were dotted around the fields, their coats grubby against the snow. It had begun to fall late the previous evening, and Liam had been out for most of the night, bringing in the ewes. The ruined byre where they stored the turf was now a rounded knoll and the hedges and stone walls were fringed white. Only the lambing shed was bare, snowflakes melting on contact with the roof, trickling down the green corrugated ridges. Around the edge of the structure was a grey-brown slush.

She heard the engine before she saw the car, if you'd call it a car. A 4×4, high off the ground and glossy black, its rear portion long, with tinted windows; a hearse on steroids. It crunched to a halt in the yard, leaving thick bluish tracks in its wake. Liam came out of the shed, wiping his hands on his arse. He stood back and watched the brother and sister get out. Trevor Rainey, his humped shoulders putting ten years on him, his nose and mouth wrapped in a scarf to keep the weather from his bad lungs. Stacey Rainey, in leopard print welling-tons, twisting her auburn hair into a messy bun. When Liam had said he was taking Trevor's sister on as an Agricultural Science placement student, Elaine had thought he meant the other girl, the one with stumpy legs and a squint. They followed Liam into the shed.

Elaine put four Weetabix into a pasta bowl and doused them in hot milk. She sat at the table to share with Grace. One for you, one for me, she told the child, but Grace was hungry and after a couple of mouthfuls Elaine amended it to two for you, one for me. Grace hadn't swallowed the last spoonful when she seized the tray of the highchair with both hands. Evacuating her bowels, her face was a picture of both horror and bliss. Elaine dropped the bowl and spoon in the sink and brought Grace to the bedroom.

She lay her on the bed to change her. There seemed to be more shite than child. She wrapped the soiled nappy tightly, resealing the adhesive strips, and pitched it across the room at the bin. It landed safely. Yes, she said and punched the air. Grace clapped. Elaine sat Grace in the shower tray where she slapped at shampoo suds. A bath would have eased Elaine's backache but lately it appalled her to see the new baby heave from one side to another, to feel the tiny heels and hands jab between her ribs.

Elaine dried Grace first, taking care with the folds at her knees and thighs and neck, and blew a raspberry on her tummy. She dressed her and put her into the cot while she got herself ready. A couple of months earlier, the bath sheet had wrapped all the way around her. Now her bare belly ballooned from it. She was colossal. In the sallow gloom of the energy-saver bulb her nipples were like cigar butts. New stretch marks made a violet lacy pattern on either side of her diaphragm. The line that ran from her bulging navel to the unkempt pubic hair that she rarely saw made her look as though she had been marked for dissection. She snapped the straps of her bra up to her collarbone and rubbed wheatgerm oil into her itchy skin. She pulled on maternity leggings, one of Liam's shirts, and Gryffindor striped knee socks bought long before a shopping trip meant standing in the baby clothes section of Penneys trying to remember what she had gone in for. There was more hair on her hairbrush than in her fringe and she spat coral-coloured froth when she brushed her teeth. A midwife at the clinic had told her she should have given herself more time before planning another baby. There had been no plan. Just enough Pinot Grigio to help her overlook the resemblance that Liam's cock bore to Grace's arm.

In the kitchen, she put Grace in her playpen and resumed her watch at the window. Snow was still falling. The shed door opened and Liam came out with Trevor Rainey. They gripped hands as if they were about to arm-wrestle, a gangsta gesture that filled her with shame for her husband. For herself.

She made tea and sat at the table to drink it. If the weather hadn't turned, she would have driven towards town. Picked up biscuits and crisps for them to snack on in the shed. Called in on Siobhán, her sister, although Elaine found the lodge depressing, with its smell of hash and mildew, the mad talk out of Sid, as if he was living on the edge of a vast frontier. For want of something better to do she stripped the bed and bunged the linen in the machine to wash.

At eleven, she dressed Grace in her pink pram suit and put on one of Liam's coats, stepping into her wellingtons at the back door. She went up the lane slowly, her boots leaving deep, deliberate prints. Grace had tilted her head back and was flicking her tongue out, catching snowflakes.

The shed was warm, the air fetid with damp wool and blood and sheep droppings. There were ewes crammed into the big pen, pawing and fretting, heavy bellies skimming the floor. In the small pens, the new mothers were nuzzling and lapping at their newborns. Stacey Rainey was filling a bucket of water at the sink by the wall, dressed in a Letterkenny IT Gaelic football jersey that was a size too small and black wet-look jeggings. She put the bucket in one of the pens and came to Elaine. She tickled Grace under the chin and the child's mouth gaped open, a slobbery, happy smile. The wee traitor, thought Elaine. Where's Liam? she said.

Stacey inclined her head at the far wall. He's watering. We're afraid the pipes'll freeze.

We're afraid – the cheek of her.

When are you back to college? said Elaine.

Monday week.

Great, said Elaine.

A panel in the false wall slid aside. For a moment Elaine glimpsed the rows and rows of plants, the cables and lamps that were strung across the ceiling, their eerie light. Liam banged the panel shut and crossed the floor to her, his feet kicking up the lime-slaked straw.

Stay in the house, I told you, he said.

I'm bored.

I don't want Grace breathing in this shit.

He kissed his daughter on the forehead.

What time will you be down for lunch? said Elaine.

Half twelve.

She put Grace on her other hip. As she passed the big pen, a ewe moaned, dreadfully. She called out to Liam to tell him the animal seemed ready, but his back was to her. He was standing with his legs wide apart, talking down to Stacey Rainey, who was crouching on the floor, bottle-feeding a lamb through the bars of one of the pens. Her haunches in the leggings were full and shiny. That one's a tramp, she whispered to Grace as they went through the door to the yard. The clouds were low and pinkish. The gritter hadn't made it and beyond the lower fields the road was a lethal grey ribbon.

Elaine left her boots at the back door, caked now with snow and wet straw. She made more tea, a bottle for Grace. She put Grace in the highchair but couldn't settle herself at the table. Stacey Rainey was knickerless and wearing false eyelashes. In a lambing shed. Elaine went back to the window and ate two KitKats.

Liam came down the hill alone. He soaped his arms to the shoulders at the sink in the utility room before entering the kitchen. Well, he said. He lifted Grace from the highchair and rubbed his nose against hers. She laughed and patted his cheeks.

Elaine slid a SuperValu lasagne in front of him. It had little meat and a crimson sauce. He ate with Grace on his knee, his arm draped easily around her.

Is herself not having any lunch? said Elaine.

She said she'd wait till after I have mine.

That's good of her.

It was supposed to sound sarcastic, but Liam said, It was.

Sorry about the lasagne. I couldn't get out to the shop.

It's grand.

It looks shite.

It's shite enough, all right.

Jesus. I said I was sorry.

You said it was shite first.

I said I'm sorry.

Fuck's sake, he said and pushed the empty tray away. Are you all right today?

I don't like you getting mixed up with that shower.

What planet are you on, Elaine? I need help, and in case you haven't noticed, I'm kind of restricted in who I can let into that shed.

He handed Grace to her and left, slamming the back door behind him.

Elaine put the lasagne tray in the bin and filled the kettle. Liam had paused at the top of the lane and was looking up at the clean roof. He crossed the yard. At the shed door, he tilted his face to the sky, as if he was asking for strength, before pulling it open. He held it wide until Stacey came out in a cropped jacket that made her legs look even longer. They stood facing each other for a few seconds, the girl putting her hands behind her head as if he'd pulled a gun on her, then liberating her hair. She turned from him slowly and began to walk away. Liam's chin went up, as if he was calling out to her, and she swung round, walking backwards as she replied to him. His shoulders heaved the way they did when he thought something was funny. He went through the door, closing it behind him. At the edge of the yard Stacey Rainey stopped and looked back at the shed. She pushed her hands into her pockets and traipsed down the lane, the leopard print boots fitting neatly in the footprints Elaine had made.

She knocked at the back door and came in shyly. Hiya, she said from the utility room. Elaine stood by the table, holding Grace, and watched the girl wash her unseasonably bronzed arms, the glister of soap and water on them.

I haven't much in, said Elaine, but I can make you a sandwich.

Stacey took a protein bar from her pocket and waved it vaguely. I have this, she said, but I'd love a cup of tea.

The kettle clicked off and Elaine put Grace in the highchair and gave her a rusk.

When are you due? Stacey asked Elaine's belly.

Six weeks, she said, dropping a teabag in a mug and dunking it up and down with a spoon.

Irish twins, they call it, when you have two babies in the one year.

Elaine felt her face get hot. We wanted to have them close together, she said. She put the mug on the table and sat beside Grace.

Stacey took a bite of her bar and chewed for a long time. The boys are worried, she said.

About the water freezing?

No. About the roof. That's how they're catching people now. The clean roof is a dead giveaway. A sign of heat.

Yeah, I know, said Elaine.

Only she didn't know. One crop, Liam had told her, to clear their debts. He'd grow it and Trevor Rainey would sell it. He'd said it as though Trevor was his business partner and not his main creditor. Elaine hadn't protested. Do what you have to do, she'd said. I don't want to know.

They're going to wait and see how long the snow goes on for. The lambing is a good cover, but the sheep don't generate that much heat by themselves, said Stacey.

Elaine was filled with pity for her. She was eighteen, twenty at most. For all her glamour, it was naive the way she spoke, repeating things she'd overheard the men say, trying to sound worldly. And what sort of brother was Trevor Rainey, sending his teenage sister to shovel shite in a grow house?

How many ewes are left to go? said Elaine.

Thirty-odd. Liam says we'll be done by the weekend.

Not so bad. You'll be glad when it finishes.

Ah no. The wee lambs are cute, said Stacey. Anyways, I'd better go back up and do a bit. Thanks for the tea.

Grace was still hungry. Elaine reheated some of the stew she'd made the previous day, flaking the meat with a fork and squashing it into the gravy and soggy carrots. She put the plastic bowl in front of Grace and watched her gather food in her fists and push it into her mouth. You mucky wee article, she said softly. She poured herself a glass of milk and sat at the table, but her gut was sick with worry and she couldn't even lift it to her lips; all this was her fault.

The men from the Sheriff's office had come the week Elaine did the pregnancy test. Liam had been bulling, roaming the place in quiet fury, hardly talking to her. On the fourth day she rose early and dressed in normal clothes, not the glorified pyjamas she'd been wearing for months. She applied make-up and took tongs to her hair, trying to look the way she used to, before she'd become sluggish and throughother. She cooked him a fry-up, chattering away as he ate. When the food was gone he tossed his cutlery onto the plate, as if he was throwing down a gauntlet. You gave me the green light, he said, in a voice so steady it frightened her. It was as if by letting him part her legs she had given a signal that he could work away at her without consequence.

Then they'd heard the engines, a car followed by a truck. Elaine went to the front door, the entrance they never used. She opened it to three of them, a slight man in a grey suit flanked by two shaven-headed men in bulky black jackets like bouncers wear. She caught the pair exchanging a look, amused, she suspected, at being greeted by a plump dolly bird with a baby over her shoulder. The suit asked for Liam and held out a plastic card, his ID.

That'd be me, said Liam, from behind her. He stepped off the porch and stood in front of the older man. You're the one with the badge, he said. I suppose this pair have the gun and the horse.

The men seemed to fill the house. One of them lifted the flatscreen TV off the wall in the living room. He'd put on gloves and looked for all the world like a burglar. The other asked her if they had any games consoles or laptops. The suit was trailing them from room to room, writing in a notebook.

Liam was sitting at the kitchen table in front of the dirty plate, a thumb pressed into the apple of his cheek, fingers splayed at his hairline. How much do they want? Elaine hissed at him.

Nine grand.

Ring someone.

Who can I ring?

I don't care, she'd said. Just get them out of this house.

Grace had finished her lunch. Elaine set about her with a series of wipes and carried her to the bedroom to change her nappy. The bed was unmade, but they got into it anyway, Elaine laying Grace on the mattress protector, which had yellowed on Liam's side. His pillow seemed to bear an imprint of his face, like the Shroud of Turin. Grace fell asleep in seconds, fingers on Elaine's cheeks. Her face creased suddenly, as if she was having a row with someone, and just as quick slumped into a drunk-looking smile. The other baby was still, and Elaine felt herself sink into the place between waking and sleeping. She dreamt, a vivid waking dream from which she couldn't rouse herself. Two guards were in the doorway of the shed. The panel on the false wall was open and the grow house looked like a strange film that was playing on a vast screen. Liam was pulling his hand from inside a ewe. Stacey Rainey was behind him, pointing her tits at his back. A car horn woke her. She jolted, frightening Grace from her nap.

A mist was curling around her father's battered Corolla. There was a mantle of snow on the roof and a new scratch by the keyhole on the driver's door, a deep one this time. She could picture him outside the Mountain Inn in the dark, a lit Carroll's in the corner of his mouth, trying to find the lock. He leaned to kiss Grace, a yeasty hum from his breath. Elaine was annoyed, yet relieved that she could only smell beer. It meant he had been in the pub drinking with other people, not alone in a torpor of whiskey and grief. You're happier to see me than your mother is, he said to Grace, reaching out his arms to her. Elaine swung the child away from him.

Are you all right to take her?

Can I not come up here without you giving me a hard time?

Elaine relented, handed Grace over.

I'm worried about you. You can't be driving round the place langers. You'll kill yourself or someone else. Or get banned.

He sat on a chair at the table and jiggled Grace up and down on his knees. He opened his legs, let her slip almost to the floor. She looked terrified then dissolved into giggles as he pulled her back up.

You're a dose, he said. I only go out for the few pints and the company.

That road must be like a skating rink.

I took it handy.

Had you anything to eat? I might put on a few rashers for a sandwich.

He came and stood beside her at the sink. The shed door opened and Stacey Rainey came into the yard and took out her phone.

He elbowed Elaine gently. I'd be laying off the rasher sandwiches if I were you, he said, and himself inside in the shed with that one.

Jesus, Daddy, said Elaine. She went to the utility room and emptied the tumble dryer, bringing the clothes to the table.

Her father put Grace in her playpen and began folding. He made a stack of Grace's things then one of white clothes, 'newborn' vests and Babygros that Elaine had laundered ready for her hospital bag. She watched him pair tiny socks and was moved terribly by the deftness of his thick fingers, the roughness of his hands against the delicate fabric.

Are you crying? he said.

No. I'm just tired. Liam's up there morning, noon and night and I'm not sleeping.

Go on up to him. I'll mind Grace.

Outside the light was fading. She brought her phone in case she needed to use the torch. There was a message from Siobhán. *Happy St Brigid's Day, you goddess. Nutter*, Elaine replied, followed by three love hearts. The footprints she'd left earlier had almost disappeared and the fields had deepened to a cold blue-white. She paused in the doorway of the shed, fearful of gleaning an ease, an intimacy between her husband and the young student. She needn't have worried. Liam was tending to the torn backside of one of the ewes. Stacey Rainey was as far away from the animal as possible, looking as if she was about to vomit. Liam asked her for more catgut and glared at her as she dithered. Eventually she handed him a piece that was too short.

It's not for flossing my fucking teeth, he said.

Elaine put down her phone and took the roll of catgut from Stacey, noticing the girl's bitten nails and the fake tan that had collected in the webbing between her fingers and thumbs. She cut a length and threaded the needle. She passed it to Liam and handed him scissors as he finished stitching.

Fill up those buckets again, he told Stacey, without looking up. He held out his arms and Elaine wiped the red, sticky mess from them. That wee fella needs a couple of nights by the range, he said, pointing at a skinny, foetal-looking creature that was squirming in a plastic crate lined with newspaper.

I'll take him with me now, she said. He wrapped the animal in an old towel and put it in her arms.

She held the lamb inside her coat. Halfway down the hill she felt in her pockets. She had left her phone behind. She turned and went back to the shed. Her eyes took a moment to adjust to the light, and at first she didn't know what she was seeing. Stacey was bent over the sink, clutching its sides. Liam was behind her, one hand on the wall, the other holding her hair. Stacey's orange buttocks were bouncing as if he was riding a pony. Liam turned towards the doorway, where Elaine was standing. He held her gaze, a look of hatred on his face.

Elaine took her phone and went outside. Phone Trevor Rainey, she'd begged Liam as the men were moving around their house, even though she knew he only had cash because he was dodgy. When the black jeep pulled up half an hour later and the television was back on the wall, she'd felt relief. Afterwards she had opened a beer and served it to Liam at the kitchen table. We'll pay him back, she told him, her fingers in his hair, it'll be grand. He flung her hand off him and it dropped heavily by her side. Are you that fucking stupid? he said.

The blue of the fields seemed to drain the air of light, and with all that she was carrying, she couldn't see her feet. She tried to turn on the torch but couldn't manage it. Her feet sank deep in the snow and each step was exhausting. A sob was bulging at the back of her throat. She swallowed it down. Her father was at the sink, holding Grace. He lifted the child's hand in a wave. Elaine raised hers in reply and trudged towards them, the lamb trembling in her arms.

THE ART OF DISAPPEARING (BEAUTIFULLY)

An interview with CONOR J. O'BRIEN by Siobhán Kane

Conor J. O'Brien has been creating music for more than twenty years, from writing songs at school, progressing to his first band The Immediate, and then to his solo incarnation as Villagers.

Four studio albums – Becoming a Jackal (2010), {Awayland} (2013), Darling Arithmetic (2015), The Art of Pretending to Swim (2018) – and many accolades later, including two Ivor Novello Awards, O'Brien has established himself as one of the most luminous, inventive, and considered artists that Ireland has produced. In many ways, his work takes us away from Ireland, and follows the John McGahern maxim (itself a restatement from Portuguese writer Miguel Torga) that 'the local is the universal without walls'.

His work is without walls, yet is searching and rigorous, a potent mixture of the intellectual and emotional, with his comportment reaching into his poetic lyrics, corresponding artwork, and atmospheric compositions, each record expanding on a vision that is distinctly his own. We talk over his kitchen table, one rainy July evening in lockdown, in the centre of Dublin.

SIOBHÁN KANE: *Becoming a Jackal was released a decade ago. You went from a band journey to a solo journey. That record, and your most recent, The Art of Pretending to Swim, have a thread for me, perhaps a mixture of the abstract and the earthy … {Awayland} and Darling Arithmetic seem like something else.*
CONOR J. O'BRIEN: I disagree [laughs].

That will probably be the recurring theme of this conversation, as it so often is between us. Why?
Probably because I'm reactionary [laughs]. With Jackal, I know what you mean about the earthy thing. With In Towers and Clouds [The Immediate's 2008 album] that was about trying to flit above earthly reality and make little dreams that you could float within. But I wanted the Jackal demos to sound different. With a song like Twenty-Seven Strangers, I wanted to use instrumentation that had reference points from a lineage of folky band music – using the Hammond organ sound for example, so the earthy is there – but then flying away from that. At the time I had the luxury to figure things out on a theoretical level. I had time and space to develop a world, that teenage feeling, a youthful sense of arrogance.

You still have that.
[Laughs] But I wasn't confronting the world as much in my mind back then. My new lyrics are written by someone who is taking everything with a pinch of salt. The way I think about the world and navigate it as a person is very different to how it was ten years ago.

How did {Awayland} differ to Jackal?
{Awayland} has got some lovely moments, but is a bit mixed up. Jackal was my first experience of having to talk about the songs to strangers with microphones

and cameras, which kind of diminishes the initial dream. I was really naïve, I had this sense that my art would change the world [laughs]. And then you get brought back to reality by playing some shitty toilet venues in America. Playing those songs from Jackal, which was almost written like a children's book, I saw that things that worked for the listener on their headphones might not work on a stage at Glastonbury. So with {Awayland} I was thinking about how songs might work live.

That awareness crept into your process.
It's a valid concern when writing music, but it can bring in a slightly cynical aspect. I was writing from a purely narrative base, and playing little tricks with words, so it made me less idealistic. I am really embarrassed about a couple of songs. I hadn't engaged enough in the topics I was trying to discuss, but I learned a lot, the songs I like were more playful, like Rhythm Composer – [sings] 'your B P M got an M R I don't know if I'm coming or going' – and that's what makes that album shine for me, but it made me realise if you want to make vaguely socio-political music you really have to think about why.

Where does Darling Arithmetic fit in?
Touring {Awayland} was a lot of fun, but it spun a bit out of control. Aggression started to creep in, with me mostly. I was losing my voice, taking steroids for it, and drinking loads. My friend Dave came to a gig in Berlin, and didn't enjoy it – he felt I was going to fall into the drum kit and split my head open.

The psychology of performing when you're not really an extrovert – if you do it for a long period of time, and at this stage, it was four years – is like going on stage in a bubble and I didn't feel in control. So Darling Arithmetic was me returning to acoustic singer-songwriter mode, then Art of Pretending to Swim was where I wanted to start flying again.

Was there a sense at that time that you wanted to 'reclaim' the Villagers project?
That is probably true in hindsight, but my main feeling was around the different colours I wanted to express. On {Awayland} everything was a full band recording in a studio, everything was to the grid, but I wanted to get back to vague brushstrokes, to be looser, and that inevitably translated to songs that were more personal. I always go into a record with an aesthetic feeling rather than wanting to show people my psyche.

But the psyche emerges anyway. Not in an obvious way, but it's always built on what you're taking in; music, films, books, politics ... What was feeding into Darling Arithmetic?
I remember listening to loads of Roberta Flack, just pure music. A lot of {Awayland} was trying to be intelligent, trying to test myself in a cerebral way. Darling Arithmetic was about feeling it out, expressing something that I was digging to get to, but I remember when the song Courage was released, it was like, 'Hey, welcome to the LGBT community', and that is not how I experience sexuality and sensuality. You are carrying a card all of a sudden, but I don't see it that way. I am a private person. I wasn't holding back on other records, I wasn't trying to make some final statement.

Photograph by Brid O'Donovan

SIOBHÁN KANE | CONOR J. O'BRIEN

You have never been interested in 'final' statements. However, your work has always had a particular intimacy. On The Art of Pretending to Swim, that morphed into an exploration of sensuality and spirituality. Your forthcoming record has this symbiosis also. Do you believe in God?

I don't think that's a valid question [laughs]. It's not a sense of believing in a god but I do have a sense of purpose which definitely strengthens when I create things. And if you take the creation narrative to its logical conclusion, it moves towards the reason why people believe in beings bigger than themselves.

So 'God' is art for you?

I don't know. I have always found it hard to tap into that in experiences and discussion in everyday life – everyday life can be so frustrating and difficult. I don't know what 'God' means. For me it's about a love of music, and trying to reignite that powerful fire that you felt from music your whole life by making your own – that's what it's about for me.

The more I learn about the world, the less I know. A lot of the writing comes from that. The title of the last record is an oxymoron – pretending to swim is really drowning, and being aware that any sort of grand narratives you've lived off in your youth have been debunked and destroyed a million times in your own brain. So where do you stand then? Grappling some sort of meaning from that is where I am now.

George Bernard Shaw said 'progress is impossible without change, and those who cannot change their minds cannot change anything.' Have you changed your mind a lot over the last decade?

About what in particular? [laughs] I think I have. I find the most interesting art has more questions than answers.

Is part of it about subverting the ego?

Subverting the ego is the act of creativity – that's what you are in service to. I like the music to exist on its own terms and I guess it is a spiritual thing to be in the service of something else. You are making sure that something fulfils its fullest potential. Quite often, it's about trusting yourself. It is a calming thing, because when you are making something, you are showing respect for what you have learned.

Do you think you have reached elements of that with the record you're working on at the moment?

If I laid all of the albums out ... The first was the 'Villagers project', then {Away-land} was confused, I sidestepped with Darling Arithmetic and the live album, and then I went back on course with The Art of Pretending to Swim. That was a foundation for this new work in a way the others weren't. It has a lot to do with listening to Duke Ellington, and learning brass. Brass hits you in the gut, it takes you away from being overly cerebral. When I started playing brass it shifted the dynamic – I was thinking about the apex of the song, where the punch in the gut would come ... The force of brass allowed me to be excited again.

Duke Ellington has meant a lot to you the last few years – is it the rigour?

We were talking about spirituality earlier. I am a very religious person in terms of structure, something you have to repeat every day. I'm addicted to that.

Is that about control?

It's Duke Ellington – self-discipline. Discipline is the reason I do this. He disciplined his own musical upbringing. He brought in classical references, jazz references, and maintained his band. He felt if you could keep them, they would get tighter and become a unit. If you listen to that version of Mood Indigo from Masterpieces (1950) it is a very simple idea. He takes the melody of the song which he recorded twenty years earlier, does it 'normally' first, then rounds it out, the instruments wavering around the theme of depression, but the third time this weird abstract thing emerges, the muted trumpet messing up the idea, but adding in close note harmonies. Even though he uses the same initial structure, the meaning shifts as he's emphasising different aspects of that melody. I like his playing with time – you take ostensibly simple ideas, and not just ideas but processes, everything you've learned because of your self-discipline, everything from your arsenal, and you impose it. That idea will shine brighter because you have infused it with that process. Every time I listen to that version of Mood Indigo it blows my mind – he thinks of these songs like lifelong friends. He shows you can get more out of the core.

Jazz is a serious and playful genre – Ellington understood the principles, but pushed outside the parameters.

Like Nina Simone, also. When I was drawing as a kid, my dad would give out to me if I hadn't started with pencil. He said you had to sketch it out first so that you had the structure, and only then start putting on the ink. Eventually I started listening to him. You have to create your own internal logic, live by that, then create a world and a song that follows that logic. It's a way of disciplining yourself, and making yourself have purpose in life, I guess.

I think of Irish traditional music in that way.

There are many songs in that tradition that are undeniably brilliant, but I've always felt I don't want to annoy the gatekeepers. Although that's not the reason why I'm not recording a traditional album. The Irishness of my music is more inherent and integrated. I have always had a complicated relationship with the idea of nationalism and being Irish. It has shifted quite a lot. It was something I rejected when I was a teenager. I couldn't wait to leave the country. I didn't want to be part of it and I didn't think it wanted me. But it means you get into other stuff. It is more interesting when you get older and realise you don't need to ask for permission to cover a tune if you want to.

You have produced all of your records, and this seems integral.

I have always worked that way. It's the same thing as shading when you're drawing. Your vocal tone will be as important as the reverb you put on the snare – I don't understand how it can't all be from the same person, it's the same expression. I mean, I know division of labour has worked well for some people.

Which people?

Er, The Beatles? [Laughs] Nearly everyone has benefited. I did this time a bit as well.

You have taught yourself everything. What's your favourite piece of kit in your studio at the moment?

My Model D Moog reissue. My Pink Floyd fetish item. 1970 to 1974 in recorded music is always worth a listen, regardless of the genre. It was the peak of well-disciplined engineering. It was by-the-book but also breaking the rules. The Beatles broke the rules big time, the impulse of breaking the rules is what people are hearing. That's why so much modern pop music is bad. We're starting to get copies of copies of things. Once the rules are forgotten completely, it's worthless, and we are at the peak of that now.

But you're not pessimistic?.

I was mixing today and got the same thrill I would have gotten as a ten-year-old drawing Batman. That sense of, 'Oh my God I've nailed it, this is something I feel proud to show people.' Adding the final thing into something you feel has a right to have an audience is heaven. When I write a song, I want to be invisible, I want people to see and hear the song … When I disappear finally, it's beautiful.

You were interested in the interview I did with Linda Perhacs in the first iteration of Winter Papers back in 2015 … Why?

She was talking about allowing yourself to be open. To use an analogy, there are people who allow the river to take them downstream and there are people fighting against the river. She said she was lost in the darkness and then saw something – in this case a female figure – and it fitted with something I was working on at the time. In a nightmarish scenario, which anyone can find themselves in, you can make it worse by closing yourself off to light. Some people can sense where the energy isn't good, while other people have to test the waters because they haven't developed that pattern of thinking.

Where do you think you are on that spectrum?

I'm weird. Since I started writing songs, I have always thought about those contexts, I've always been taking the notes, that's home to me. You always have that with you, even if it's a dark time – you can always use it, it's a constant.

Art as bloodletting?

It is of therapeutic value, to a degree. The thing that I hold most closely beyond anything or anyone is the idea of creativity, and the idea that you should probably devote your life to that.

When did you first feel that sensation that you were an artist?

I have a strong memory of when I was three. I got the role of the bus driver in the creche play, I was the only person with a line, and I felt so proud. I also remember making a plasticine figure … I just couldn't believe I could put two legs on it and it would become a thing. When I saw An American Tail, I was hiding my tears as it was so affecting, I was obsessed with the melodies, and I sang those songs a lot. Moving on a few years, my sister Maeve used to listen to The Kinks, I thought it was 'girls music', but I would sneak away, put headphones on and listen to them, I knew they were a genius band … It was like a continuation of An American Tail for me [laughs].

When I was in primary school, our principal was our music teacher. He died when I was ten. He was very cool, a good influence. We could choose our instruments. The fact that we had a choice blew my mind. I felt like I was high, being able to choose a colour to give to the overall sound ... I took the triangle or something, actually it was the tambourine [laughs]. And then I remember seeing my older brother play guitar when I was nine or ten in his school concert – he was really good – and that's my first memory of live music.

And then you wrote your first song at twelve.
Yes, 'Psychic', [starts singing] ... 'When I'm walking down these streets I feel like a monkey in the arctic / city dwellers staring into my eyes, and it makes me wonder if they possess psychic powers like you / not a chance, your mind controls over everything / I never feel safe around you, I want to block you out of my mind / I try to refrain from asking if it is everlasting, so I say nevermind.'

When I moved schools, it was a different world. I asked for an electronic drum kit for Christmas, and with my friends, Dave and Arthur, we had a band called Penguin Presidents, and I thought, 'This is me now'. I entered the Jacobs song writing contest but didn't get a reply or a 'special mention' or anything! It ended up being released as B-side for The Immediate, This Mirror in the Hall. I was trying to sound like that Elvis Costello song, New Amsterdam, the chord structure, the way he sings, the acoustic guitar rhythm. It was very evocative of a romantic sense of hope and escape. I wrote lots of songs in school with different people, Pete and Dave [Toomey and Hedderman, of The Immediate] in particular.

I have been thinking a lot about artists who begin young and continue to produce at a high level. Björk and Radiohead instantly come to mind.
Björk meant a lot to me when I was younger, her playfulness, her voice, so incredible and mysterious, and the production on her records was insane. Homogenic was my world for about a year. I tried to copy all the songs a little bit, the techno one especially, Pluto. I tried to replicate the breadth of her vision when I got home from school with guitar pedals.

You probably return to Radiohead the most?
Probably. They were my first gig, at fourteen. You could get so much out of their records depending what you focused on. The emotional level in Thom's voice, the fragility and strength, that tension, the musicality, the two to three leading melodies going on in each song. I return to In Rainbows the most, it's so warm. I probably just overplayed the others. When In Rainbows came out, I thought they were geniuses, that they could still do an album like that after bringing out Kid A and OK Computer. Radiohead exemplify a rare thing, the antithesis to popular bands. You can hear the emotional journey. It's most likely a journey that you have gone on as well.

Radiohead were a great band if you felt like an outsider. I never felt part of any crowd, they were talking directly to me, and I was hooking it to my veins. Not just their presentation but their lyrics. They made me feel that you could use it as a strength, a sense of being unique rather than left out of something. That you can be part of something bigger than the social contract which you are meant to be indulging in with everyone else. That's why music is powerful – it's best when directed towards an individual.

Did the lyrics from Talk Show Host influence Set the Tigers Free? They both reference sandwiches.
[Laughs] Maybe.

What is a favourite song of yours from the last decade?
Hold Me Down from the last record is a really natural song even though it
went through a bizarre process. Cormac [Curran] did an arrangement that was
the complete opposite of what I asked for, but it turned out to be brilliant.
I listened to it recently, as I was thinking about ways to do old songs, and I
enjoyed it from start to finish. It's symphonic but really close to your ear, whis-
pery, but really widescreen at the same time. It's an authentic song.

What does the word 'authentic' mean to you?
Honesty is a dangerous word. Authenticity gets closer to the core of what you
should be striving for when you are in the throes of a romantic entanglement
with the creative process. The connection only happens if you are making
work that is open-ended, where you are learning something in the process. If
I am getting into a song, and feel it will be something people hear, the process
involves researching things, and getting lost in reading. You are trying to get
into a subconscious space, it's a more natural way of learning about things ...
It's a betterment thing, to a certain degree.

You have always been very considered. Do you think you have placed more impor-
tance on intellectualism in the last few years?
There is a quiet majority that's not happy with the way the world is moving ...
People are staying silent because the world is being shaped by the internet, and
by group-think. People aren't properly disseminating ideas. It has changed the
social landscape, and social contract, so you have to navigate this compromised
world.

Do you think then that you fetishize language more because of this shift?
Language is being used for reasons related to power games. I have noticed that,
so I struggle. I imagine releasing these records back in the '60s, because of the
way pop culture was structured, when there was no internet. Now, when you
bring something out, you're asked why it's 'worthy' of people's time. It diminishes it for me, and I have to work twice as hard to bother doing it again the
next time. It could be a personal thing, as I don't like talking to that many
people. I find it tiring, especially in the context of a press interview, so you have
to realise you are not doing it for a machine, you're doing it for yourself.

   As you get older, you are confronted more with complicated and contradictory situations, situations where you have to hold lots of truths in your mind
at the same time. When you are younger, you have this idea that you know
everything. But as you get older, you see a grey area in every conversation.
If you're a writer, there is no way that can't influence you. It complicates the
initial impulse, you just don't have the same sense of benevolence. I'm always
questioning my right now to speak on any subject. I think that's positive,
personally, but it goes against this modern sense of everyone being an expert
on everything ... Because we are surrounded by that now, it almost feels like
you're kicking against the pricks by being nuanced.

   That Keats idea of 'negative capability' is attractive – holding on to two
different ideas but peacefully, without feeling like you have to rashly shout a
slogan or put a hashtag on something. Being able to be nuanced and change
your mind, being able to have discussions about things in a rational, fair-
minded manner, and still having empathy and respect for people that you
disagree with. The space for arguments and debates these days has changed

to this anonymous online world, it's changed the dramatization of the act of arguing in itself – the fact that we are not using body language in arguments, because we're not even in the same room.

You and I talk about this a lot, and recently saw that After Dark [British late night live discussion programme that ran from 1987 to 1997] episode with Andrea Dworkin and Anthony Burgess among others. The way they communicated was inspiring.
There was so much disagreement in that room, but it was so respectful, and when people were being so-called 'disrespectful' to each other, it was done with such articulacy, people listened and didn't feel the need to shout. Body language was a big part of that conversation. Everyone should watch the Andrea Dworkin episode of After Dark.

What value do you place on happiness?
I think happiness is an umbrella term. Contentment is probably more useful in the long-term. Contentment should be your ability to be sad when you're sad, and music should be the thing that allows you to be sad, a licence to not feel alien to these emotions. I want the songs to have that legacy. Music and art serve a purpose. People have to suppress a bunch of things in order to just keep it together, and music can be the place that is cathartic, not just for happiness but for a whole range of emotions, and flush that out and flesh it out, and flish it out, you know?

That's the epitaph? Flush, Flesh, Flish?
[Laughs] I recently found this poem that I wrote in 2007. It's interesting to find something from back then ...

> The glass
> the misshapen candle
> the friends betrayal
> the humming crowd
> the cash register
> the friends betrayal
> emergency lights
> new shoes
> awareness of ignorance
> choosing to ignore
> learning to ignore
> being eaten by the very same monster
> the same god
> the same ground
> the friends betrayal
> making songs
> something where there was nothing
> I have something to prove
> I have something to prove
> I have something to prove.

DEATH AND THE FAMILY

John Patrick McHugh

Within the space of a year, my cousin died and then the grandad. They were at the extreme ends of things as deaths go: Grandad was ninety-one and his mind was smashed in by Alzheimer's, while David was eighteen and had recently sat the Leaving and was all set for college. In terms of the act of dying, they were opposites, too. One death was protracted, periodically climactic, fiercely draining and, in the end, a relief when it arrived. The other was abrupt as a head meeting a piano in the other room.

I was at the laptop when Dad shouted up that David had had a heart attack. My first instinct was the wrong one: I assumed he was referring to our David in Achill, my older cousin. Still a shock, still shocking, but the David in Achill was in his thirties, a hardy farmer, a sleeves-rolled-to-the-elbows buck – it was conceivable that his heart might suddenly give out. I pictured this David in the midst of a heart attack, his pool table frame sprawled over the wheel of a tractor in a sodden field, grazing sheep fanning out from him, but even in this first feverish dreaming, David was never dead. Altogether shook at his home, or possibly wired-up in the hospital. But not dead. People you know and love never die.

Downstairs, I trailed behind Dad as he threw on a coat and fished for his keys in the bowl while relaying the necessary and unnecessary instructions in a perfectly calm and composed manner. Look in after Granny and Grandad (who lived next door in a converted granny flat; the house was originally theirs). Talk to your sister. Put out the dogs in a while. I nodded along, not fully processing, and when he was out the door – his puffy coat on, the keys held in a fist – I thought to ask after Mam.

He said she was at the hospital; he was meeting her there.

'Already?' I said, 'In Castlebar?'

He answered, 'It's not that David.'

After the car pulled off, I phoned my sister, I hugged Granny, I checked on Grandad, I sent a flurry of messages and then silenced my phone, I stomped about the house, and then I decided I should make a lasagne. An activity which carried me along for an hour, and it was as I teetered over my excessively cheesed creation, the dread building in my stomach once more, that I received a call from Dad. His voice was seemingly normal, but the reception was patchy, so I moved outside. He asked how next door was, how I was doing, if Sister had arrived over yet. And I enquired about how he was, how Mam was, and we both pointedly avoided what the call was truly about. In the trees, the leaves were see-through like shredded plastic. The dogs were sniffing behind me. The grass was cool and wet beneath my naked feet. 'I better go,' he said, and so finally I asked – 'How is David now?' There was sunshine too, I recall. A lazy breeze. The rustle and whistle of overgrown hedges. Birds. Prickly weeds gleaming throughout the garden as if dusted in silver and gold. Lovely day, really.

'Oh,' Dad said after a moment, 'Oh, John. He's dead.'

The news of Grandad's death shouldn't have surprised me. There had been near misses. Off-the-post jobs. It's a gruelling business, Alzheimer's. It digs in ferociously, like a tick, and offers no chance of reprieve. On one particularly bleak occasion, I had arrived back from London to a full-on vigil around his bed. Solemn hellos. Squeezing of forearms. Dad had already decided where and when the wake would be held (the front room at the rear of the granny flat, Sunday). The priest had been informed. My aunts had travelled from Dublin to join their brothers. Candles burned in the hallway. The deranged experience of being impatient for a person to die, repeating stage whispers to one another, about how it be best if he did slip away, how he'd nearly be lucky to go, as if he might hear and heed our advice. Later, I was given time alone with him to say my goodbyes.

And I did. I thanked him. I wished him well on the journey. I told him I loved him, and despite not believing in anything otherworldly or holy, I found myself blabbering about others I knew who had died in case he wanted to say hello to them and the dogs I had loved who would definitely go for walkies with him. I was utterly sincere. The sole light was from a lamp on a dresser, and its rot-orange glow cast the room into a shadowy, baroque composition. My grandfather's face was the point of drama and in his weathered, wrecked state he didn't half look like the rattled St Peter from Caravaggio's topsy-turvy crucifixion painting. The crinkled stress marks between bushy eyebrows. The weary agape mouth. The stubborn muscles still bulging along the shoulders and arms, mighty and strong, albeit useless considering the circumstances. He lay there to confirm our agonising vulnerability. His lips were badly cracked and swelt. My mother had applied Vaseline to sooth them, and in the tawny light, they shone like oil, rendering the inflamed lips cartoonish, as if the man was allergic to dying. There were tufts of hair atop his head, but the scabby skin beneath was now mostly visible. His face had melted somewhat, but it was still decisively him. I held his warm hand and I listened to him breathe, a wheeze and then this arid clicking, I listened to him struggle to stay alive.

Yet he held on that night, that entire weekend, and when he did pass, weeks and weeks down the road, it was a quieter affair: he simply floated away in the nursing home one bright Saturday morning. No vigil this time, no family members scampering to stand guard, no fuss. As pleasant and dignified as a death can be, one guesses. I had made coffee and was back up to work in my bedroom in Dublin when the phone rang. I knew before it was said – just hearing my father's subtly lowered voice was pronouncement enough. (Death does not occur until it is told to you factually over the phoneline on a Saturday morning.) Huddled on the floor, I cried. The coffee went cold. My housemates awoke. I packed and drove down to Galway.

David, like his identical twin brother, was autistic. He was brilliant in all the ways you'd expect – he had an encyclopaedic mind; he was an ardent believer in and efficient administrator of order; he had an uncanny ability to soak up information – and, as may also be expected, he strained under certain social pressures. People could confuse and overwhelm and mystify him. He rubbed uneasily against the intricacies of situations and norms, and he had to be taught, from a young age, to interact with the world in our pre-established mode – to talk about how he felt, to explain himself, to empathize more conspicuously. This is not to say, of course, that David did not innately care about people: he did. I think of him following Granny around the kitchen as they baked. Or his impulsive laughter when his father would tease him. And I say all this not to trivialize David's condition, or to idealize it and sing prettily of how his disadvantages were his advantages: I say all this because it is fact and it is what David, with his family's tireless support, worked to both live with and overcome.

My own one-on-one chats with David were superficial at best. When he would be over at the house, growing up, I'd smile widely at him and lift my eyebrows and maybe ask him about school, or how he was in general. He would reply economically in a nasal voice which broke like static over vowels. (A voice I can hear flawlessly now: the mewing lilt at the end of a sentence, each word said with an exact syllable-by-syllable enunciation; an exactness only shattered by David's own glee.) In these brief encounters, I was the uncomfortable and nervy participant. I never sought to engage deeper with David. I could have asked further questions about his day. I could have encouraged him to reminisce about the musicals he adored. I could have interrogated him about his school and teachers, which was my old school, who were my old teachers. I could have asked anything beyond the easy and the casual but I did not.

I told myself that this distance between us was justified because I didn't understand David's brain and I might carelessly upset him. It was better to be stand-offish and frigid. I was acting for David's own good! But, brutally, I was more worried that I might upset myself. I was scared talking to David. But of what exactly?

Can there be any solace or lull from Alzheimer's? Perhaps if you are willing to focus on the perceived knowledge that the individual who has the disease does not comprehend the true extent of it and so, in an odd paradox, is saved from experiencing the brunt of the torment and misery. If you can subscribe to this cuntish idea, then, maybe, you can cope more easily with the remorseless nature of Alzheimer's. It is what I tried to do. I wanted to be impassive. The old man next door was Grandad, obviously, but I started to imagine him as some poor unfortunate stranger I was kindly helping. Cowardly thinking for sure, cold anthropology, but it was bearable, it was manageable to watch the steady diluting of a person I loved if I did not think they were that person any longer. But the ploy does not grant a total absolution. The worst thing about Alzheimer's is that you can occasionally glimpse flashes of self-awareness in the sufferer, an out-of-place emphasis on a word during a spiel, or a familiar echo of the previous unfaded self in a shift of arm or neck. For that flashing moment they know something is off and astonishingly wrong, they understand that this is not at all right and they are scared, too.

It reached the point where Grandad could not walk or stand or be trusted on his own. He was bedridden and the single room in the granny flat was now his. And this small change in circumstance granted, in my strange mind, a new addition to the family. All my life I had thought – innocently? shallowly? – of Granny and Grandad as one whole being, and now, all of a sudden, they were separated. They were two.

In the coffin, David lay bedded within banks of cream satin. Glasses removed, hands steepled on his chest. (Were there rosary beads woven within his fingers?) The playroom had been cleared. There were mismatched chairs lining the wall, but no one was sitting. There was a feeling akin to the excitement before a first kiss as I stared down at him, a whirling which started in my gut and surged to my throat and nose and was then overtaken by the sensation that I was about to puke. There was no malice in David, only good. His brother was upstairs in his room – he had welcomed us earlier. His mother was being held by her daughter. His father smiled at everyone and his eyes were pink. It was night, and through the large windows, the sky was not black but the delicious purple of a copper beech leaf. It was unreal looking down at David as it would not be in a year's time looking down at Grandad. My brain thought only in platitudes – we were lucky to have him, isn't it desperate, the poor lad, there was no malice in him only good – but what was so inaccurate in those statements? I made a flustered sign of the cross and marched on.

When I was eight, I was told by my parents that a dear friend of theirs had died and at this news, I collapsed into tears. Beyond knowing the friend's name and having visited them on two separate occasions, I had zero relationship with this person, and yet, for five minutes, I was utterly devasted. I suppose I took as my own my parents' sadness, or their expected sadness, which sounds awful noble and thoughtful. And at first, maybe it was. But in the days after, I recall being treated very nicely by my parents, and by the mother of the family who minded me as Mam and Dad travelled up to the funeral, and even though, deep down, I knew I wasn't that sad anymore, I milked this kindness as best I could: I pouted glumly, I squinted at the sky, I stilled myself at the mention of anything moderately death-related.

My initial fear was that I was doing the same with David. That I was latching on to another's grief, that I did not deserve to mourn to this extreme extent, that I should not be rocked so hard. That in fact I was in love with all that grief offered – sympathy, excuses, story.

Every day, I'd be tasked with sitting in with Grandad for an hour or so. Ostensibly I was there for company and for Grandad, when he awoke, to meet a friendly face, but I was mostly perched across from that bed to make sure he didn't hurt himself. As I watched over him, in fitful sleep, or when his eyes were wide and bloodshot and absorbed by some unshakeable, unexplainable idea, I thought (predictably) about how this may be the last time I see him alive. I began to take notes. I began unknowingly to start writing this essay. I jotted the few phrases I could make out from his mad rambling. I described how his body seemed to dwindle day by day, how his hands thoughtlessly curled the knitted tassels along his blanket. I conjured up gaudy similes. I felt that however suspect this may appear from the outside, this is what I must do, this is my duty. In my notebook, I wrote down how I felt after each of these 'sessions' and the gist of these scribbles could now be summed up as, 'It is sad to see Grandad like this, it saddens me.' Not ornate or complicated but truthful all the same.

I often wondered if my presence at the side of his bed bestowed some peace to the man. I often wonder if the collective presence of his revolving band of watchers seeped into Grandad's crumbling mind and spread over it a degree of contentment and familiarity, or, for the briefest instant, a cooling respite. I wonder whether he felt our love in the same way I sometimes wonder whether my nephew is aware of my doting intent when I stand over his cot and ogle. It is nice to think Grandad did feel our love, that he appreciated it. It is certainly nice for us to think that, anyway.

Grandad's speech declined in the way you'd expect, and at the stage when he required constant minding, he was constantly telling stories that were set both in the present and the past, stories which were patterned with narratives that did not line up with known history or logic or basic plot rules. There was a phantom game which was about to be thrown in that afternoon, that very second, but the pitch was in a forest in Wicklow fifty years ago, and he was playing centre forward and, also, he was not playing. Wood needed to be urgently chopped and restocked, but then there was a bus and he was the man who was to drive the bus someplace. Amid these winding tales, this dreamscape, there was an undercurrent of real memories and events and detail – his forester career did begin in Wicklow, he did have to chop wood for the stove in the kitchen, and being a county footballer he had played numerous games of football and likely one was held in Wicklow, though perhaps not in a forest – and as he told these stories to us, we sought at first to chip away the falsehoods and help him reassemble the narratives in their correct order, or the order that we judged correct, and then we just encouraged him to fit any sort of resolution, bizarre or credible, on to the end of these meandering yarns, and, finally, we just sat there and listened.

Three weeks before David passed away, he wore a bowtie and a short-sleeved dotted white shirt to my sister's wedding. My sister, not known for minimalism, had organised the perfect day. Laughter, loved ones. In the wedding DVD, you can spot David speeding across the dance floor as soon as the first song is concluded and clapped. He is pursued by his mother. Clearly, David had given his word to stay until the first dance and, now that it was over, there was no demand or reason for him to stick around. Sensible, logical.

Three weeks after the wedding, we all gathered again for the burial. It was by now September. Schools and colleges were reopening. Jackets and coats were zipped up. Around the graveyard, the trees were already yellowing, and their leaves were drifting in lumbering arcs to the ground (but that can't be right?). The crunch of tyres on gravel, then the heels and the dress shoes. Alloys were reflected in puddles though there was no rain. Bodies stood between headstones, fanning out from the coffin. The wind moved the unmowed grass as if they were the tips of flame. There were low greetings and nattering and exhausted tearless tears. Music was played. Dirt was flung. He was buried dressed in a bowtie and a short-sleeved dotted white shirt.

The last lucid conversation between myself and Grandad happened a month or so before a tumble in the kitchen from which – and I don't think I'm being melodramatic here – he never truly rose. What lead to this conversation, or what lead to the conditions of us being alone together for the conversation, was that Granny had gone into the hospital that morning for a routine check-up – my grandad had bowed unironically as she exited through the backdoor with my mother; Granny had scoffed and called him an old fool; I watched this and thought Love. At lunchtime, I went next door to help Grandad with the Indo's crossword, which he would normally have raced through with Granny. We sat in the kitchen. A fire glinted through the iron grate though it was only half twelve in the day. Being dyslexic, being a dummy, I knew I would be next to no help with the crossword, and if anything, I might exasperate a competent regular. But Grandad only half-minded my uselessness as we scanned the clues. Intermittently, while flexing the paper in my direction, he laughed in his dry scratchy manner. I chuckled, too. He brought the tip of the pen to his mouth as he pondered. I looked out the window at the hedges. After about forty minutes, when the grid was messy with his curvy penmanship, Grandad ruffled the paper and put it aside, crossed his arms, and without making eye contact, said: Do you ever get lonely?

It was a startling and unexpected question; it was terrifying. It was the kind of rich, vulnerable question which had never even vaguely been voiced by either of us. Our relationship was good and loving, but not complicated. But here now was intimacy, here was fragility, and it was all wrong.

Before I shame myself, let me say that now, in the years after his death, I view this question only with regret. A bitter, sighable regret. I believe Grandad was extending, in that horribly naked sentence, an opportunity for us to strengthen our relationship. To dig down together and uncover nerves and emotions and untouched feelings. To talk about something which may or may not have bothered the other person. A mature and unyielding conversation between two people who love each other, basically.

But at the time, I panicked and saw the substance of this question exclusively through the male egotist's glare: was this not an indirect knock against me and my penis?

I had wanked in my room about half an hour before gliding downstairs and joining Grandad in the granny flat. Suddenly, I was petrified, and then paranoid, and then convinced that my onanism had not been as discreet and tactful as I assumed, that my humming laptop and my haggard tugging had been incredibly loud and perhaps, somehow, the whole ordeal had been audible to Grandad next door, and who knew but maybe my countless teenage masturbation sessions had been overheard for years and years, and thus, within this significant question about loneliness, there was not a mushy candour but, rather, a forceful, belated challenge: you are an adult, John, so would you stop wanking so feverishly and thunderously.

Was Grandad glum or morose as he asked this question? I don't recall any marked difference in his expression or any tense adjustment in his body language. He sat there, back straight, looking out at the garden. There was no crack in the voice, no desperate grappling for my forearm. Just that simple, scary question, ringing around us. I went red. I squirmed in my seat. It was a silence which brought to the fore other sounds: the snap of wood breaking into fire, the fridge purring coldly, the clock. There was no reutterance of the question. He seemed, to me, satisfied with the silence of my not answering. Eventually, I excused myself – I had work that afternoon in town – and stood to leave. Grandad laughed then but at me for fleeing so quickly? At me for dodging the question? I don't know, but I do recall it was unlike the laugh I had heard and chuckled along with earlier. As I hurried from the room, Grandad was carefully folding out the newspaper to read the sports section.

What bothers me now is that I can't help but wonder whether Grandad shared the same panic that afternoon. Was asking the question painful? Was it as surprising a question for him to say aloud as it was for me to hear? Was it on his mind throughout the crossword and the morning preceding, or did it form spontaneously as he put away the paper? Was it inspired by my granny being off to the hospital that morning? Or was it a question he had been lugging around his whole life? Had I disappointed him by evading it? Did my hesitation and subsequent scrambling hurt him? Was this an abiding fear of his? Was he himself lonely?

As obvious as it is, as blatant, it is still remarkable to think that once someone is gone, they are gone for good. And those questions we have will be left unanswered, even unsounded. I suppose this is where fiction emerges.

There are many who could write about these deaths, these two men, with more acute insight, with more aching sadness, with more knowledge. It should be my granny, it should be my uncle and aunts, it should be David's family, it should be my parents, it should be an expert on autism, it should be an expert on Alzheimer's, it should be an essayist, it should be someone who doesn't automatically assume an emotionally charged question refers to their genitals. I wrestled with why I was the one who gets to write about them – I do not think myself special in terms of my grief, in terms of my voice – but, in the end, I am writing about them and everyone else is not. And that is enough.

My last conversation with David is uncertain. Probably it was at the sister's wedding. He was collecting everyone's signature that day, so I would have signed and asked in a cheery, condescendingly amplified voice: Well, David, are you having a great time? But it might have occurred after the wedding, at the house, when he would have been over visiting Granny and Grandad. If so, I would have asked: How you getting on, David? And likely he answered, Good, before one of us hurried out of the room.

Funerals descend in a similar sequence regardless of whether you are a member of the deceased's family, or have just rocked up to pay your respects: you shake a lot of hands, you listen keenly and encouragingly if someone speaks, you nod a bit. Sure, there are a couple of bonuses if you are part of the deceased's family – speeches, front row pews, no guilt if you laugh – but, by and large, it is the same for everyone bar the priest and, of course, the dead. So, you know the drill. We cried, we stood stoically, we held out our hands, we prayed when it was time to pray, and afterward, we ate catered curry at David's house, and at a Granny-approved seaside restaurant for Grandad.

I visited Grandad on rarer and rarer occasions when he was in the nursing home. It was too hard. It was too miserable. I did not want to remember him like that. This is what I told my precious self. But also there was a tedium in visiting him. A sameness which brought apathy. Why go visit when it will be like last time? Why go visit when the man is happily unmoored? It was both boring and dispiriting.

Here is how it happened: David was at the piano. It was the 31st of August. It was the morning time. His mother was in another room. There was no one else at home. She heard a bang. An aneurysm ruptured around David's gut and in a blink of an eye, in the pressing of a key, blood pooled into his stomach cavity, and from this trauma, from the lack of flowing blood, there was cardiac arrest and he was no longer.

Here is what I will never know: What was he thinking about as he played the piano? Did he feel any discomfort? Was there a moment of reflection and realisation before his body stopped? Was he frightened? Was David as happy and fulfilled and content as he could be as he sat by the piano that late summer morning?

In their last year living together in the house, their home since 1988, Granny had come to resent her husband. She was frustrated by him. She had no patience. I recall her animated and noisy – traits I do not typically associate with my bookish, sharp grandmother – in the kitchen as she explained to Mam how she was at the end of her rope. That he had to be moved into a nursing home today. She was sick of it. She could not deal with that man anymore. As this was taking place, Grandad was sitting in the front room. There was a decent chance he could hear this eruption from down the hall though it was unlikely he could understand. It was painful to witness this, to see the true cost, and it doubly stung because we all recognised that Grandad's time at home was coming to an end. Regardless of Granny's wishes, his departure was inevitable, but we craved to pretend a while longer yet. It was all a mess. Objectively, Granny was, in her demands, her treatment of Grandad, cruel and heartless that day, but it was not at all hard to understand why or to sympathise or to concur.

By then, Grandad was tough to manage. Mood swings, babyish pranks, strops. He'd wear you down – physically, emotionally. On an average day, I only helped in small ways but still it wrung me out completely. Beside the all-encompassing exhaustion of caring for someone with deepening dementia, I cannot imagine how mean it must have felt to wake each morning and confront anew the fact of your husband being undone methodically, crudely, in front of you. For all your piled-up decades to fade to dust in standard time. Granny did not stop loving Grandad: he simply passed away from her long before he did from us.

In A Grief Observed, C.S. Lewis remarks that no one informed him grief 'felt so like fear'. I'm not sure I was scared in the immediate aftermath of either death, but I am certain I did my best to not face up to grief and, more or less, sought to bypass it altogether due to fear. I was numb after David's death and this indifference arose not only because of the senseless waste of an eighteen-year-old's life, or because of brief nihilistic aftershocks, but because I was ashamed of how carelessly I valued my own life. In the wake of David's passing, my own fraternizing with suicide – however theoretical rather than practical – was suddenly so wrong and selfish and disrespectful to David, and, in response to this newfound perspective, I switched off the self-critical part of my brain which had considered it, and for a long while, I never sought to flick it on again. I paralyzed my brain because I was fearful of what I might unearth if I waded clumsily into its nets and traps. Grandad's death allowed this stupefied condition to continue. I tried and largely succeeded in ignoring certain passes and loops in my memory which might lead me to think obsessively about Grandad and David. I kept a distance from the depths that could have led to a release of some kind. And in doing this, I lost interest in everything and casually, boringly, I lumbered through the nothing days. I did not write seriously. I did not read. Man Utd no longer ruled my weekends. I worked a job I despised. I harmed personal relationships. And when I could not duck and weave from grief and its mirrors, when I was struck unexpectedly from a blow outside my controlled and deadened self, I found myself crumpled and weeping and blinking hard at the wall for hours, and then I would rise up and paw at my snotty cheeks, disregard the collapse, mark it a secret, and suppress it all once more.

I'd like to be able to say I solved this numbness through miraculous insight brought about by a spiritual awakening, or a therapeutic pilgrimage which plucked my unseen demons or, even better, by the disciplined writing of this essay. But I can't. I hobbled along and eventually, with knowing and unknowing help from friends and family, I allowed myself to think about it, and this enabled me to move past it and, finally, to see it – depression? grief? – for what it was, or what I was in relation to it. What was so large was one's own shadow, et cetera. There was no bright epiphany. No rhyme or reason. It did not make sense how I overcame it. It does not make sense that David died. It does not make sense that Grandad should have fallen apart in the way he did. That's life.

Grandad was informed about David's death by my father. His mind was totally scrambled by then. He didn't seem to know who David was – he no longer comprehended the innate connections between himself and anybody else at this point – but, afterwards, sitting in the living room, his feet shuffling, he commented upon a nearby photograph of David. With a wheeling finger, he gestured at the photo and said, The poor lad. No one had to steer him. Naturally, he empathised. Over the course of the weekend his grandson was buried, he would repeat this line. The poor lad.

DADDY

Oisín Fagan

There is no one waiting for her at the bus stop. Dara glances at her phone, shading her eyes to see the screen. The family WhatsApp is silent, and her mother, Ruth, has left the last eight messages unseen. She examines the time-table on the post box. It is a sheet of yellowing paper stuck in a plastic folder; moss grows there in small islands where rain has leaked in. The bus arrives at 9:47, 15:12, 15:58, 21:02. After twenty minutes of waiting, she begins to roll her suitcase along the backroads, carrying it onto the grass verge whenever a car passes. Over the two hour walk, most of which is uphill, three people offer her a lift. She should remember the second woman's name; it is the mother of Áoife Madden, who was a year above her in school.

I like the walk, she says.

There are burrs on her tights, sweat on her back. Her wrist is sore from the bounce of the suitcase. A swarm of midges circles her head, and a butterfly drifts repeatedly against the windshield. The Madden woman smiles and there is a quiet sympathy in her look which annoys Dara; she returns the smile.

By the time she gets home the sweat has gone through her underwear and even the cuffs of her blazer are moist. The laurel hedge that hides the house is now almost three metres high, so heavy it looks like it might topple over at any moment. When she goes around the back she sees her father's face in side-profile in the kitchen window. The room is unlit, and his cheeks are the sole bright point in the room, his skin starkly pale under his dark beard and hair. Though he is looking at nothing, his eyes are angry. He sees her and frowns, disappears from the window, and then the back door opens. He stands there in an open dressing gown, wearing only grey briefs beneath. His beard is huge and he is so skinny she hesitates before coming any closer. He looks like a skinned wolf, and emaciation has enlarged his eyes.

What are you doing here, Dar? Cian says. Did your mother tell you to come?

It's the May bank holiday, Dad.

Oh, is it?

Why haven't you checked your phone?

Got rid of it, he says. That's a lot of luggage for one weekend.

A taut swelling in the lower half of his belly looks like something trying to escape from him, and she tries not to stare at it. She hauls her suitcase in, kisses him on the cheek. He smells like he always did; like autumn smoke and wet plants, but when her lips come in contact with his cheek she feels like she can taste the skull.

Just my work things, she says, her voice cheerful. I might have to make some video calls in the evening. Where's Mam?

Don't know, he says. Greenhouse, probably. I don't know where that woman goes.

She hauls her suitcase into the kitchen and then walks down the garden and into the greenhouse where her mother is watering the beds, her thumb over the mouth of the hose so the water fans over the soil, rainbows flashing and disappearing into the earth.

Dara, Ruth says, and there is an unburdening in the saying of her daughter's name that makes Dara feel dizzy. She looks for something to lean against, but there is only the plastic sheet slapping against the concave metal poles. It is too hot. The waft of the wet soil is making her nauseous.

It's impossible, Dara says. He needs to go to hospital.

I have to turn off the hose, Ruth says. Sit down.

She points to a rocking chair at the end of the greenhouse. Cian made it ten years ago with intentionally long bands so that sitting on it feels more akin to being on an amusement park ride than sitting on a chair. It is one of the many practical jokes he has sewn into the fabric of their lives.

The hose turns down to a drip. A little later her mother comes back in, smoking a cigarette.

We can't stay out too long or he'll get suspicious, she says.

He has to go to hospital, Dara says again.

You've gotten a shock, she says. It's very difficult, but this is the way it is.

So we just have to watch, Dara says. For how long? A day, a week, a month?

You don't have to watch, baby.

When they come back into the kitchen the lights are still off and every cupboard is open. Cian has closed over his dressing gown and is smoking in the conservatory, a cup of black tea in his right hand. He built the conservatory when Ruth said she wanted to stop smoking, but she only managed to quit for five months. For a while, though, they both only smoked in the conservatory, but now Dara sees half-filled ceramic ashtrays on nearly every countertop.

Is it just yourself, he says to Dara. Or should I be expecting all my progeny?

Just me.

He nods and drinks off the tea in three long gulps.

Are the cherry tomatoes ready, darling? he asks Ruth.

She nods.

Very nice, he says. We'll use them tonight.

They talk about the upcoming referendum for a while, both her parents more astonished than angry at what is happening. At one point, there is a gurgling noise, like a cat's cough, but so brief Dara wonders if she has imagined it. She looks around the room and sees nothing that could have caused such a sound. Her father is still in the chair, rolling another cigarette, but next to him the mug is full of tea again, though she is certain he finished it. The pot is still next to her on the table. She goes over to the sink, supposedly so as to wash her hands, and sees the surface of the tea has a certain viscosity to it, like petrol spilled on the sea, and she realises what has happened. Trying not to change her expression, she goes back to her chair, but he is staring at her now, brazenly, his huge eyes challenging her. He gets up and throws the tea out in the sink.

Dinner in an hour, he says. I'm cooking.

Cian, Ruth says. The word is brief, flat.

Chicken chorizo pasta, he smiles. Dar's favourite. Cherry tomatoes, to boot.

Thanks, Dara says.

I'm cleaning out Pat's room tomorrow before I fix the shingles, he says. Will you help me with the dresser and cupboard, Dar? You know, with your mother's neck, and all.

Of course, she nods.

She showers, and then tries to connect to the wifi, but the signal is too intermittent so she tethers her laptop to her mobile and sets up an invite for a Skype with her siblings, scheduling it for the next day at six o'clock. Immediately, Niamh is video-calling her, her image pulsing against the screen, and Dara answers, accidentally accepting the video as well as the call.

What is it? Niamh asks. Now. Tell me now.

It's bad.

Niamh's face disappears and Dara is left staring at a white empty room on screen for a while. She wraps a towel around her head, and waits, her bare arms getting cold.

How long? Niamh asks, before she has appeared again.

Weeks? I don't know.

Should I come?

I don't know.

I'll come.

Do you need help with flights?

Niamh appears on screen again. Too close to the camera, her face is huge. No, she says. I don't, but offer Sorcha.

Okay, but I want you to tell her, and I want you to talk to her and Pat. If they ask any questions just tell them I don't know anything else. I don't.

There is a knock on the door, and Dara jumps with fright.

Dinner in five, her dad says in a sing-song voice.

She didn't hear any footsteps, and wonders if he has been waiting outside.

I'm naked, she calls.

She waits until she can hear him walking down the hall, then shuts the laptop and puts on a tracksuit.

On the kitchen table, there is a vase of wildflowers, whites, purples and greens arranged together; the centrepiece is a dangling, old-fashioned rose that looks like it's about to fall apart. It sits next to a black candleholder, gothic and curved, in which are planted three candles. Cian is still in his dressing gown, but now he is wearing a huge chef's hat, which he puts on whenever Dara visits because it annoys her so much. He is smoking a cigarette, stirring a saucepan over the cooker.

Sit down, he says, with a wave of his arm.

At her place, there is a little platter of pitted olives, thin slices of spicy chorizo, a wedge of Manchego cheese. Whenever her mother gets drunk, she talks about falling in love with Cian because she had never met any man who knew so much about food, who had learned so much about plants, herbs, spices, soils, natural medicines. Dara eats an olive and it reminds her of summer holidays, cycling with her father in seaside towns, the salt on the wind.

Your mother has opened a white, he says, but I've put two small beers in the freezer for you.

There is a floating ember glow in the conservatory and she notices her mother out there, smoking in silence.

It's ready, he calls.

He ladles the pasta onto three plates, gestures towards the parmesan and the grater on the table. Dara pulls a beer from the freezer. They all take their places. Cian sits down last, at the head of the table. Steam from the freshly served meal billows up in his face. He raises a glass –

Here I sit, he says. The patriarch; lord of the manor, ruler of all I survey, the last surviving member of the Fourth International. Comandante Lynch, suppressed leader of a ravaged global proletariat. Multilingual lover to a thousand heiresses, father to a million children. Death to the CIA, the MI5, the FAI, the IFA and the IOU.

He takes a sip of wine, tosses his head slightly to the side so his chef's hat crumples, and then glances out the corner of his eye to see if Dara is laughing. She bites down a smile, but Ruth is covering her face with her hands, and her lips are moving. For a moment Dara thinks her mother is praying.

I don't want this, Ruth says.

Eat up, my darling, he says. I like you nice and plump.

Ruth and Dara eat their meals slowly, Dara shaving parmesan and crunching pepper on nearly every forkful. For a while Cian just drinks his wine and smokes a cigarette leisurely before putting it out, half-spent, in the hollow of his pasta spoon. Over the candlelight, he sits, watching his wife and daughter eat, and then he picks up his cutlery.

Well, he says.

Ruth stops eating and looks at her plate. He twirls a forkful of linguine around till it is tightly wound and then swallows it whole, chewing perhaps only twice. Raising his eyebrows, he nods in appreciation, and soon he is eating ravenously, his head low over the plate, his beard brushing off the tablecloth. This goes on for maybe half a minute, and then he puts the fork down and sits up straight.

Fuck, he says.

In one long stream, he vomits everything he's eaten back onto the plate, the consistency of the pasta and sauce barely changed, though slightly discoloured by the wine. Dara and her mother draw back their chairs and shoot up to escape the splatter. Cian creases his face in annoyance; there are two long threads of pasta and half a tomato in his beard.

Daddy, Dara says.

Bedtime, Dar, he says.

What?

Bedtime, Dar, he says. It's well past your bedtime.

Yes, baby, Ruth says. Go to bed.

Her father has taken the half-smoked cigarette and is relighting it off one of the candles. Dara goes to her bedroom and sits on the edge of the bed, waiting until all the noise in the house has stopped.

When she returns to the kitchen an hour later all traces of the dinner are gone. The lights are on; the dishwasher is running. A part of the floor is swiped dark from where her mother has mopped up. The candles have been extinguished. The wooden clock ticks loudly on the wall, but its big hand isn't moving. The digital clock on the cooker flashes 20:11. Dara pulls a second beer from the freezer and opens it; it is nearly entirely frozen, and vapour spills out over the edge and little tubes of yellow ice pulse out of the green rim that she catches with her mouth.

He's gone to bed, Ruth says, standing in the doorway. Let's watch something.

By the time Dara has picked a comedy show on Netflix, Ruth has fallen asleep on the couch. Her head is back, her mouth slightly open, and a little crescent of white remains visible under her closed eyelids. Dara looks at her, and sees in her mother's unguarded expression something that terrifies her.

Leaving the TV on so as not to disturb her, she sneaks out to the conservatory where she takes one of Ruth's Native American Spirits from the packet and then she goes to the backroom. She looks inside the glasses bin and sees forty or so green bottles of Jameson, along with the occasional empty bottle of white wine. She has expected this, but what surprises her is that so many of the bottles are still half-full, some even three-quarters full, and she understands that her father has been regurgitating whiskey right back into their original bottles, perhaps as fast as he can manage to drink it. There is an opened cardboard box of Corona next to the washing machine, next to several stacks of old newspaper. She takes another beer, and then, on a whim, moves one of the stacks of newspaper and finds they are covering several more stacked baskets of half-drunk Jameson.

She goes out the back door, and pretends to herself to be smoking the unlit cigarette, inhaling, tapping imaginary ash off the end, blowing air out her nose. The stars are bright and the greenhouse at the bottom of the garden reflects brightly the moonlight. A sheep in the bottom field bleats sadly. Dara goes back inside and places the American Spirit back in its packet. When she goes back into the sitting room, her mother jolts awake and smiles at her, delighted to see her daughter.

Bedtime for me, Dar, she says, reaching out and holding her hand.

Dara drinks four more beers in the sitting room until she can neither follow what is happening on TV, nor on her phone. She is glancing between the two screens too often, and it is only when huge noises awaken her in the next room that she realises she has fallen asleep on the couch.

She is shivering with cold. The TV is still playing, and her phone says it is 23:57. Out in the hall, she sees a dresser emerging from Pat's room. Then she sees her father behind it, sweating, and she doesn't know how such a diminished man has remained so strong.

What are you doing?

Cleaning up.

She turns on the hall light and he covers his face with his forearm.

Off, off.

That's Pat's, she says.

Turn it off, he shouts.

She does and he shuffles around in his dressing gown pocket for a cigarette. In the flame of the lighter, she sees his left eye is half-closed and so red it makes her own eyes water.

Where's Mam? she asks.

I told them to clear their stuff out. I won't be held responsible anymore.

He touches the dresser fondly, and then disappears down the hall. Dara, still dazed from sleep and beer, follows him, and when she gets into the kitchen, she sees through the conservatory window her mother, lit up by moonlight, carrying a cardboard box, trying to kick a pile apart in the middle of the garden. Dara steps out the back door, and the first thing she notices is the stench of petrol.

Out of my way, Cian says.

Ruth, clasping the box to her chest, stands between Cian and a random assortment of items belonging to the children; she sees one of Pat's intercounty medals, some of Sorcha's denims, a drawer, a lamp, some of Niamh's old fantasy books. The rest she cannot make out.

Ruth, Cian says, my darling, you are going to get hurt. All burnt up with nowhere to go.

Stop. Go inside.

You're being unreasonable, he says.

He moves around her and throws his cigarette on the pile. Flames bloom up, and the hem of his dressing gown catches fire. Laughing, he takes it off, stamping on it in his slippers. He stands naked in the moonlight, skeletal and silver, the knobs of his spine visible against the curve of his back, looking over his shoulder at Dar.

I've figured it out, he tells her.

He looks like one of those faeries he used to describe to her and Niamh at bedtime. Nothing gave her more pleasure as a child than his terrifying her, and now she wonders if all this is just another portion of his wonder, his endless fun.

Figured what? she asks.

The fire is blackening some of the lower leaves on the chestnut tree. He picks up his dressing gown, shakes it out and puts it on. It is still smoking around the hem. He goes over to the tree and pulls a bottle of whiskey from out of the hollow. He unscrews the cap, tosses it on the fire, and then with his middle and forefinger he forces his left eye wide and presses the rim against his eye.

One doesn't get sick, he says, in a posh British accent, if one indulges one's thirst in a more, how shall I put it, a more ocular fashion.

Ruth goes into the conservatory and smokes alone in the dark while Dara waits out with her father who drinks from his eye every now and again, looking at the fire, laughing to himself occasionally. When the fire gets lower, glowing a deeper orange, he slouches against the tree, suddenly looking confused and lost.

Daddy? she asks.

Nothing, baby, he says. That's enough of that now.

The next day Dara stays in her bedroom until she is sure she can hear her mother's footsteps in the kitchen.

I'm doing the big shop, Ruth says, drinking a cup of coffee.

Will I come?

Stay here with him.

What am I supposed to do?

Just be with him.

But what do I do?

Sit there with a book, or your phone. He won't need anything. He doesn't get up until evening, usually.

Once she has seen her mother out, Dara checks the garden. There is a burnt patch, rimmed by a halo of crisp, brown grass. No other trace of the fire remains except for some blackness on the trunk of the chestnut tree, shining like treacle. Her mother has even cut back some of the scorched, lower branches. Clothes flap on the rotary clothes line, the pole held up by half a breeze block. It is only her mother's clothes there, she notices.

She stands outside her parents' bedroom door for a long time. Eventually she opens it, and sees everything is as she remembers. The carpet is rich green laced with threads of gold; the walls are covered in a dark pink wallpaper. In front of a dressing table sits a small cushioned stool with two drawers built into it. Horsetails hang down from hooks above the window; three pots of sage sit below them on the sill. Outside the glass, a blackthorn hedge bounces up and down in the wind like a jockey. On the nightstand, lies a vase of five late daffodils, and a pile of old paperbacks. The earthy smell of the room, mixed with her mother's perfume, is overpowering, and Dara wishes she could open a window, but she is afraid of waking him.

He is sitting up in the bed, the duvet covering only his lower half. His chest is naked; his skin, against the white sheets, looks jaundiced. He has a slightly wet appearance; Ruth has washed him, rubbed Vicks on his chest, oiled his beard, and spread a sheen of Vaseline across his lips and eyelids. His hands lie outside the blanket, palms facing upwards. The eyes are closed, the mouth half-opened and his teeth seem as long as a horse's, blackly rimmed, the gums receded to almost nothing. His face seems enormous atop the diminished neck, but what scares Dara most is the unrelenting vigour of his hair and beard, which throws into relief the decimation of his muscle, the thinness of his skin. Each breath against his small frame seems a huge rumble inside him, and there are little whistles from his nostrils, producing strange shudders in his throat. If he were to wake up and ask her for a kiss, Dara thinks she would be too scared to touch him, but she knows he would never ask this.

He draws a deep breath and opens his eyes and immediately they become the focal point of the room. He lifts his lips at her and snarls, and she realises, a moment too late to disguise her fear, that this is his smile now.

I always know when it's you, Dar, he says, but you don't always know when it's me. Do you remember, you were four, maybe not even, I shaved my beard and you didn't recognise me. You ran away and hid down Burke's field. You wouldn't speak to me for a week and you didn't let me carry you until it grew back.

She forces herself to sit on the stool, facing him.

You're such a mad bastard, Dad, she says.

He laughs happily.

You know this is mental, she says. All this. All this sickness, all this secrecy, all this everything.

Sure we're the same, he says. You and me. Pat a bit, yeah. But, mainly, it's just you and me. The others don't see it.

Dad, she says. You're fucking crazy. This can't happen; it just can't. You're like a dying wolf or something with your little stick body and your big head. I've never seen anything like this.

Her father draws up the blanket so it is covering his mouth and nose. He darts his eyes from side to side.

All the better to eat you with, he says.

What about Mam? she asks.

He drops the blanket down over his waist, and smiles again, but even more tiredly this time, resting his head against the backboard.

The big secret she keeps from all you sprogs is that she agrees with me, all the way. And so do you, Dar.

Dara turns away, looking out the window.

You could just see a doctor and not be fucking crazy, she says.

He sticks out his tongue, rolls his eyes back, rotates his head like someone in a cartoon trance. When she doesn't laugh or even smile, he stops and waits, staring at her, but she won't look back.

Try not to worry, baby, he says.

Her throat is sore from not crying; it feels the same way it used to after those parties where she'd be in someone's room for four or five days, smoking cigarettes and drinking, keeping herself awake with cocaine and pills. Soon, he closes his eyes. His breath slows down, his head falls to the side, his nostrils begin whistling again.

When her mother returns, she helps her bring the shopping in.

Well, she asks, did he wake up?

Whatever has been building up inside of Dara breaks and she is sobbing, covering her eyes with her fists.

He's starving to death.

Ruth goes to her, arms outstretched.

Don't touch me, Dara says. You're worse.

We should go out to the greenhouse if you want to talk, she says.

After about a minute of crying, Dara catches herself.

How long have you been doing this? she asks. You've quit your job, haven't you?

Ruth doesn't answer. Dara takes out her phone, and thumbs in the pin.

I'm calling an ambulance, she says. I won't be a part of this.

Ruth shakes her head. It's not your choice, baby. He wants to be with me, here.

What if it makes a difference, though. What, then?

It's too late, Dar.

I'm calling them, she says.

She has to unlock her phone again, the screen has gone black. She taps in the wrong pin three times and has to wait some more, and staring at her phone she realises that although she has been anticipating this moment for most of her life she still doesn't know what to do.

Then, as always, her father surprises her. Light as a bird, he steals into the room, his burnt dressing gown flapping around him, pulls open a drawer and starts rooting around.

What are you doing? Ruth asks.

I'm not going, he says. One thing I've asked. One thing. Plotting against me in my own house. Sick of it.

Daddy, Dara says.

He pulls out a set of house keys.

Put morphine in me, pump me full of chemicals, he yells, so I can't feel it. So I can't see my mother when I go, nor Jamie, nor Mary. They took Mary, and you'd put me in there with those bastards? Harvest my organs for rich Americans; put me in a vat with foetuses; fuck cotton into me so I'm closed-off, bury me under concrete in a graveyard run by fucking paedophiles. They stole children from their mothers. And that's what ye'd have? What are ye fucking doing to me?

Stop it, Cian, Ruth says.

A change comes over his features, a type of realisation. He stares at nothing, holding a key for the front door between his forefinger and thumb.

I've had enough, he says. That's all. Look, I'm sorry I shouted, but it's time ye left. I need a bit of headspace.

And then he is shepherding them out the corridor, decisive and soothing, leading them out the front door. Dara doesn't know what is happening until she is almost outside, and then he is locking the door, and Ruth and Dara are outside. Momentarily, the two women are speechless.

The back, Ruth says.

Dara runs around to the back door, just in time to hear it locking. Then, from the backroom, her father says, Oh no, Jesus no, and it is the worst sound she has ever heard. He keeps repeating it, though it becomes more muffled as he walks away inside. She reaches for her phone, but somehow it has been left inside. She goes over to the conservatory and sees it on the kitchen table, along with the shopping bags. She scans the sides of the house; all the windows are shut. She sees him there, standing between the conservatory and the kitchen. He is baffled, leaning against the wall, and then he looks directly into her eyes.

He begins vomiting black stuff silently behind the glass. It is a glistening liquid, not blood and not bile. She has never seen anything like it. It is coming out of his mouth and his nose, and he's crying. He falls to his knees and clutches at the door frame. He is getting sick for so long she doesn't know how anyone so small could be so full, and she is transfixed, but what brings her back to herself is not her mother beside her, but her father looking up at her before lowering his head again. He is still completely lucid, she realises.

It is happening now, she says.

She knocks over the washing line and drags out the half a breeze block from its base and carries it back towards the conservatory and swings it against the glass. The block bounces back and almost lands on her feet. The window is only cracked. She does it again and this time the glass collapses in a shower of blue hailstones and she climbs through the window. Her father sees her coming towards him and his eyes are illuminated with fear. He tries to escape her by crawling away into the kitchen, but he slips on the black stuff and smashes his side against the door, and falls flat on his front. When she reaches him she flips him over and holds him in her arms.

Look at me, Daddy, she says. I'm here.

He tries to flail away, like a trapped animal, still gurgling black stuff from his throat. It is all over his chest and beard. She wipes some of it away, and then sees his hair is covered in blood, and she wonders if he banged his head in the fall, but then she realises it is her hands that are bleeding from the broken glass, matting his hair with blood. He manages to turn on his side and only now does he start vomiting blood, bright and red, across her lap. There is no force to it. It trickles out his mouth, across his cheek and drips down onto her. His eyes are alive, and they go from side to side between Dara and Ruth, who is inside the house now, on the phone, speaking to someone. His chest rises and falls; a popping liquid sound gurgles in his nose. His eyes go up in their head in an effort to look at Ruth again and then the knowledge leaves them.

Let me have him, her mother is saying, standing above her, and it takes all Dara's courage to kiss what is left of her father on the forehead. Ruth sits down next to her on the floor, and Dara slides her father over, and then she sits on one of the kitchen chairs, looking at the stains on her tracksuit, feeling very annoyed with herself because she forgot to say she loved him.

Fuck, she says. It's so fucking disgusting. I was supposed to tell him, but once I was there it was so fucking disgusting.

Ruth doesn't answer; she is whispering something into Cian's ear. The front door is open, Dara can see it from over the top of the shopping bags. For a moment she thinks he has opened the door, and is coming in from work, peeling off his boots and overalls. It is one of his tricks, she thinks, but he is still lying in Ruth's arms, breathing wetly, his face turned into her lap. Two paramedics have come in the door, an older woman and a younger man, and Dara stands up and shakes the woman's hand. Neither are taken aback by this, or by the black shining liquid everywhere, streaked brown and thin where her father had tried to crawl away. They check her father's vital signs, shine a light in his eye, arrange him flat on a stretcher, strap him down, clean his orifices with antiseptic wipes and intubate him, the older woman speaking discreetly into a headpiece all the while.

When he is carried into the ambulance, Ruth climbs up next to him, puts on her safety belt and tries to reach for his hand, but can't with the pull of the strap against her shoulder.

I have to stay and clean up, Dara says, standing beside the mechanical ramp.

Her mother is looking at the tube in Cian's mouth.

That can wait, the woman paramedic says. Come along.

She stretches out her hand and, in response, Dara folds her arms.

I broke a window, she says. Someone might get in.

Is there anyone who could stay with you now? the paramedic says.

I don't need any help.

I'll call Julia, Ruth says, suddenly paying attention.

When they load the ramp and close the door Dara can see herself reflected in the back window, covered in black stains and blood. The ambulance disappears behind the laurel, the red and blue light flashing off the leaves without sound, and she goes back into the kitchen.

The shopping bags are still lying on the table. The black stuff on the floor is becoming hard. The flower pots outside the conservatory are reflected in parts in the shards of blue glass. His slippers are beside the chair in the conservatory, his pack of tobacco lies open on the table. The clock is very loud, but she does not check the time. She fills up the bucket with water and washing-up liquid, wrings the mop in it, and then leans on the handle for a long time, looking out at the garden.

Hello? someone says from the corridor.

It is the woman who offered her the lift yesterday. She and her daughter, Áoife, are standing in front of the open door, looking around, carrying bags of cleaning products. The woman is already wearing rubber gloves, Dara notices. Before they spot her, she slips out the back door, out to the garden, running low so it is less likely she will be seen. She passes the greenhouse, hops the wall, and then crawls under the electric fence and sprints across three fields until she comes to a hollow she doesn't recognise.

A herd of bullocks have noticed her. Tails wagging and chewing their cud, they converge around her. Devil's bread and nettles sway at waist height, blue-bells and mayflowers shine up at her, and the smell of it all is stifling in its sweetness. A tree shades her, its name she can't remember, its every branch is almost entirely hidden by clusters of small, white flowers. Dandelion clocks have exploded around their own stems, covering the hoof-printed dirt in webbed bunches of feathery seeds. Looking down at her hands, she realises she is holding a mop. She closes her eyes, and, still, she sees him. It is a moment of calm, strange as anything she has ever felt.

I KNOW, BUT ONLY JUST

Claire-Louise Bennett and Ruby Wallis

snakes and ugly creatures · multiple locked vessels within me · you gasped you grasped · nature's revenge

loss · forgo the apple · unleashed · spinning out of control · I catch a glimpse · cacophonous sounds

a strange dark room · mother-of-pearl · shopping list ticked · uncharted territory fear sometimes beauty · back to the shadowlands

a whirlwind · Never open · spill · shine a light · flashing eyes · SECRET · there are very few landmarks · a world of trouble · your all too human hands

a shiny apple · carefully folded · a world · anything at all · fantastic · open · delve · freefall · stop crying · literally anything that someone else needed

trying to · Here Be Dragons · a stirred hornet's nest · Mexico City · grassland houses and hills · her vagina · all trailed their desperate coloured tails

a huge pocket · undoubtedly nice interiors · a pair of trousers · first peek · rage and jealousy · standing on a log · rusty nails · façade · infancy

keep the box closed · breath · she opens her legs · freefall into the void · dances too freely · between lavender and tissue paper · faint whiff

we're all in there · purple smoke · suffering and illness · flapping by the wind · silver lining · those bracelets · four bald smiling figures

worst nightmares · memories of the · imagination · gorgeous sumptuous · binary · never look · god knows why · crudest clearest sense

multiplying on the coffee tale · pile of corpses · personal information · layers · upon layers · without risk · unravels · conceive

the exact opposite · unconscious · looking into this abyss · the whiff of evil power · wellspring · she lives within me · out flew

she enters a room · HER · keeps nothing · read about it · layers · much bigger than that · extremely discounted shoes · no way of closing it

a massive black one · peering out · tools · brilliant and sparkly · bated · layered · contours · dust them off · a can of worms · the first place

every · song awaits · toolbox · hummus · defining feature · imposed order · kicked out · cursed be

the maw of hell · squared off over the centuries

☾

I look around my flat and I see boxes, dozens of boxes

cuttings, photograph, 21.0 × 29.7cm, 2020

Þ

The first morning of the world is brilliant and sparkly, dazzled by its own newness. All of creation awaits their naming. A hush falls – the bated breath of the divine – and a box is opened. From it emerge cacophonous sounds: of a storm, or a stirred hornet's nest, of chaos and catastrophe. With that first peek into unforeseeable contents, the infancy of humanity ceases

ɜ

Adventurers leave their homes, which made them, to find these unmapped places and face dragons and monsters – they face their own fear

ɰ

I had Pandora in my head so I started to wonder if she had a box. And if she did what colour it might be. I decided pink like her cardigan. And gave it flaps

Ọ

God knows why, but a whirlwind of purple smoke engulfing a landscape which settles over everything – grassland, houses and hills

Ф

I remember the first time I heard the term Pandora's Box, I was pretty young, and someone, I can't remember who now, said it to me sort of vaguely, we were both standing on a log in the countryside somewhere

splittings, photomontage, 22 cm × 8 cm, 2020

Þ

Who opened the box, releasing negative forces into the world?

♱

It's the Ark of Covenant stored away in a warehouse. It's in the box at the very back of the top of the wardrobe in your parent's bedroom. It's what Freud would say about that. It's Tutankhamun's tomb. It's a bunker in Switzerland

ω

All the gifts Zeus never wanted, he put in the box he gave to you

Along with the blame passed on to you, the woman, created for the task, by a male pantheon

∍

Some things you should not look at because they ruin your happiness

π

And that's what it is isn't it? Another of these classic myths that through the centuries of sexism boils down to 'curious lady dooms humanity'. Cursed be she who questions the imposed order even if it doesn't really make a lick of sense

α

Pandora, Cassandra, Jocasta, Medea. We know them but we don't know how we know them. But we intuit that somehow they are bad...else their names would not still live

Ж

I am not familiar with the myth

I am aware that Pandora was depicted as a beautiful woman. I learned this from reading The Beauty Myth by Naomi Wolf

Ђ I'd like to associate that box with the hope that Pandora finds at the bottom of the box once all the rage and jealousy and disease has made its escape Ћ My question is, why was this box so easily opened in the first place? It seems to be a bit of a set-up. If you want to keep your afflictions locked up, perhaps it's better to find something less accessible? Ќ It evokes memories of the imagination that I had, for I believed that the box contained pretty jewels and things of great Beauty, that Pandora could perhaps open the box and find whatever she was looking for, anything at all Ђ Pandora's box has a magical quality and always has had from when I was a child Ф I always found something about the words Pandora's box a bit irritating, maybe I don't like the name Pandora, or else I'm irritated by the vagueness of the possibilities of what it means Ж I remember when I read that book thinking, why is it always women who are depicted as wreaking disaster – Eve in the bible for instance – when in fact decisions made by men have caused more sorrow and pain to humanity than women α When she opens her legs – annihilation Қ I used to wish that I could fix all problems and it took the form of a pair of trousers with a huge pocket in which there were tools and literally anything that someone else needed – to make them happy – and that I could do this. I didn't call them my Pandora Pantalones but they could have been that Ȣ When I think of Pandora's Box I don't think of the myth, I think of the iconic silent film from the 1920s. In my mind's eye I see Lulu peering out from her monochrome screen world Ƃ A disruption in the façade of the normal Є Berlin, Mexico City, London Ќ A Myth to my young mind was little more than a fairy story, a story which I changed to make me feel happy whenever I thought about it ѡ Horrors, nightmares, tempests, curses, plagues, pestilence, war, disasters ɘ The transmission of wisdom Ћ Choose the right container, casket, trunk, suitcase, coffin, urn, lunchbox, envelope, package, shipping container, safety deposit box, pocket, safe

handlings, photomontage, 22 cm × 8 cm, 2020

Ƨ

She is disarmingly naive when

she's not being entirely calculating

Ҟ

I know, but only just, that the box is meant to spill out problems

ә

My daughter Emer when asked about Pandora's Box told me it is an online
shop where she buys very pretty jewellery

α

For me the whiff of evil power associated with Pandora still sticks to those bracelets even though they are marketed as the exact opposite – girlie, desirable, collectable. I like when I catch a glimpse of one on the wrist of my niece. Hahaha, I think, you're out of your box!

Ф

I wonder about Pandora, who she was, was she young or old, and just what she opened up for herself and the world. I wonder whether she was punished for opening the box, or did she thrive from the wonders and lessons that the box opened, were they positive or negative lessons? Was she sorry she opened it?

З

Lulu is a simmering, smoldering, sexy, celluloid, screen siren. She is the embodiment of 1920s glamour with her slinky black bob, flashing eyes and carefree smile. But Lulu is a world of trouble

Д

Pandora is misunderstood and it's not Pandora's shop on Shop Street as my husband thinks

Щ

As silky as a slinky snake

She won't be boxed

In the next frame, she is home

feet up, tea cupped,

in a soothing ritual of rest

З

Men lose their minds, their willpower, their morals when they are around her

ҭ

If you find you don't care for this binary, could you accept that we already contain everything?

Д She is the rebellious disobedient one and someone to fear. She looked at her lovers head on you see. You look at her when she enters a room π I think an apt update would be lazy entitled bigoted man doesn't just open the box – he has the power to close it but chooses not to because it might slightly inconvenience him and besides – I mean – couldn't he use all the chaos caused by these plagues or scourges or whatever to his own benefit? ᴈ Pandora's box immediately makes me think of opening the door of a strange dark room Ọ A feeling of anticipation, excitement and wonder of the power within. A temptation with a fear of something prohibited and irreversible Ɛ You could say these unopened boxes are the 'what ifs' in my life. An arrangement of 'what ifs' arising from a fear of not being able to return the contents to their place. And so I keep them tightly shut, carrying them from home to home, unopened boxes multiplying on the coffee table Φ There was a very particular time in my life when the description opening Pandora's box fits perfectly. I'm not sure if there is an adequate word to describe the profound experiences that opened up and I was absolutely unready for. I longed to return back to the time before it all kicked off, but I couldn't, and I'll never forget the moment that I realised that I could never go back to the way I was before ᴈ This analogy of the dark room, uncertain ground, is something I have used to describe what it's like to venture into a new part of my psyche or emotional being, testing out new areas of feeling which are not straightforward or pleasant – it can be frightening, like looking into the abyss Ќ I was eventually to find out that my version belied the Myth surrounding Pandora's box, I found this entirely unsatisfactory ᴈ Without risk, there is no growth Φ The lessons have been incredibly deep and profound and have changed me forever π Stop crying about it already and find the silver lining to the mounting pile of corpses ɑ And of course that box in its crudest clearest sense is her vagina

 б

Some try and go back to where it was before the disruption,

some flow and thrive and are able to co-create a better world,

others get stuck in sadness, depression and doom

✝

Open and closed are opposites, but maybe they don't need to be

Д

I fear to let go of the tight grip I have on multiple locked vessels within me. A woman is not allowed to become hysterical. Keep a lid on it and all that

Ф

An opening up of something that cannot be put back to the way it was before, but an opening up of what? Something tremendous most likely, layers upon layers of new energies, experiences and emotions that perhaps we weren't ready for

Ҭ

Is that the doorbell? If it's your bad news letter, don't open it. It's in an email about the SECRET of how to lower your blood sugar. It's in a vial in a lab, quivering. Put a lid on it. This message seems dangerous. It's buried treasure. Similar messages were used to steal people's personal information. Is there truly a difference between inside and outside?

Ь

With Pandora's act, layers of complexity are added to the world. Human becoming is initiated by the loss of innocence; the contours of the self are known not just through love and joy, but also through suffering and illness

э

The unknown box is also the knower and the process of knowing

С

I bought it for fifteen pounds from an antiquarian in Camden passage

Ҳ

projections of others
Pandora keeps nothing in her box at all. It is full of the imagination and

Д

She lives within me

Ш

Don't shoot the messenger

Б

Shines a light

Є

(some are gifts from my mother)

Є Ь э Ш Q Ф Ҭ ω э п а Ж Ђ Ќ Ҕ Б 6 Д Ҳ

Chloe Phil Sarah Mary Louise Róisín Suzanne Ruth Áine Jessamyn Alice Mary Michal Karole Kate Sarah Anne Vicky Deborah

tearings, photomontage, 22 cm × 8 cm, 2020

foldings, photomontage, 36cm × 45cm, 2020

CLAIRE-LOUISE BENNETT | RUBY WALLIS

PAISANO

Tim MacGabhann

The dead are very close to the living, and I do not see them as separated by some frontier.
Victor Serge, World Without Possible Escape – Memoirs of a Revolutionary.

Things remained strange for me well into my first year off drugs and alcohol. I blame Mexico City. Huge and claustrophobic at the same time, the din, the cram, the heat, the brownish perma-shimmer of smog, all of these lend ordinary walks the lysergic urgency of a panic dream. Apart from going to NA meetings, I did most of my socialising on Sunday afternoons, when the volume on everything goes down about half a notch.

One such Sunday I was in the Centro, on a street whose name I can't remember – one of those gloomy rows of tezontle-stone apartments, their eaves like frowns, their stonework dried-blood red, quarried from the wreckage of Tenochtitlán's old temples and palaces, which were in turn made from stone hacked out of the long dark tongues of magma that swiped in over Cuicuilco in the fourth century AD, swallowing it forever, making the present city a matryoshka of wreckage, one ruin hidden inside the other, all the way to the core. The air was cool on my skin. There weren't any vendors yawping around the place. The thud of electrocumbias was at least three streets away. Trees swayed above a small park where a man lay on a bench, his beard like an old Brillo pad, his face ruddy with street-tan, his eyes the yellow of old cue balls as he watched a kid kick flies away from the eaten patches of pink around a mangy dog's arse.

I pressed the buzzer, which was set in a scrolled brass plaque inlaid with fasces, the old Porfiriato-era eagle rearing above the letters SPQM, the serpent flailing in its beak. I was there to meet a photographer I'd met on assignment in Oaxaca, covering a left-wing indigenous uprising that hadn't, in fact, wound up crushed by the police – this was a rare glimmer of hope during a presidential term when forty-three students had been disappeared, when protesting teachers could expect to be shot in the head, and when two of my friends, driven mad by the atmosphere of repression and despair, had vanished: one a probable suicide, the other a footsoldier in a Marxist group in Chiapas.

The uprising had settled down by the time I arrived in the village, early on the first of November. There were no direct buses from Mexico City except for the night route that left from the Fypsa terminal, out near the airport, in a warehouse of mildewed brick and blue neon. The people I was travelling with were going back home for Day of the Dead, fathers wearing padded flannel shirts over jeans, their work boots squeaking on the rain and muck and gravel tracked over the lino, mothers wearing hoodies over old-style floral skirts, kids giggling at phones or kicking their heels against the wooden benches. The names of the towns spelled out in white letters hooked onto the noticeboard looked like the names of mysterious painkillers: Xoxocotlan, Tecomavaca, Culiapám. The vehicle carrying us there was a repurposed US-style schoolbus, gleaming pale blue under the glare, lit drops of rain teeming down the bonnet. Inside the bus was a warm fug of rained-on wool and leather that made me think of the pubs of my childhood. People loaded net bags of onions and brand-new toasters and microwaves from Woolworths into the storage space above seats. The rocking of the bus on its suspension plus the stuffy air had me nodding off fairly quickly, whatever the speed we were going. I woke to a yellow-green sky and the squeak of brakes as our route coiled down towards the village at the bottom of the valley. When we stopped, a rain-loaded gust almost tackled me from the steps out of the bus, and further gusts pummelled me along the road to the town, over cobblestones as slick as the backs of bullfrogs, down a narrow maze of crumbling 19th-century tenements, their porticoes scrawled all over with red spray paint, spelling out words like RATEROS and FUERA CORRUPTOS and hung with anarcho-syndicalist flags. The alcaldía was in ruins, smashed glass lying in a snowy nap all over the square, old police files flapping in the wind like dirty seagulls, blackened and smashed desk chairs littering the square, burnt-out offices visible through the gaps where windows had been. The news said that the mayor had been allowed to leave the town unharmed, only for his car to go off the road on the tight bends above the valley, in an accident that nobody was going to say more about. Now quotes from Lenin and Flores Magón were spray-painted all over the toppled busts of Félix and Porfirio Díaz. Teenage kids had replaced the police, wearing red paliacates and black hoodies, some of them armed with old hunting rifles and shotguns. Rain pattered on orange-tiled roofs. Knee-high fog hung above cobbles that shone blue in the dark, turning the alleys into a network of caves, slick-walled and slippery and dark. Some of the buildings had that colonial look, dark stone, deep windows, but others were improvised things of stone and whitewash, some of them shops with sun-faded Coca-Cola and Victoria signs above the entryways. An old woman stood in a doorway across the road from me, chasing rain from the step with a broom made of dried palm. When she saw me she propped her broom against the wall and waved me over, gesturing to her mouth, miming that she was eating.

'I have to feed you,' she said, with a solemn blink. She must have been close to ninety. 'Tradition. At this time of year, you might be a ghost.' I saw gold-capped teeth with stars imprinted into them when she opened her mouth to talk. Over her shoulder, inside, a man in his fifties was sitting at her table, munching on a sweetbread. He toasted me with a clay cup.

I thanked the woman and let her walk me in. The house felt like a sea cave. A bowl of lit copal resin smoked under a Virgin of Guadalupe garlanded in orange sempasúchil flowers. The concrete floor was dark with recent scrubbing, the air thick with cocoa powder and soap suds.

The man sitting at the table put out a hand. He had a huge Nikon camera and a PRENSA lanyard around his neck. Stringy, tanned, with shaggy grey hair and a beard, he might have passed for one of those draft-dodging acid casual-ties still bouncing around every provincial town in the country.

He told me his name in Mexico City-accented English, then added, 'Nice to meet you, I'm sure.'

The old woman pulled a three-legged stool from under the table and gestured to it like a head waiter. I sat down beside the man and introduced myself.

'You're here for the whole pachanga with this uprising, then?' he said.

I told him I was, and he chuckled when I mentioned the outlet.

'The imperialist world service,' he said.

'Les tengo que alimentar,' the woman said again. Now she was lifting a wire rack loaded with cakes shaped like children.

'Who are you here for, then?' I asked. The woman handed me a cup of café de olla.

'Just myself,' he said. 'I come every year.' He thanked the woman and took a cake from the rack.

'Que coman, que coman,' she said, miming eating again until I broke off a leg, after which she nodded so hard that her long grey braids whapped her apron.

'Extranjero?' she said to me, then nodded and said, 'Su casa', gesturing around the smoky dark. Her wave took in a shelf above the hearth, where a band of skeleton mariachis made of clay serenaded some black and white photos: a dark-skinned Mexican man in a straw hat with a rifle, and an older black man with his arm around a woman I guessed was Chinese. Before the photos stood ceramic gee-gaws made to look like tacos and chicken drumsticks in a bowl of brown sauce.

'Su familia,' she said, pointing at the photo of the black man and his wife. 'Aquí son sus abuelos.'

'They take the "Mi casa su casa" seriously here, eh,' said Tona, around a second sweetbread. 'Even give you their grandparents.' He pulled off a leg of the skeleton. 'American?'

'Absolutely not. Irish.'

The leg of the skeleton stopped half way to his mouth, but then he nodded and bit into the leg, wagging a finger gently at me as he chewed.

'When you're back in the city,' he said, and swallowed, 'you should come meet my friend and I. We knew a paisano of yours once.' He held the other leg in his mouth while he took a business card from his wallet, wrote an address on the back of it, then drained his coffee, shook my hand, and thanked the old woman before stepping out to the street.

The rain had begun to ease, fog burning off and rising from the forested cliffs that made it seem as though the town was held in the palm of a rocky hand. The photographer continued towards the square, stopping to talk with a family spreading blankets and laying out their wares, crates holding wooden ornaments and mandarins and avocados and livid red tamarind sweets propped by their feet.

'Buen hombre,' the old woman said, nodding. If she hadn't said that, I'm not sure I'd have looked him up. I reached for my wallet to pay her, but she swatted me away, then handed me a tea towel leaking steam.

'Tamales de frijol,' she said, pulling back the towel on a bale of coffin-shaped parcels wrapped in corn leaves.

'You're spoiling me here,' I said.

'You could be dead for all I know,' she said, then accompanied me to the door and waved me off before resuming her sweeping.

An 'S' of smoke frayed up from inside the woman's house, following me out the door, the same shape as the gecko that skittered up the wall of the house that the photographer had sent me to. From inside I heard two voices and two pairs of feet approaching, and then the lock clicked open.

'There he is,' said the photographer, and pulled me in for a handshake. 'This is Oscar, the other friend of your paisano.'

'Pleased to meet you,' said the man standing behind him. He was around the same age as the photographer, but taller. He sounded like he was from the US. 'Come on in.'

'I'm pretty curious about this paisano of mine.' I followed them along the cracked tiles of the corridor. Oscar walked quickly, with a slight limp. The air smelled coolly of dust and vegetation from the overgrown courtyard garden, where huge ferns and banana leaves nodded in the dirty sun.

'It was Rory Gallagher,' said Oscar, and my foot caught on a loose edge of the stairs. A chip of pink ceramic went flying. The photographer steadied my elbow.

'That's impossible,' I said.

'You have two witnesses,' said the photographer.

'And proof,' said Oscar.

'1985,' said the photographer, as we began to climb again. 'Just after the earthquake. My parents had a guesthouse at this time. He stayed with us in San Rafael, near where Che and Fidel lived. There were lots of rock bars, cellar ones, near Monumento a la Revolución, and we got him playing in one. Ruta 61 it was called. Everything has to be a versión chafa of what they have in the US. Ruta 66 menos cinco. He made the house band sound like his. I don't think they knew who he was. I know he didn't die for another ten years but it looked like he was about to drop any second. He kept getting these fits where he'd have to lean against something, a pillar, a wall, a piece of furniture, the fingers of his other hand clawing in the soft of his middle. I asked him what was wrong once and he told me a story about a show he played where bombs were going off in the background. Eleven of them, counting down for New Year's Eve, boom, boom, boom, counting down to midnight. And how he was sure the twelfth would take the whole venue out. And how he just kept playing, because at least now he would die playing. And he told me that the twelfth bomb was in here.' The photographer tapped his belly. 'He said he could feel it ticking sometimes, counting down.' He waved a hand. 'Oh, he told me lots of things, you'll see.'

I had never heard about Rory Gallagher doing a tour of Mexico and told them so.

'Yes, well, this was no tour,' said the photographer.

I felt dizzy. We were between floors, on a landing at a bend between staircases, and I could see how the doors of the apartments on this floor had been pulled off, their interior walls knocked down, their bathrooms stripped, leaving only ceramic shards and green profusions of weeds spreading over what remained of the tiles. Across the courtyard, a metal staircase clung to the wall, rickety and fragile against the orange sky of evening, making shapes like Bach fugues in my head.

'We'll show you some things,' said Oscar. 'It could change your mind.' If his voice hadn't been so gentle I might have believed this was some kind of scam. Neither of the men looked like they needed money, but the dereliction of the building was making me wonder.

The top floor was colonnaded, the air thick with the riverine smell of busted pipes. I could hear them dripping in the walls. Swallows zipped and flirted in the air above the courtyard. One divebombed the overgrown privet hedges where clothes had been stretched out to dry. An old woman in a shawl knelt against her walking stick to add more newspapers to a fire lit under a big pot. A younger woman dipped a cup into the heating water and then dumped it over the head of a toddler who stood wailing and naked in a paint bucket. The crinkly grey smell of burned newspaper made my nose fizz. The courtyard flagstones had been rucked up by years of earthquakes, subsidence, and swelling tree roots. From the street came the clank and skirl of pesero brakes, the shrill whistle of a camote vendor, but they felt like they were beaming in from years and years away.

'Used to be a convent here,' Oscar said. 'Dr. Atl lived on the roof for a while, when he couldn't live anywhere else.'

'And now you do?'

He shook his head as he led us over to a scatter of greyed plastic beer chairs with the Corona logo peeling from the backs. A small table held olives and caguamas of beer.

'I used to rent a place as my office,' he said. 'But I've been moving my things out. It's getting too weird in this area. I'm an anthropologist. I don't want my collection disappearing. Because that would be those pieces gone for good. It's all Afro-Mexican culture I work with. People here don't even know it exists,' Oscar said. 'It's all the one struggle for us in America, north to south.'

The photographer took a chair and poured himself a glass of beer. He replaced the bottle on the table and raised his fist in a Black Power salute.

'Don't you start,' Oscar said, and went to pour me a beer. It took me a second to refuse. The heat of the day and the sad brown gloom of the place had made my throat all tight and itchy, and I was still so shaky in early recovery that I feared even the most prosaic triggers for relapse.

'Jails, institutions, death,' said Oscar. 'Yeah. I got you.' He unscrewed the lid of a bottle of Peñafiel instead and poured us each a glass.

When I sat down I saw a tape recorder next to the bowl of olives, its window yellowed and cracked, the black paint lost to years of dings and scuffs.

'I bought this after the earthquake,' the photographer said. 'I was helping out, same as everyone. I can't lift a pickaxe, because I'm too thin, but that means I can get into the tight places.' He scratched under his chin. 'I did this for some days. Then, one day, I was jumping on a buried door for about an hour until it broke. Helped a mother and her kids out. But just this hour made my lungs bad, from the dust, so I had to switch. Sorted the clothes at a collection centre. Interviewed the people digging. So, when your paisano arrived, well, I wasn't going to pass up the opportunity.' He picked up the recorder, and pressed play. The voice that rose from the speaker, I'd have known it anywhere.

'Would you call it running away? You would? Right, right. Well, I wouldn't have thought of it that way. It was just a holiday for me so it was.'

That voice, so jittery, restless, lilting, gentle, like he was three-quarters afraid of whoever he was talking to, and yet so brassy and furious and clear as a bell on the fourteen hours of bootleg live recordings that a friend's da had put on a hard drive for me – that voice had rattled my earbuds on secondary school bus trips, had roared in every room I'd called home over my years out of Ireland, had called up pictures of foaming seas and misty forests and open roads and skies the blue of old photographs.

'I mean, can people even run away when they're thirty-seven, like?' said the voice on the recorder, and even through the crackle of static there was no mistaking him. 'Would that not be kids' stuff only?' He laughed. 'Sorry, it's supposed to be you asking the questions. But I mean, I don't even know what I'd be running away from, to be honest. You can't call hotels home – they're the opposite of home, and they're basically where I live. The few stacks of books, the VCR, the paintings, none of them heavy enough to weight me in place.'

Oscar picked up the recording and pressed pause. He and the photographer were both looking at me.

'That's him alright,' I said. 'That's Rory Gallagher.'

'He had become obsessed,' the photographer said, uncrossing his leg to lean forward for the caguama, 'with the colour palette of a film he'd seen.'

'The Long Goodbye,' Oscar said. 'Robert Altman version.'

'It's hard not to blame him,' the photographer said. 'You see, there's a trick the crew did with the colours for this film, where they underexposed the reels for most of the movie, so there's a greyish, stepped-on sort of papel de aluminio feeling to the light, as though the Elliott Gould character, the detective, as though he's Theseus in a greenish labyrinthine supermarket, a headachey feeling in these scenes, as constant and nauseating as the consciousness of one's own heartbeat. But then he gets to Mexico. And boom.' The photographer clicked his fingers. 'Here, the colours wake up. Because the reels of all of these Mexico scenes have been unravelled and left expuesto to the sun for one full day.'

'And so, you know, being a rock star and all that,' Oscar said, 'he got himself a flight over, to find the locations where they filmed those scenes.'

'He felt good here, I think,' said the photographer. 'Like he was in a film.'

'That's how it is for everyone when they first get here,' Oscar said, and spat an olive pit over the parapet.

'Finding the locations was the easy part,' said the photographer, with a wave of his hand.

'My friend worked as an artist for the movies. Set design, stuff like that,' said Oscar. 'She was still living here at the time. Moved north. Had a kid. And this guy right here' – he nodded to the photographer – 'he calls me, and I tell him to bring the tape to a party we're having.'

'A good party. On this big ranch – an avocado farm, wasn't it?' the photographer said. 'They pulled a piano out on the grass, people were playing guitars, bossa nova music, all so nice.'

There was a floaty feeling in my body, like I was blowing out of the chair and the building and the moment and back into their time. I don't know where the pictures were coming from, but I could see all of it, like I'd been there – the earthen oven under its reed ceiling, a man with a moustache over a harelip fanning the flames with a dried palm branch, waiters in shirt sleeves loosening their bow-ties and trying to swipe tacos and leftovers from the old women tending the big clay pots, getting swatted with flannels and dough-gloved hands for their trouble, two hefty suited bodyguards yawning and smoking, their eyes tracking back and forth across the people spilled out on the slopes and dips of the garden, while, in the house, Rory Gallagher stands by the TV, his foot tapping, his arms folded, waiting for the artist friend to identify the place, while ferns and banana leaves sway outside the window, ripples of sun like water lights on the terracotta tiles.

'And we slot in the video,' the photographer said, 'and she knows it immediately. "They make a lot of stuff there," she said. And so boom. Onto the bus, straight from the party, the four of us.' Oscar leaned forward and pressed play.

'The bus left us on the edge of town, the dust cloud boiling up silver around us. The sun's last red fade-out was lingering on the ground,' Rory said. 'We were starving. There was a single light on in the whitewashed bulk of the market. We stumbled our way over the path there, tiredness and the fact that the ground was all humpy from stuck rocks and the roots of banana and date palm trees. The air was cool and heavy, almost like it was water. Inside the market all the stalls were shuttered, and people were swabbing the tiled floors with soap and water, patterns of suds spreading out like galaxies in the dark. We stepped over the puddles all the way to the one place with a light still on, where a family was wrapping papayas in newspapers, laying mangoes in egg boxes, drawing long towelling material over bunches of cilantro. They sold us a few bits and pieces, out of pity, I suppose, and I handed over a bill and looked beyond them to the mural on the back wall, one showing Zapata lying dead on his back underground, shrouded by the entwined roots of a walnut tree whose branches held images of the future he'd died for, laboratories and classrooms where kids of all shapes and sizes and skin tones sat bent over their work. Outside, a single electric light flickered, orange-toned, turning the single oak tree that stood by the road a deep red, waiting for the family to finish shutting their stall. After that, they took us the rest of the way to town in the back of their pickup.' He laughed. 'And, you know, it wasn't until the following morning that I felt like we'd found the place. I think I was too exhausted. But I was looking out at this pure blue air over the cemetery, this perfect, faded tint, pure Panavision, straight out of old photos, and a kinda peace floating out of it, and I remember thinking it might be worth sticking around in this life long enough to somehow play that colour on my guitar, and that way keep it there for long enough to feel it settling over my skin. I think I'd be okay to give everything up if I could do that even for a minute, like. I think you can love a sound or a colour with the same heat as you can love a person. Maybe I'm not terribly human, but all I ever really wanted was to play notes that sound the way a feeling does when it rises off the light hitting a given wall, or a body of water, or whatever, you know? Just the feelings of things, to give them sounds, I think that's all I've ever been trying to do. And I think waking up that morning in Mexico, looking out over the cemetery, at the sky, at the mountains, I think that was when I finally realised that.'

The photographer reached forward and stopped the tape.

'Y pos ya,' he said.

'Is there a way I can hear the whole thing?' I said.

'Your friendly local archivist,' Oscar said, reaching into the pocket of his flannel shirt and pulling out a memory stick. He handed it over. 'There's no way this guy's giving you his tape recorder. Most expensive thing he owns. And I think he's only with me for tech support by now.'

'At this point, yes,' the photographer said.

'I might have more questions,' I said, 'if that's okay. After I've listened.'

'Call either of us,' said Oscar, leaning back and stretching in his chair. 'We spent a lot of time with the guy.'

I stayed for a polite spell, but I was already itching to be in my car, driving home, the memory stick hooked up to my stereo. By the time I excused myself the sky was dark, the street was empty, and the air was as close to quiet as it ever gets. When I pressed play on the files, Rory's voice rose out of the speakers, and the slats of the fan rattled in sympathetic vibration as I coasted home along Lázaro Cárdenas, then Bucareli and Ciudadela, tree shadows and streetlights flowing along the bonnet of my car.

'I don't know why that film speaks to me so much,' the recording said. 'I think it might be the ending, the way he's dancing and kicking his heels, even though he's lost everything. Even his cat has him messed up, like. But it's all okay with him. The more he loses, the lighter he gets, the freer he gets, the more peaceful he gets. I guess nothing could break you, if you could live that way ... The drifty sort of camera as well, the way the takes are so long and rambling, I don't know, it's like a centre of calm that people only tap into by accident. But yeah, I'd have known the odd version of that kind of peacefulness now and again, definitely. There was a train trip me and the boys took when we were on tour in Japan. A young fella from the fan club was our guide. This was '77, maybe. He took us to the English Garden at Shinjuku Gyoen, just this empty white sky, firs curving against it, a calligraphy of them, and the arcade of bare poplars either side of us narrowing towards a vanishing point of pure fog. The fan cub lad told us that there's a tradition in Zen where 'sky' and 'emptiness' are the same word. I sort of liked that, you know, paradise being that point where you have nothing more to let go of.'

I don't know what got in the way of me calling the photographer back. By the time I did, his number had been disconnected, and, when I went back to Oscar's building in the Centro, a construction job had hollowed the place out. That happens a lot: the city eats itself, it's a machine for forgetting, confirmed time and again, like the morning I tried to find the rooftop where I first realised this whole heroin thing was probably going to be a problem for me, only to find that the whole building had gone, was now nothing but a pit of oxide-red dirt bristling with rebar, floored in heat-warped boards. Chunks of the walls' tattered lagging of concert posters and union notices went blowing past my ankles, paper curled at the corners by the parch and drench of wet nights and scorching days, the pavement dribbled with an almost cursive of run ink that invited me to try to read it even though it was impossible. White puffs of thistle seed floated through the gaps in the fence.

Maybe I didn't want to find out too much more about Rory Gallagher's trip, in case a detail turned out to be false, and the whole story fell apart, which means I can still put on the MP3 of Rory's voice, on nights where the rain comes down seething, as though the old lake is trying to take the city back. The dull roar of the traffic crashes in waves, muted by rain and distance. The file is at the bit where Rory is talking about listening to the radio under the covers, breathing through a cardboard tube of kitchen roll poked out from under the covers so that he could breathe and still keep the radio noise quiet, while his thumb rolled along the glow-in-the-dark dial of the transistor, his eyes moving between the names of the cities the transmissions were beaming in from – Rome, Luxembourg, Stockholm – his ear chasing after any jangle of guitar, feeling like the hunt was taking him all over Europe without even moving from the warm hub of that childhood bed, dreaming the little tuning bar to a skiff riding low over the black crash of the static between stations, the yaw and bend of the signal brightening out of its theremin waul, clearing and sharpening into the clear still bay of human voices, human music, like a port, a still point in the crashing storm of noise, and down he would cruise into sleep, borne down out of view on a tiny raft of sound. From the roof I watch white cataracts of water tipping down through the broken siding of the Periférico, catching the light. The TV shows rust-coloured grass and fir trees that look scorched, rock-faces whitish with calcite, and billowing grey smoke low over Ayutla, a Mixe town in Oaxaca, now entering its fourth year without water. Old people and teenage sons and daughters queue up to fill buckets from trucks whose leaky pipes drizzle litre after wasted litre over the dirt road. Lights bob and waver in the rain fog. They could be the boats of the long-gone lake city, and my rooftop is one among them, a little coracle. Looking at the map pinned to my wall, so dense that it looks like a bone in cross-section, reading the names of streets that, district by district, log every lake and river in the world – Tanganyika, the Rhine, Constance, the Danube – and every fruit tree that can't grow here – jacaranda, guanabana, alhelí – and every philosopher and writer that nobody has the time to read anymore, Descartes and Dante, Kant, Rosario Castellanos, and it feels like the whole city is an encyclopedia on fire, the pages curling and yellowing, the black mesh of the bindings showing through then flaming away in a shower of orange sparks, just like what's left of the dictionaries and reference books on the shelves of Trotsky's house. All the damage is legible but I can't tell what it means, but then again all damage is the beginning of the legible, because all writing is the pressure of one thing on another, pattern attributed spuriously to the resulting marrings, from the motion of crows to the whorls on a plant's leaves to the motion of crowds to the dings and dents of years and years and years of booted feet left on a pavement, what is it saying, what is any of it saying, what am I saying when I show up at my meetings and narrate the markings, run words over the scars, what is it but the counting and recounting of the same old searings and markings and scarrings and leavings. Afterwards, though, if the rain clears while it's still dark, I can look up past the counter glow, see again the same old stars.

CONNEMARA CHRONICLE Nidhī Zak/ Aria Eipe

I

You will remember it like this:
he will be telling you of Gráinne Mhaol, pirate, woman who is called Grace
O'Malley on the brand of heatherinfused gin feels like silk in your throat

while the smoke which you inhaled
from the slickrolled skinthin spliff in the alley by the speakeasy stretches
its wings like a sleepy bird in your sternum slowly starting to wake, jazz

chords still teasing your tympanum
from the band that went before, making the tired hotel bar seem strange
-ly intimate in the sudden hush, you can count only three couples there

you've had two firsts with him tonight,
your first smoke and your first joint and he has bought you another drink
though you've both likely drunk enough; he shifts a stray wave of curl

from your cheek, he calls you princess
because you are named, Ariadne, after one who gave her heart away
to one who did not love her back – nothing new there, this is a story

as old as the hills upon which
those shipsick Andalusians fanned out in formation then bred
with foreign beauty to form offspring of famed gentility, he tells you

I want to talk about us, about what you're doing
with me. I'm concerned about you; you wave it away, (t)his concern
– there's no need to worry about me, you say, I'm fine – he tells you

of his first child, delicate daughter
who you are young enough to be (mistaken for, and since you have
no next of kin you have put him in place of your father), he tells you

how she has run away to Spain, how
she blames him; you will remember, the postcard you sent from Jerez
de la Frontera, its sonorous Spanish lyric: the man who does not love

a horse cannot love a woman, he tells you
it needs to end, you have to let it go, we have to be friends from now
on we can no longer go on like this, like lovers, like love – he tells you

how his partner is now in the vital stages
of this pregnancy, the fetus' features coming clearer into focus
on marblewhite scans: an eye here, an ear there; *I cannot be divided,*

I need to go deep into this with everything
I have my child will suffer otherwise – and what about me? you want
to sling back. Is my suffering any different for that I'm not *your* child?

2

Your fingers follow the stem of the glass, careful crystalslitted gashes down
past pools of condensation overswimming the rim. Your chin quivers, tears.
You cannot *look at him.*

Come, he says, softer now, *talk to me. Would you rather go up to the room?*
You nod wordlessly, slide off the stool, only taken two sips of the glossy G&T,
the bartender watches your back.

On the short ascent, silence and you, cannot bring yourself to meet his gaze,
you struggle to find the keys, turn them in the lock; inside, you are not alone,
three wildhaired hags leer at you

from a painting above the hearth, suddenly seized with the wish for home,
for the one hung on your wall – young girl leading the bull-boy by the hand
through a night blinded by stars

inside, he heads for the bathroom while you lean your slim and shaking
sheerstockinged legs on the long edge of the vast plush bed fit for kings,
and wait for a sentence.

He comes out, sits down in a highbacked chair, facing you are set against
each other – *speak, say something you don't say anything,* he throws at you,
eyes aflame.

You laugh, a fast, unhappy laugh, in a voice thick with hurt. What do you want
me to say? It has always been like this, you say – you lay it down, you tell me
how it's going to be

between us, and I say okay, and then that's the way it is, what makes you
imagine it would be any different this time? – he remains rigid, unmoved.
I need to know that you understand.

You shrug, in a defeated understanding. What does it matter, you think,
if you understand something that doesn't make sense to you, in which
you have no say? The truth is

you knew this moment would come, these things always end but what you
couldn't know is it would come so soon; what surprises you is how fiercely
you are rooting for this very horse

running in him, the one that will put his unborn child before you, yes; you,
back arced over the track rails bloodyelling yes, willing it to gain ground,
cheering it on with the full ho(a)rseness

of your lungs and all the while they are being crushed under the punishment
of everything that he is prophesying. *Do you understand, love? Tell me.*
I need to know that you understand.

3

You

leave me   *deserter*   my beached body
                        supine on the sheets

stealing into a night in which

                                        we are both beyond
                                        pretending
                                        we can sleep now

I wander this city a wreck this city

                has always been the possibility

                        of encountering you

city on her side, flanks heaving, laughing with your mouth

                city on her back, knees raised, dark water for a heart

She
        speaks to me

        in your voice, now she Echoes

                                every/where I look to the river to find
                                                your face
                                /where I turn she says your name

        and the water like the water
        of the river where I was born
        flowing from the black hair
        of a viole(n)t-throated god

                                and the water like the water
                                of the river where you were born
                                bisecting a state divided by hate

rushing over the bones of all the dead horses and the bones of the dead
hopeless and the bones of the dead crusaders the bones of the dead invaders
and the bones of the dead and the bones of the dead in the dead of the winter
where you left them, where you came from, dead bones flung over the borders,
dead bones in the streets, dead bones of all our dreaming the dead, the dead,
there was snow all over Ireland, the snow fell, all over Ireland, Mad Ireland,
she hurt you, and the dead all hurt you, and Ireland has her madness and her
weather still, raw towns, dark cold, and the ghosts of all the horses and dead
dogs barking across Europe and how hard it must have hurt you and how
much you have hurt me, hard-hearted, and how you have hurt me now, again,
                                                        into poetry.

4

I understand that I am nothing

but a toy, amorous play/thing in your hands

You

wind

your words around me, spin me a|part of your story yo-yo yo-u reel in close,
then, when I am not watching send me s-a-i-l-i-n-g out into unbordered sky

I tire of moving to this rhythm, always away from you. I want you to let it rest
now, keep me, close to your chest how I wish you would stay your delight to
unravel me, love,

you lift my face from your shoulder, like a child, *look into my eyes*

you have to

let it go, *you have to*

let me go, you say

and so I let you

I let you let me go

but not before I –

Take this glistening gossamer red. Thread one end through your tail.

The wrong way up

like love.

Because, you see, I have taken a life
time to finally understand:

this is where the story gets it wrong –

Love is not the man.

Love is the minotaur.

Notes: The painting referenced in section 2 is Pablo Picasso's Minotaure aveugle guidé par une fillette dans la nuit, from the Vollard Suite. The final verse of section 3 draws on lines and imagery from The Dead by James Joyce and In Memory of W.B. Yeats by W.H. Auden. The line 'The wrong way up like love.' in section 4 is quoted from Watermark by Sean O'Reilly [The Stinging Fly Press, 2005].

LIFE FORCE FREQUENCIES

Roisin Kiberd

There's a video I come back to sometimes on YouTube. It captures a shark trying to chew through the internet backbone, a cable which transmits information around the world. The shark appears through fogged turquoise water, and hovers a moment before it bites. It persists, but the cable won't break. Finally, the shark turns away – I detect, in its wide eyes and rictus jaw, a certain exasperation – then it swims off, fading into the blue distance.

Stories about sharks eating the internet were popular online a few years ago. The video became something of a meme, enough that the International Cable Protection Committee published a report titled Sharks Are Not the Nemesis of the Internet. The report lists no shark-induced damage since 2007, but does detail the first recorded incident of this sort, in 1985, when a fibre optic cable was damaged near the Canary Islands. 'The culprit was the deep-dwelling crocodile shark (*Pseudocarcharias kamoharai*),' it reads, explaining that the attack 'led to design improvements of the cable's protective sheathing that effectively eliminated the problem.'

To me, the story was not so much that a fanged sea creature would conspire to chew the cable, but that the cable was in the sea in the first place. I'm not used to thinking of the internet as a physical reality; I'm used to it floating through the air. I'm used to envisioning the internet as a 'cloud', as an ethereal fifth element, or talking about it, in a vaguely metaphorical way, as something that drapes over me like a veil of frenetic meta-reality.

This sense of the internet as magic was challenged earlier this year, when my boyfriend and I moved into a flat in the south Dublin suburb of Blackrock. We were renting at a steep discount from relatives while they hunted for a more permanent tenant. The flat was ideal; it was big, with great transport links, and the beach only a few minutes away. But it was also an internet black-spot; there was no wifi, and we couldn't use our phones as hotspots – as soon as we were through the door, all coverage disappeared.

During our time in that flat, I felt the internet reconfigure time and space around us. In the mornings we sat by the window, waiting for connectivity bars to appear on our screens. We hovered in the doorway on cold February nights, holding our phones up as though in prayer, or as ritual, begging the gods for data.

'Digital detoxes' have become popular in recent years, but I suspect their effect is only relaxing when it's desired, and anticipated. Time passed slowly, nervously, inside the flat; without music, or videos, or ready access to information, we were forced to sit alone with ourselves and with each other. By day we worried about falling behind on work, or about friends thinking we were ignoring them. By night, sleep felt deeper, somehow, in the knowledge that no emails could arrive. We took up residence in nearby cafes, downloading furiously from their wifi during the day, and we spent the nights in a branch of Wetherspoons popular with students and raucous elderly men. Eventually, after three weeks, we gave up and decided we needed to move out.

It felt terrible to leave a perfectly good flat, not least in Dublin, where such things are rare and almost always unaffordable. But the situation, we felt, would drive us either to madness or to Wetherspoons-induced liver damage. Depression set in by the end of our time there; I have rarely felt so idiotic, or frustrated, or futile, as when I went into the Eir shop for the third time to ask if there were any short-term broadband deals (there weren't) and if they knew, even vaguely, what had caused the complete lack of connection inside the flat. The responses the man at the desk provided sounded unlikely, improvised; it might be damage to phone masts, or lead paint, or topography, or maybe the walls were made from very thick cement. It might simply be bad luck, he said. (It's worth noting, also, that he neglected to mention shark attacks.)

What I learned from the flat was that, as much as I like to think otherwise, I'm not sure I can live comfortably without an internet connection. What I also learned was that I know next to nothing about how the internet works, despite writing about it for almost seven years, and that this has almost certainly informed my attitudes toward it.

I tried to understand. I read that a mobile phone is like a two-way radio. It sends information to a base station, or a mast, which passes it along to other phones and networks. The masts need to be close to phone users; lower frequency connections, like 3G, are able to travel long distances and penetrate buildings with thick walls, so there are fewer of them, while 5G, the new generation, has a more limited range due to its high frequency. It comes down to 'spectral efficiency', a phrase I tremendously enjoy; 5G can deliver more data per hertz than 3G, or 4G, but it needs a higher number of masts to do so.

When the man at the Eir shop mentioned 'damage to masts', I envisioned storms and high winds, an internet at war with the elements. But since I started researching this essay a news story has emerged, appearing alongside headlines about the pandemic, police brutality, racism and recession, like some dark punchline to these global calamities. In mainland Europe, and in Britain and occasionally in Ireland, members of the public are attacking phone masts. In England alone there have been seventy-seven attacks at the time of writing; some involve cement poured on the masts, but more often it's arson. Infrastructure workers have been harassed and spat on, and filmed by bystanders who accuse them of playing a role in a deadly conspiracy. The arsonists and bloggers and believers come together on social media, and sometimes at protests, to voice their passionately-held concern that 5G is dangerous, and fatal, and part of a plot to cull the world's population.

While anti-5G sentiment was around before, the pandemic lent it a new volatility, and momentum. This latest phase began with claims that 5G was first trialled in Wuhan, China, where the virus originated. It then coalesced into a set of theories: that 5G is spreading coronavirus, that 5G *is* coronavirus (the symptoms are caused by exposure), and that lockdown is a government ploy to keep us indoors while 5G masts are installed, allowing them to kill a portion of the global population once activated. There's also the idea that Bill Gates is involved, either to profit from a vaccine, or to microchip the populace and create a global surveillance state, or, possibly, to reduce the global population as part of a Malthusian bio-terror plot.

I came across the idea of electromagnetic hypersensitivity (EHS) a long time ago; it's a condition where the sufferer can 'feel' electromagnetic waves, which come from devices, and, when exposed to them, they experience symptoms like headache, muscle pain, sleep disturbances and stress. It has remained mostly under the radar as a phenomenon, in large part because sufferers are seemingly intolerant of the internet and other technologies.

Doctors dispute the existence of EHS, adding it to Morgellons, Adrenal Fatigue and Wind Turbine Syndrome on the list of conditions which might be delusional, or a psychosomatic allergy to modernity. But what strikes me about EHS is how convincing it seems; I'm certain its sufferers are experiencing *something.* In a 2015 Washingtonian article titled The Town Without Wi-fi, writer Michael J Gaynor visits Green Bank, West Virginia, a town where mobile phones, wifi and other technologies fail to function due to interference from a government-owned telescope. The town has attracted a large number of electrosensitive people as a result. Gaynor describes an electrosensitive woman meeting with a group of sceptics, during which her hands gradually turn red and her wrists swell up. She guesses – correctly, it turns out – that one of the men hasn't left his phone at home.

Over the years, thinking that one day I'd write about EHS, I've checked in on it in the Google News tab. It continues to be defined as a 'questionable disease', but it did appear (sometimes comically, sometimes tragically) in the TV series Better Call Saul. There are 'quiet zones' without wifi and phones in an Italian national park and in the city of Zurich, where a special four-storey apartment block was built with radiation-absorbing walls and hypoallergenic decor. It's difficult to find first person accounts of it online, understandably, but EHS sufferers seem to have carved out a community for themselves, enduring something that seems incomprehensible, and dubious to many, with a certain dignity.

The current wave of 5G activism goes a step further, imagining connectivity as body horror. It depicts 5G as a disease, preying on the elderly and vulnerable. It's politicised, versatile, encompassing parallel conspiracies about China and Russia and 'global elites'. It's insistent, seeking out new converts with YouTube videos and meandering all-caps blog posts (5G AND OXYGEN: WHAT THE MORONIC MEDIA ISN'T TELLING YOU). It has been endorsed by David Icke, of the antisemitic lizard-people beliefs, in a one-hour video which subsequently got him banned from Facebook and YouTube. A university researcher in Qatar, Marc Owen Jones, analysed 22,000 Twitter interactions mentioning '5G', and found evidence of what he termed 'inauthentic activity', indicating a state-backed disinformation campaign. In the UK, where 5G is currently being rolled out, the conspiracy gained such momentum that the cabinet secretary Michael Gove addressed the issue in a briefing, calling it 'dangerous nonsense'.

The 5G backlash reads like a darker, more sensational version of the EHS phenomenon; one with more intense, life-threatening symptoms and with the addition of a scheming villain, Bill Gates, lurking in the background.

It's predictable, of course, that a pandemic would drive people to find a scapegoat, and that conspiracies would flare in an American election year. But I think another factor in this transition, from alternative medical belief to arson attacks, is its shift to social media. It's the first time I've seen this kind of viral selective Luddism, not only rejecting technological progress (while accepting other versions – 3G and 4G – of exactly the same thing), but attempting to understand, however misguidedly, how the internet works, and reeling in horror when they realise that technology is extremely complicated, and mutable, and man-made, and embedded in the fabric of everyday life.

As I write this, I'm sitting on a sofa with my laptop connected to the internet through my phone, which I'm using as a hotspot. The connection is passing from my phone to my laptop, *through my body*. This makes me wince a little each time I think about it, though not enough to stop me using my devices. For this reason, I have some sympathy for the anti-5G protestors, though not those who practise violence, or threats, or barely-latent bigotry. What I sympathise with is their need to question the properties of this mysterious thing – the internet – which occupies the world around us as well as our minds, and our emotions, and our time.

Over the years my relationship with the internet has been uneven and often troubled. At times I've been addicted to it. At times it has very nearly driven me mad. I used to write a column about internet subcultures, and it went to my head; in 2016, the year I was writing, I watched every platform devolve into conflict and conspiracy and political extremism. I became severely depressed, and paranoid, and eventually I had to quit.

These days, I try to stay level-headed in my dealings with the internet, but at some level, like those who tweet that 5G gives you brain fog, or cancer, I too am reeling at its presence in my life. That's why I choose the internet so often as a subject in my writing; I'm confident that, in this area at least, life will always be stranger than fiction.

Another true story that's stranger than fiction: in 1941, a Hollywood star named by MGM as 'the most beautiful woman in the world', and known for filming the first on-screen female orgasm, worked with an avant-garde composer on a communications technology called 'frequency hopping', designed to help Allied ships communicate with torpedoes without the signals getting jammed by the Nazis. The two inventors, Hedi Lamarr and George Antheil, moved a radio signal between multiple frequencies to avoid detection, using a piano roll (a paper scroll filled with perforations, usually used to operate a player piano). Today, this technique is recognised as an early template for Bluetooth and wifi.

The number of frequencies in the universe is potentially limitless. Birdsong has a frequency of 1000 to 8000Hz. The keys of a piano range from 27.5 to 4186. Sometimes I think I hear frequencies higher than most people can hear. I hear the ultrasonic insect repellers; when I walk into a room, I can almost always tell when one is on. During a college exam, years ago, I had to ask the invigilator to turn off a similar device meant to drive out rats, because it was distracting me. Lately, I can hear the sound of my phone charging, which creates, for me, a strange kinship with technology, and a sense that it might have a life of its own.

When I read about the 5G attacks, I wondered how people were able to find the phone masts. It turns out there's an interactive map online, for Ireland at least, compiled by the government group ComReg. It displays 10,332 masts nationwide, with 3,691 in Dublin alone. Ranelagh, the suburb where I grew up, has ten of them in a distributed grid. I've been surrounded all this time, passing but not noticing the internet all around me.

We are swimming in connectivity, which is what brings me back to the flat in Blackrock. Now I'm standing outside it, on the street, and holding a small box-shaped device. It's an Electromagnetic Field Radiation Detector, also called an EMF meter. Conspiracy theorists, and EHS sufferers, and even real life engineers use them to test for electromagnetic waves, including wifi.

In the spirit of understanding the internet, I bought this device on Amazon for the bargain price of £22.99. I planned to use it to measure waves of electricity around the flat, but now that I'm here, I realise I've no idea what a normal number of electromagnetic waves would be. I stand back a little in case someone sees me. I am trying very, very hard not to look like a crackpot. I turn on the meter but nothing happens; the screen just flashes '0.00'. Someone, the new tenant, is inside the flat sitting at a desk, staring into a desktop monitor. I'm guessing they've had wifi installed. The EMF meter remains the same.

Feeling sheepish, and annoyed at myself, I walk a little up the road and cross over the DART bridge which leads onto the beach. We used to walk here for a break from the flat, but my appreciation of this place was marred by a compulsion to check my phone, downloading everything possible before we went home again. This afternoon the tide is far out, almost invisible, leaving behind a landscape of seabirds and taupe and grey puddles.

Our coast is another critical site for the physical internet, one far less visible than phone masts or wifi routers. Ireland is surrounded by eighteen active undersea cables, thirteen of which land at coastlines in the Republic of Ireland, and five of which connect to Dublin. They land at Rush and Lusk, and at Sandymount, down the coastline from where I used to live.

Ireland's subsea cables connect to Britain and to the United States. We're well-positioned on the internet backbone, one of the reasons why Silicon Valley companies love to open offices here (the other being their ability to avoid paying taxes). Ireland was home to the first transatlantic telegraph cable, completed in 1852, which ran between Newfoundland, Canada, and Valentia Island in County Kerry. A piece on Ireland's subsea cables in the Dublin Inquirer, written by researcher Paul O'Neill, details how, in 1916, news of the Easter Rising was sent across the cable to New York long before they knew of it in England, thanks to a telegrapher employed at the Valentia Island Cable Station who was also a member of the Irish Republican Brotherhood.

There are sharks in the Irish Sea – the basking shark, the world's second-largest fish, is known to appear here in the springtime. I've not heard of any trying to eat the cables, though the networks have been subject to other interference.

In 2013, NSA whistleblower Edward Snowden revealed that GCHQ (Government Communications Headquarters, the British government's intelligence, cyber and security agency) had targeted undersea cables with landing points in Ireland. The operations are fabulously named; 'Mastering the Internet' is one, 'Global Telecoms Exploitation' another. They worked with 'partner cables' which allowed them access to data travelling over their networks, including the ESAT2, which lands in Sandymount.

The practice of extracting information from cables is called 'fibre tapping'. During the Cold War, America's 'Operation Ivy Bells' involved a purpose-built submarine and a team of divers sent to tap Soviet communication lines. More recently, the GCHQ operation used 'intercept probes' at the cables' landing sites, which allowed them to take 'vast troves of data'. (It's worth including Snowden's warning here that British surveillance practices are far worse than those of America. Speaking to Der Spiegel, he said, 'Well, if you had the choice, you should never send information over British lines or British servers.')

In February this year, stories emerged of Russian intelligence agents spotted at landing sites along the Irish coast, apparently noting the precise locations of cables and checking them for weak points. I find the lack of detail in these reports, published in the Irish Times and later in Business Insider, alternatingly irritating and intoxicating. I envision the agents dressed like cyberpunks, Johnny Mnemonic extras in leather duster coats, all steely gaze and mumbled code words. I picture them ambling casually along the coast, perhaps stopping to buy an ice cream at Teddy's in Dún Laoghaire.

This is a paranoid history, one made all the stranger if we visualise 'hacking' not as something done on a screen, but as a physical act. Fibre-tapping, in particular, takes on an almost Promethean sense of transgression; it involves opening the cable without breaking it, and *stealing light* to later analyse as data. This is also a history which has left its detritus behind. Unlike software, which upgrades and erases its past with each new iteration (creating the unnerving impression that technology is always getting younger), undersea cables continue to litter the ocean beds long after they fall out of use. In a Guardian interview from 2016, Arne de Jong, founder of cable-recovery company CRS Holland, estimated that 94 per cent of unused cables remain in the sea after their work is done.

There's something forlorn, and eerie, about the thought of dead wires intruding on the lives of dogfish and sunfish, the conger eel and the basking shark. They'd be right to chew through these remains, the debris of technologies past, if only they could. Tech CEOs talk about changing the world, almost as often as politicians do, and that's exactly what they are doing; *changing the world*, physically as well as behaviourally.

The language employed by tech companies ranges from the eccentric ('bounce rate', 'dogfood' as a verb) to the procedural ('web native', 'actionable analytics') and to the mysterious ('bit rot', 'plonk', 'shadow ban', 'Internet of Things'). The term most often used to describe the Irish tech industry is 'ecosystem'; it's an economic construct with delusions of joining the natural world. Then there's the complex, subject-specific languages of coding, and UX, and connectivity, and marketing, all of which lead me to believe that technology cloaks itself in jargon in an attempt to retain its value, and, in a sense, to resist its own democratisation.

Writing this essay has been something of a wake-up call, though I'm still not sure where to begin to assemble a more holistic understanding of the internet. At least I now know how much I *don't* know. Try as I might to think better of it, I still understand the internet as metaphysical; this is an impression conjured from years of living with it but knowing very little about how it functions. It's a kind of complacency, one which goes hand in hand with the resentment I feel towards Silicon Valley and its products. I associate Google and Amazon and Facebook with power and momentum – the ability to 'move fast and break things', and laws, and people, too, if they choose. This leads me to envision technology as capitalism unmoored from humanity, a force so powerful it has taken on a grim organic life all of its own.

I recognise now that this thinking is at once correct, and very flawed. The internet is at once abstract and material. For better or worse, it is part of our landscape now.

In April 2020, Glastonbury Town Council issued a report asking MPs to establish an inquiry into the safety of 5G. The supplementary materials provided included a list of 'Recommendations', including the use of shungite, a grey-black mineral traditionally used as a Russian folk cure, and believed by the town council to be 'a cheap and helpful preventative' solution. There was also mention of a device called the 5GBioShield, a USB stick intended to block 5G's effects, costing £283.

The website for the 5GBioShield features a picture of a lion, and a smiling woman enveloped in a bubble. It reads 'Proprietary Holographic Nano-foil Catalyst Technology.' The device's creators claim it provides 'plasmic support', 'quantum oscillation', and provision of 'life force frequencies.' Mention of the 5GBioshield has since been redacted in the Glastonbury report, after it was revealed to be nothing more than an ordinary USB stick.

My parents have a 5G internet connection at home, where I've been staying during the lockdown. I don't own any shungite, nor do I have a 5GBioShield, but I do have some orgone, the material used for esoteric life enhancement by Wilhelm Reich, and lately promoted as another cure for 5G, or coronavirus, or the Bill Gates world domination plot. This piece is quite modest; a circular slab that fits in my palm, containing layers of metal and crystals in a transparent resin disk. I was given it by a friend, during my nervous breakdown several years ago. I can't tell for sure if it's helped me, but it lived at the bottom of my handbag for a while.

First I try the wifi router in the hall. I hold the EMF meter in front of it. Electric field: 46 volts per meter. Then it rises to 50, and a magnetic field of 0.1. I get the orgone and put it between the router and the EMF meter. Nothing changes.

After this, I try the same procedure on my laptop, and the results are instantly alarming. The magnetic field is 0.0 microtesla (µT), but the electric field is 254 volts per meter. The EMF meter starts beeping, and a tiny red light pulses on its side. An alert – 'HARMFUL' – displays at the bottom of the screen. I'm surprised, and worried, though I also don't fully understand what I'm worried about. I pick up the orgone, though I almost laugh at myself as I do so, and place it in front of my laptop to see if anything changes. The counter goes up: 260. Apparently the orgone is making it worse. Finally, I decide that my casual experiment is over, and I turn off the EMF meter, but not my computer.

Later I look up – on my laptop, again – what a dangerous level of exposure would be. The first search result is a health website which advises that 'there's disagreement over EMF safety' and that scientific studies have proven inconclusive. It lists safe numbers of volts per meter in household objects – 10 V/m for TVs, 14 V/m for microwave ovens – but declines to mention phones and laptops.

Still, I don't really need an EMF meter to warn me that the internet is harmful. The 5G conspiracy theorists are a product of a filter bubble, a trap that many, perhaps all internet users fall into in less noticeable ways, which inherently keep us from seeing a bigger picture. Like someone inside an orgone accumulator, or trapped in a flat with lead paint and cement walls, the conspiracy theorists are blocking themselves. They're willing to discuss the internet as a physical reality – an unusual thing, given how often I see this reality taken for granted – but instead of accepting it as a flawed product, built by flawed humans, they weave it into an apocalyptic plot. They approach the kind of understanding of the internet that could empower them, but they turn away at the last minute, unwilling to accept that it might be anything less than magic.

What does the word 'internet' even mean? What we use everyday to access information is the World Wide Web, the hypertext system proposed by Tim Berners-Lee in 1989. The word 'internet' refers to the network which supports it. More recently, the web has been defined in strata: there's the 'surface web' (everything that shows up in search engines), the 'deep web' (material hidden in databases, private records and behind paywalls) and finally the 'dark web' (home to criminal marketplaces and criminal acts).

No one user experiences the internet in full. Not even GCHQ, or the NSA, who have long been gorging on our private information, and have consequently harvested way too much of it to sift through. Like the conspiracy theorists, what most of us experience is a filter bubble: a timeline and a set of algorithmic search results, which very rarely stray beyond a narrow template. My own filter bubble is an anxious one, which no amount of orgone seems to help. In the first month of the pandemic, with stories of death counts and contagion pouring in, I deactivated my social media accounts – all of them, Twitter, Instagram and Facebook – with the goal of improving my mental health.

It's been a few months now. Sometimes I get a fear of missing out, or even a fear of being *seen* to miss out. But I needed a break; too often, I accepted the internet as something I couldn't turn off; as being invasive, not only in terms of technological surveillance, but in terms of the internalised surveillance we live with, and often suffer for.

It's little surprise to me that anti-technology beliefs have taken a turn for the absurd, and dangerous, and are of themselves evidence of an extremity which is symptomatic of life with technology. There is no 'HARMFUL' alert for spending too much time online; only neurosis, paranoia, noise, and a tendency to act in the interests of content-generation rather than instinct, or goodwill.

In early June, I consult 'FindStarlink.com' for the date, the time of night, and the location for viewing Starlink, Elon Musk's 'satellite constellation' designed to bring high-speed internet access to the world.

Musk has been in the news lately. His girlfriend, the musician Grimes, just gave birth to a baby they named X Æ A-12, and his company, SpaceX, recently launched two autonomous drone ships named in tribute to novels by Iain M Banks; they're called Of Course I Still Love You and Just Read the Instructions. Starlink is part of a trend in airborne internet; Amazon's Project Kuiper is a similar satellite system, while Google's Loon uses stratospheric balloons instead. Starlink goes further than any undersea cable, or local phone mast, in its environmental intrusion; it aims to enmesh the planet in a rotating layer of satellites. As I write, the number stands at 540, with plans to launch sixty more every two weeks of this year. The goal is to have at least 12,000 in orbit, increasing later to 42,000. This will bring connectivity to locations that have never been served before, and raise enough money to fund Musk's ultimate goal, his mission to Mars, and its colonisation.

In my mind, Musk occupies a place somewhere between Mr Burns, Mr Robot, and the socially awkward engineering types I sometimes end up talking to at parties. It is only in reading about the satellites that I begin to properly resent him for his hubris, and his plan to take over the night sky. Still I want to see the internet in lights, at 1:10 A.M., from my parents' back garden. I'll look from the southwest to the east, at an elevation of 23 degrees, and find the chain of satellites among the stars. Perhaps I'll even experience awe, and excitement about our technological future.

The time comes. I stand outside, wearing slippers, dodging a convention of snails that has gathered around a piece of bread which my mother left out for the birds. It's different at night; birds – or are they bats? – move as shadows above me. Light from inside the house catches on puddles of rainwater, and the glitching movements of insects.

I think I write about the internet because it remains, to me, intangible yet utterly mundane. I'm writing in an attempt to understand the thing that would eat my humanity if it had the chance.

I look up, but the sky is too clouded even to see a star. I wait.

1:10 A.M.

1:12 A.M.

1:15 A.M.

Nothing appears. I look back at the snails. There are more now, slowly making their way to the bread from all directions, leaving in their wake a mandala of slime. I decide I'm going to stay here a while, watching, waiting for nothing in particular, except silence.

L–R: Niamh Algar, photograph by Christian Tierney; Nicole Flattery, photograph by Conor Horgan

STRAIGHT OUTTA MULLINGAR

NIAMH ALGAR and NICOLE FLATTERY in conversation

I've known Niamh Algar since we were both thirteen. We went to school together in Loreto College, Mullingar in County Westmeath. When we were both eighteen, as part of a group of five, we travelled around Europe together, which was easily the most disastrous trip of all time and the most fun I've ever had in my life. It's not a surprise to me (although nothing on that trip indicated that any of us would go on to achieve greatness) that Niamh, only in her late twenties, has already developed such an interesting and varied on-screen career. In 2019, she had her breakthrough role in Shane Meadows'

The Virtues, and made memorable appearances in the drama-comedies Pure and The Bisexual. She worked with Ridley Scott on his upcoming project Raised By Wolves and was named as a 'Breakthrough Brit' by the BAFTA Academy. I would love to have been able to conduct this interview in the manner befitting a Hollywood starlet—in a swishy high-ceilinged hotel suite as both of us pick absentmindedly at salads but circumstances won't allow it. Due to the coronavirus, both of us are back in our parents' houses, in Mullingar, and this interview largely took place in my parents' back garden with the appropriate amount of social distancing. My mother brought out the good biscuits.

NICOLE FLATTERY: What's the question you've been asked most this year so I know not to ask that?

NIAMH ALGAR: 'What's in the water?' Everyone keeps asking me, 'What's in the water, Niamh?'

NF: What's in the water of Mullingar to produce all this talent?

NA: I want to tell them that we're all in a cult.

NF: It's strange – I think this is the most amount of time I've spent at home since I was a teenager.

NA: Same.

NF: Did you like being a teenager? I mean, did you like school?

NA: School was ... I found different ways of entertaining myself. I think I enjoyed elements of it. I didn't consider myself very academic. Although it was an all-girls Catholic school, I never necessarily felt that religion was forced down our throats.

NF: I feel, because we started in the early noughties, we missed a lot of that. My primary school was much more religious.

NA: Our teachers were really approachable.

NF: Definitely. I have teachers I think back on fondly, and say, 'They really encouraged me.' I feel indebted to my English teacher. I had her all through school, from first year onwards.

NA: Yeah, you were good at English.

NF: It was my thing! The thing I was good at. Which really becomes your identity at that age. In secondary school, you get your identity thrust upon you by the thing you're good at. So I was good at English and that's suddenly who you are. Did you feel that at all? You were so good at sport?

NA: I was. Of course, then I was compared to my sisters, who are so athletic, which I kind of hated. I rebelled against that by not wanting to do any sport. When you're compared to siblings, it's tough. When I was in first year one of my sisters was doing her Junior Cert and the other was in her final year. It was so fun to have them there but they were so focused. I wasn't like that. I joined the Pioneers because they put on plays. And because it could get me out of class.

NF: Everyone joined the Pioneers! And then when you found out what it was … you were like, 'Oh no, I don't want to be involved in this at all.'

NA: They used to announce your name over the intercom.

NF: I swear when they were trying to coerce us into the Pioneers, we all just heard 'field trips' and nothing else.

NA: Well, anything to get out of academic work. And, God help my parents, they put me in for after-school study and grinds and all that, but it didn't work. So I played a lot of sports. I was on the equestrian team.

NF: For a long time, I didn't know we had an equestrian team.

NA: I was only on it for a year. I played hockey, too. I think I got a belt of a hockey ball in the face. Like I said, anything to get out of class.

NF: I was definitely academic but I remember feeling a huge sense of point-lessness, even at that age. Just sitting at home thinking, 'The Junior Cert, does it mean anything?' And now I know it doesn't mean anything but I was still always striving for that sense of achievement, for reasons I don't even really understand. I did after-school drama classes and one thing I think they gave me that school didn't was a sense of play. You got to have fun, you got to be silly. In school, in order to be taken seriously as a smart, academic person, you had to shut down that side of your personality. The freedom those classes gave me was so enlivening.

NA: It's so true. When I stopped doing certain sports, it's because it started to feel like work and all the fun and playfulness was gone. And that's when you go off it. Any of the jobs I've had as an actor now, it doesn't feel like work. When it starts to feel like work, you need to question why you're doing it.

NF: Did you have any idea you wanted to be an actor when you were younger? I remember seeing you in the musicals in the Mullingar Arts Centre?

NA: They were great. Sean Lynch, the guy who ran it, never made us feel like kids, which is why I think a lot of us loved going there. You weren't babied. It was a different environment. He always said, 'I'm not a teacher, teachers are who you go to from nine to four.' I think when you're given responsibility at that age, you respond to it. I loved the freedom of it. Although I never got a leading role. I was tall so I was always in the back with the boys.

NF: What do you think the musicals gave you that school didn't?

NA: I suppose you're listened to. You're not listened to very often as a teen-ager. I mean from the start of the play to the end was the only time you could have lots of adults sitting in silence watching you. The plays we put on weren't children's productions. We did Les Misérables. I played a sex worker and a nun.

NF: Both?

NA: Both, in the same play.

NF: You're so versatile.

NA: I also got lost in the stories we were trying to tell. I've been reflecting on this because I've been at home. When you grow up in the countryside, you really learn about the world through stories – you don't see very much on your doorstep. A lot of my teenage years were spent watching plays and films and allowing myself to be affected by what I saw.

NF: I agree. Boredom is such an underrated aspect of creativity. I grew up in Kinnegad near Mullingar, which is a very small town, and I remember my parents telling my sister and I to 'amuse ourselves' a lot. Not because they were bad parents or anything, I must stress, but because there was just nothing to do. We got the occasional trip to Dublin, and my parents brought us to galleries and we read a lot. We were not impoverished by any means but we didn't have a constant stream of stimulus. We didn't have the algorithm telling us what to read, what to listen to ...

NA: You really had to seek things out for yourself. I remember going to Xtra-Vision as a treat on Saturdays and trying to trick my way into getting a 15s or 18s film. I used to say they were for my dad. They must have thought he was a huge indie and horror film fan.

NF: The culture you absorb at that age is so formative and important. You feel everything far more than you do as an adult. You haven't developed those critical faculties and you're not cynical. What was the first film you remember loving?

NA: I think it was Dog Day Afternoon. I know that's quite a naff thing to say. My brother Ken always had a lot of DVDs. You know when you've watched all the usual teenage junk and you're just ready for something new? He had Dead Man's Shoes and it was violent but I immediately recognised it as a different type of violence than I was used to from films. It wasn't gratuitous. It was quite real. It scared the life out of me.

NF: I remember mine was This Is Spinal Tap. That scared the life out of me too but for different reasons, I think. Then we started going to discos, living a life of debauchery, and forgot about films.

NA: I don't think I've ever come across the same carnage as I saw in those discos.

NF: I still have visions of them. Sometimes a memory will just come back to me. I remember one night a friend of mine wore this all-white outfit. She had these high, white boots, a white top and a little white t-shirt. I will never shake that outfit from my mind. It marked me.

NA: Strapless bras, that's what we were all wearing. Boob tubes. The heat in there was very bad for the strapless bras.

NF: You know what really reminds me of school? Derry Girls. More than anything else I've watched, I think it captures it.

NA: The nun in Derry Girls! I remember a nun shouting at us in school, 'Ladies should be seen and not heard!'

NF: The idea of anyone looking at us and calling us ladies. We could barely dress ourselves.

NA: They had to get rid of ties because we couldn't knot them properly.

NF: I'm ashamed to admit I had one of the elastic ones. So after school you went to Dublin to study design?

NA: Yes, I studied design in DIT. I didn't love it. A lot of the work was done on computers. I'm very stubborn so I continued on. I had to see it through to the end, but I wasn't sure what I was going to do when it was over. I found it hard to find my feet in college. But I loved Dublin. I had so many part-time jobs in Dublin and I really fell in love with the city. I started working in Cineworld on Parnell Street and one of the guys in the cinema began involving me in the film premieres and the Q&As that were happening with different directors. I found it so interesting. I knew something was up when I preferred working in the cinema to turning up for lectures. That's when I started getting passionate about it. I met the actress Seána Kerslake at the screening of her film Dollhouse in Cineworld and she was doing these improv classes in Clondalkin. That's when I really started to get involved in that world.

NF: It's a big transition from school to college, from the midlands to Dublin, even though we're really only coming from down the road. I had no idea what it was going to be like. I didn't expect it to be such a jump either. I had no idea that Trinity – I just had no idea, I was so naive – was so cliquey and so many of the students went to private schools. One of my main memories from early Trinity was people asking, asking straight out, where I went to school and I would answer 'Loreto' and they'd be like 'Dalkey or On The Green?' and I'd be like ... 'Mullingar'.

NA: I don't think I was very happy in college but then when I finished college and started acting training in The Factory, I felt so much better. It was like being back in the shows in the Arts Centre except I was able to audition for the lead now. It really didn't matter about your credentials in there. It was all about creating your own work. They brought actors and directors in to give us talks.

NF: I think when you meet people who actually do what you want to do, it's a real lightbulb moment. I did my MA in creative writing – it was fantastic, I learnt so much – but, at the same time, it wasn't applicable to the real-life skills required to be a writer. When I had work published, I was meeting people, real-life writers, who were doing it. That was so useful – those conversations about money, how they divide their time, all that. It's what should be taught in college straight away. You should get to meet these people and learn how you get better, or learn, more crucially, how you can fail, and how failing is often part of it.

NA: The fear of failure is crippling. It prevents you from trying. But I learned in The Factory that, like in any kind of creative job, you can't wait for stuff to happen to you. I realised that pretty quickly. And that you can't rely on other people to elevate your mood. You have to learn to do that for yourself, particularly as an actor, during the periods when you're not working. You can't go around blaming people saying, 'Oh, they didn't give me work, they wouldn't cast me.' You have to have a word with yourself if you start thinking that way or else you'll just be bitter. The Factory taught me that I could create my own work. It also taught me not to compare myself to others but collaborate. There's more to be gained from sharing. You have to be open-minded and understand that you don't know everything.

NF: I think that's a real moment of realisation in any kind of creative career – the only person essentially stopping me from doing this is me, the only person who can produce my work is me. I can't force anybody to take me seriously, I have to do it myself. It took me a long time to learn the self-belief that's crucial to sustaining yourself.

NA: Yeah, there was a time when I was getting sort of disillusioned. I couldn't get an agent in Ireland. I was getting frustrated. I was told I didn't look Irish. In order to get roles, you need to get credits, and in order to get credits you need to get work and if you can't get work … I was doing as many short-term courses as I could and I was working for free. But I wasn't looking for anything more, necessarily. I wasn't looking for anything huge. I felt fulfilled by doing the work and that's what I'm struggling with in lockdown. That's what I've found challenging. I'm motivated by work. It's hard for me to sit still.

NF: Who do you think gave you permission to do what you wanted to do? For a long time, I felt so constricted by my idea of what a writer is. I couldn't be loose, or have fun, or write what interested me. It took me some time, my whole twenties essentially, to see there's no strict way of being something. Do you feel there's anyone who did that for you? A person who encouraged you?'

NA: I would say Shane Meadows. I've never done anything as intense as The Virtues. I always had such a strong emotional response to Shane's work. I still remember watching This Is England when I was sixteen. He was someone I always wanted to work with.

NF: Tell me about how that happened.

NA: I went to London and I gave myself thirty days to make something happen. My thirty days were nearly up, I was temping in different offices and I was auditioning a lot. Then that role came up. I got an email saying, 'Shane Meadows wants to see you for a role.' It wasn't a scripted audition. It was improvised and there was no real brief for the character. He immediately encouraged me to be open, not to be afraid to experiment. The scene went a different direction than expected but I could tell Shane trusted me, that he was invested in me. I knew from watching his other stuff that you had to be open to being vulnerable.

NF: Did you find your work on The Virtues emotionally draining? I mean it was a tough, but rewarding, watch.

NA: It was draining because I was totally invested in the character. I just wanted to do my best, give it my all. Before filming, we did a lot of improvisation. There was a lot of full-blown feelings involved, nothing phoned-in or half-arsed. In that way, it was exhausting. But it was always safe. The workshop area had this lovely sitting-room vibe. There were couches and a kitchen where we could make tea. It was collaborative but Shane was very much at the helm of the ship.

NF: Did you feel a connection to Dinah, your character on The Virtues?

NA: Obviously Dinah isn't me. I don't have an illegitimate child, I've never hit a man, I don't have that kind of toxic relationship with my mother. At the same time, I felt like I understood where she was coming from – constantly blaming herself for stuff, having these conversations in her head that never happened, someone who definitely hasn't progressed emotionally since she was a teenager. The minute she steps back into her family home, she regresses.

NF: As we now know from experience.

NA: Yeah, our experiences over the last few weeks. Dinah's background was different from mine. But it made me think about my own life, and parts of my adolescence, in new ways. I remember, for instance, being in school and if someone got pregnant, it was the talk of the town. They were ostracized.

NF: It's horrible when you think back on school and remember people who were excluded for certain things. We all judged each other so fiercely for nothing at all. It's easy to be nostalgic but it's important to acknowledge that.

NA: During the workshop, Shane and I talked about how Dinah got pregnant. The shame that affected her whole life came from people's attitude towards her unplanned pregnancy and the fact that she had to hide it. She had to carry it, not the father. We talked a lot about whether there should be a scene in The Virtues where she sees him? It ended up not being included in the script but we discussed a scene where Dinah is buying cigarettes in the local shop and he, the father, comes in, and she is either embarrassed or she's scared. There were two ways I could have played it. If she was scared, maybe she was raped. If she was embarrassed, maybe he never knew about the child. It was the time of Repeal and I was reading a lot of stories like that at the time. I read an article about a girl who got pregnant, went away that summer and had the child. When she returned to school there were lots of remarks about her weight. She just carried that around secretly for a long time. She went on to become a barrister and no one knew. Her aunt raised the child.

NF: I felt there was a lot of that at the time, a lot of internalised misogyny and shame, and we just didn't talk about it. I was aware in school – and in an all-girls school it's hard to escape the fact – that young women in Ireland were dealing with a lot. I refuse to give my sixteen-year-old self too much credit but I think I was aware, in a way I certainly couldn't articulate, of the unfairness.

NA: Definitely. I think that's why now I shy away from roles like 'The Girlfriend'. I encountered a lot of stuff like that at the start but I think it's beginning to change now. Those roles just don't reflect my own experience. I love flawed characters. I like characters that have a lot held against them. I like a good outcast. Not villains, because no one ever thinks they are a villain, but characters who are unapologetic. I'm drawn to the more gritty, ugly stuff. I love film-makers like Andrea Arnold and Lynne Ramsay.

NF: Lynne Ramsay! Morvern Callar is an incredible film. I admire her a lot, too and her films have informed my writing. You can tell from a single frame of one of her films that's she a perfectionist and that's such an underrated quality in this era of constant, relentless content production. I love the layers in her work. When I was writing the holiday sequence in the story, Abortion, A Love Story, I was thinking of the holiday in Morvern Callar.

NA: Yes, and her characters aren't your average heroes either. It's a lot more interesting. Often her leading characters don't say a whole lot and a lot of what they are feeling is expressed between sentences.

NF: That's something I think Calm with Horses did brilliantly, too. Colin Barrett's story, from his collection Young Skins, which was really an important and formative book for me and a lot of other Irish writers, is much more thoughtful and sensitive than the average gangster drama. There is a lot of care shown towards those characters. It's like what you were saying earlier about Shane Meadows – it's violence, but a different sort of violence. I think the film captured it.

NA: I remember you told me to read Young Skins before the audition and I just loved it. It's really not a gangster drama. At its heart, it's about a man and his divided loyalties. Ursula is another character who has suffered from people's perceptions of her, and is trying to break away from that and have a fresh start. She has an edge to her personality but she's vulnerable. She's fully human. That's the work I want to keep doing.

NF: So working with Ridley Scott – was that the most nervous you've ever been?

NA: The most nervous I've ever been in my life was doing The Late Late Show.

NF: I watched. Was the white suit you wore a nod to Joe Dolan, the original Mullingar superstar?

NA: Everything I do is a sly nod to the town. Just trying to figure out what's in the water.

OFF YOUR CHEST

Dave Tynan

He was sure that was the cancer now, bristling away in his sack. A young man boiling in Army Bargains, convinced of the tumours ahead. From behind the cash register he felt the shopkeeper watching him, so he made a point of fingering the balaclavas. He read the sign beside them, insistent in thick permanent marker – *Don't Try It On* – and the shopkeeper offered an explanation.

The hygiene, he said. Some of the heads that are in.

The young man looked up at him but did not respond. The shopkeeper saw a young fella, early twenties, shifty barbed looks under the knobby rinds of his forehead. He paid the shopkeeper for everything in cash and shoved it all into his rucksack and was gone. To his left the street narrowed towards the old fruit market. To his right Capel Street blared its ragged day. He lit up and sucked on a smoke. He thought of his mam every time he had one. They had blood and lungs in common. She had only tried to warn him off them the once.

It's an itch on the inside, she'd said. An itch you can't get at. You don't stop now, it's hopeless. This is the only time it's ever easy.

That one time she had gone on holidays, that window before everything, when she tried new things, she brought back Duty Free cartons for the two of them and that was it. On the street, he put on his headphones, the dearest thing he owned, and returned to last night's show, right from the top.

– You're listening to Off Your Chest with Clive Geoghan. We're talking to Niall, who's separated from his wife. They've got a young lad and for a play in school their little man was dressed up as a fairy. Would you have a problem with that? We'll hear from Niall next, who's absolutely hopping about it. –

He'd been onto Clive for a while now. He had the measure of him. He pictured Clive, smug and certain behind a studio mic, the kind of man who liked fitted shirts and younger women. Online they called him Jean Claude Van Ham but fuck them too, soft and safe behind their screens. The world was plastic and plastic could be bent to will. He slid his pinky underneath the cellophane of the fag box and worried the corners.

– Niall, you're live on Off Your Chest. You're fuming, are ya? – Steaming, Clive – You're a steamer, Niall? – Don't act the maggot with me – Listen I'm only yanking your chain – No, listen, I'm ... sorry Clive. I'm fucking furious to be honest with you, Clive. Let me ask you, would you want it? – I've no kids, Niall. Or none I'd own up to, let's put it that way – But if you did ... – If I did, the rules would be clear under my roof – The rules would not be allowing for any fairy dressing, d'you know what I mean? –

He moved through the slate city. He stuffed his hands deep in the pockets of his anorak and went past the Korean restaurants and their karaoke caves, past the nail bars, the head shop, the sex shops, The Brothers Dosirak and the student-packed coffee shops. The traffic lights held him back. He ran one nail under another, a thin worm of grime he couldn't get at.

– No, you can't be carrying a shagging crossbow around in public – I can. I can, Clive, and I will. It's nothing for me to say that I will walk that crossbow into your yard and then we'll see who's a big man, won't we? It's nothing for me to say that nothing at all – Try it! – I'll bring a world of murder to your door ... – Go on, I'll stick the kettle on ... – I'll find you. Only small, Dublin. And I do be everywhere ... – That's enough you, apologies for that listeners – Everywhere I do be ... – Can't be ... – Everywhere ... – Threatening other callers ... Maybe there's other stations you can do that, but there's no place for that here, that's not us. We've got some standards on Off Your Chest. 1800-46-46. Call us. We'll pay some bills and get back into it –

He would never have to see his manager again after this morning. First level complete. No more taking deliveries off grunting Russian lads. No more stockroom. No more Baltic basement. He only saw his manager when his manager wanted something from him. Before he saw the light of Christ his manager had gone hard for a decade in speed and squats. Now reformed and six years clean, he had no mercy for anyone, which made for a prick of a boss, a disembodied voice shouting catalogue numbers into his skull. Getting the sack hadn't taken long once he stopped responding to the orders. It was so simple, something he could imagine his dad doing to his mam years back. Maybe that was where he had got it but he was sure he would remember. He remembered everything. He knew nobody else in a Dublin stockroom knew catalogue numbers like him. Ian, who he had to share an hour with on swap over, Ian barely knew how to tie his own shoes. It was Ian who first put him onto Clive's show, who said the stockroom was like being in solitary otherwise. He hated the shared hour with Ian, preferred when it was just himself and Clive coming out of the shower radio, suction-cupped to the wall as he made short work of the boxes. After four years he was dynamite with the Stanley, the solid weight in his palm and the blade eating everything in front of it. Alone in the mornings he was samurai slick, slicing and running his blade through the hordes in front of him. This morning he'd finished everything earlier than ever and stood still in the centre of the freezing room. He stopped responding to the orders coming in from the bright shop above. After half an hour his manager stormed down the clanking steps and flung the door open.

Right what's the story? Why d'you ignore me?

When?

What the fuck's wrong with you?

I just. Don't hear you.

You don't or you can't? Is it medical?

No.

An hour later, with the shop humming during lunch hour, he did it again and his manager finally snapped – he heard him coming from above as he took the stairs down two at a time, charged in and fucked him against the wall. That was an hour ago now. He followed the tram tracks that led past the National Leprechaun Museum and he took the escalator up into Jervis and went into Currys.

– That's not fair now – D'you really believe that? Listen an alien wouldn't believe that – We're all aliens Clive, when you think about it – D'you reckon so yeah? Elaborate on that for me now – To someone else we're all aliens – Come here till I tell you something, can I say one word – If you kept it to that I'd be delighted. – Would ye give me a fucking syllable here? – I'm going to say one thing, right? Just let me say one thing – You've another thing coming – Who are you anyways? Here, are you doing a line with the crossbow fella? – Come over here and say that – I don't believe she has any affiliation with Crossbow Joe – Don't be encouraging him. He'll be back on – Ah you're grand. I'm happy in me nappy here –

He swerved the young lads at the Luas stop. Half of them kept a hand down their kaks while smoking, the weed dank and reeky in the breeze. He didn't want their attention, knew how they saw him, knew what they could do to him. He remembered walking back into his estate the first week of school. The first time they asked if he wanted a go. The second time they didn't ask and there were many times after. His dad had insisted he wasn't going to the local school which was a good way to get the head slapped off you just before you got home. He listened again to the city angry.

– This is it now, Clive. Between Pluto and the dinosaurs, nothing's what it was – Run that by me again now – It's all change, Clive, the dinosaurs we grew up on don't exist anymore they've changed all the names on us they're only cut-and-shunt jobs by the archaeologists – What has this to do with anything, Clive? For the love of all that is sacred and divine, tell me – Taxpayer's money is what I'm concerned about – Dinosaurs don't pay tax, you sap –

Someone had cried live on air once. A grown man giving it the large portion, up until Clive called him a bad father. A chesty roar and ugly wracked sobbing.

– Should we ban pyjamas from shopping centres and forecourts? That's the question for the next half hour. What do you think? Let's be honest, it's young ones that do this, isn't it? And sometimes not so young. But it's not men doing it. Now I get the feeling, just a hunch on my part, that decent people are sick of it. But maybe you feel differently. For me, this is about toe rags and skangbags. –

He went past the deep freezers and blue ice neon of the Asian shop and into Spar and he got a can of Monster and he had the new box of smokes already ripped open before he was out the door. The stench of petrol and sugar roared up out of the big can, his third of the day. He lowered it down his throat and it fizzed back up from his belly and he let a huge gurgly burp ripple out of him. His mam hadn't rang him today. She'd be off work at six. He checked if she had put anything up on Facebook today. Nothing yet. He had been scaring her more and more recently. Last week, when he had returned after days of not being home, she stood, smaller than ever and further off, looking out the window at the concrete blocks of the garden wall they'd never painted. When she turned, he'd seen her eyes glassy with tears. She never said anything to him after that. Now he got what she used to get from him and even with his dad gone round and round they went, like blood down a sink. She hadn't been onto Clive recently. Last time they laughed at her and told her she couldn't be on every night. That was three weeks ago. He had good battery on his phone.

– Young ones can't be going around doing that and expecting men to behave normally in public – It's a free world or at least it used to be – And you'll be out there tonight parading it round with everything hanging out – You don't know what I'm at tonight – I can see you already – Are you fucking clairvoyant are you? – Common sense clear as day is all I have – Not that common is it but? – Open your eyes – My eyes are open they're never shut – Are you a fish, your eyes never closed – A what? – Yeah a fish and a fucking prick too. –

He lost a few minutes on Grattan Bridge watching a man empty his suitcase into the river. The contents took to the air. A woman went over to the thrashing man, but he pushed her away with a clumsy shove, then looked up at the sky as the papers swung wild on the gust, finally coming to rest on the dark glass river. The sluggish Liffey chewed them up. He waited at the quays. When the 145 pitched into view he lined up, stepped on and pulled himself up the stairs, the steps steep in his face. He sat upstairs, his rucksack on the seat beside him, as the bus rolled into traffic.

– I know your type – I'm not a type. You don't know the first thing about me – There's thousands like you – Excuse me? – Getting your hole and getting the state to pay for the results – Excuse you? – Here, you're the one up in my business – Wouldn't want to be near your business, wouldn't know what I'd catch – How dare you talk to me like that! – You can probably walk down both sides of O'Connell Street at the same time –

It went on and on as the bus left the old parts of town. There were rumours of a huge black cat wandering through Stepaside and the low hills of the Dublin mountains. Was it right now roving the retail parks? Was it right now sniffing the tyres of a Lexus while an affair heaved in a bungalow beyond? Or hosing out a massive piss in a granny's garden, the steam lifting through the leaves? Clive had a lad on who kept a pair of tigers, six vipers and one Gila monster, the exact location of which in Westmeath he would prefer not to disclose. You could rely on Clive for these lads. The man with all the beasts said he should be able to keep whatever he wanted. Bang on, Clive agreed. He ripped out his headphones every ad break. He despised the jingle. The bus powered up the dual carriageway. The smell was at him again. He sniffed the air and knew he was manacled to his own history. In that everyone had the same hot bad intestines, in that there was always shards of wrong snagging inside him. The bus shook and chucked its way along. He watched kids in school uniforms get on and they swarmed the top floor and all around him they talked Irish and he didn't understand a word of it and he put his ears back in.

– They're only spongers, d'you hear me Clive? – A pox – A God-honest pox. My God – Thousands coming across the Med – Listen to you, 'the Med' – It'll fill right up – What's that? – Stacked right up. Octopuses and Muslim scroungers and the rest of them – Let it fill up. I don't care. Fill it up – Then they'll only drive over – You be careful with your mouth and what creeps out of it – This is it and when they're bringing afflictions of all kinds into the country – We won't recognise our country soon – My poor head is wrecked. I do it for you, listeners. I'm a martyr. Back after these … –

The bus left him off at a concrete bunker of an old shopping centre. He had time to waste. He slunk across the car park towards the diner, floodlit bright and headachey inside. He pushed open the door and the blast of frying animal fat made his nostrils flare. He sunk into the red vinyl booth. His table shone with grease. The waitress scratched out his order, hot dog, no sauce or onions and a large Coke. Only a father and his son in the rest of the diner. The father drank a coffee and swiped things on his phone as his son picked at lurid cheese fries. The waitress clanked a second milkshake vat down in front of the boy, the fake cream nozzled on top. He could listen to the show again but he knew he wouldn't. When she came back with his order he bit into his dry dog, the mottled pink showing within the casing and he ate and looked around him. The kid had pushed away his smeared bowl. He stopped chewing when he saw what the boy held in his hands, the weight of the book unwieldy. He hadn't seen one in years. The rest went distant now. He was back in his youth spent scuffing the carpets of Games Workshop, dodging friendly lads who worked there, ponytailed back then, acne-cursed. He spent hours in that small shop on Liffey Street. On the bus home, scared to read it out in the open, he would anxiously sneak peeks at the drawings in the Codex. This was when he first saw into another world, felt it expand beyond him, planets and legions swarming in battle. The huge lore of 40K between the pages. Hopeless mortals ruined in broiling seas of war, crushed under the hordes even as the towers fell above. But as he looked at this new cover he felt no echo of familiarity. He was knocking on air it all looked false nothing like what he remembered it was just shiny fake CG all gloss and bollix, all cheap nothing now all the shadows flushed out no room for fresh magic and no new stars to reach. He fell back into the sanctuaried space of the classroom at lunchtime poring over rulebooks with Hambo, an orcy lunk of a lad with the worst underbite in Dublin 14. When we was mates. Until the door handle was plunged down and the two gentle boys on the floor shrank. Until clumps of mud flew from lads' shoes into the figurines. Until they stamped everything to bits, his armies lying smashed beneath him. Intricate brushwork meant nothing after that. Then it was all swept into the bin of classroom C3 and the bell rang and Hambo said he was done playing and he stuck to it, too. All he had now was the ruins of what had been. He saw it all again but amongst the wreckage, a talisman from an earlier age. The huge axe of a Knight of Chaos, a Hero Quest classic, the first game he ever had. Now the paint-daubed figure held a crude majesty over him and all he knew, cathedrals of hurt, towering cities bleached and raging, untold billions lost in worlds of ash, every war a grain of sand lost across the cold galaxy. The Axeman rose, the warp storms raging.

Out in the suburbs everything was still and the colour of seaweed. He heard his own breath, saw it turn to live frost then nothing in the black air. Past the Butler's Pantry and by now he was used to the houses around here, each of them grandly named, too good for numbers. A brittle, windless night and the moon fringed by clouds. His mam had been on Clive's show eight times. She had been mocked on air and in Tesco Express since, even in her beloved local, the Coach House. Her fingers clicking like insects on the counter, the nails chewed to the quick. He thought of her clutching the counter, her skin tight from the fags, little bubbles under the eyes, a desperate woman left on hold too long. She would ring in and they would take turns with her.

– I am and you're lucky to hear from me Clive. You called me scum – You must have deserved it – You let me say my words – You're not able, nothing to do with us, love, help yourself – You're not being fair to me – It's only shits and giggles love, yeah? – Would you listen – All right, calm down there, bottle bank ... –

His mam became a sour joke they kept telling. He remembered her in the kitchen, pleading with him that if she got a few minutes on the air that'd sate her.

I'm allowed a bit of switch off time, she told him, the ashtray between them.

Doesn't switch you anywhere though, it's only winding you up.

Don't worry about it, she said, and tried selling on a weak laugh.

I do, Mam. I am. Worried.

Don't be. Just I ... just need my words out. Alright?

He was moving across the green when he saw her. Her eye was a shining emerald in the dark. He stood transfixed. He watched her and the panther watched him back. She was the colour of midnight and all grace and power and everything immaculate muscle under a cloak of perfect fur. She purred and it felt to him like nature rumbling. Humans had none of this, he understood. She melted back into the leaves. He had stood before her and he had not looked away.

He turned onto Brooklawn. Everything looked darkly Californian. He felt the rule of all he had laid carefully in place. He already had Clive on strings, a puppet to the future. The beginning was so long ago now. The first night, he had hidden near the station's dumpsters, his mouth tacky from the smokes and sugar, until Clive strode out of the revolving doors and winked good night at the security guard. He had watched him vanish inside the multi-storey. Next time, he waited by the exit of the car park and watched his Saab glide off, moving like pure confidence executed. As the seasons changed he kept going back. Every trip he knew more. Every night he was closer. Every night he went back to his mam. He reached the driveway. One lamp was on deep in the back of the house and when he stepped closer a security light flicked on. He looked up and noted where the motion sensor came on. He let himself go still, waited until it went off, tested it again. He went to the window and peered in at cream carpets and huge sofas. He took his time taking everything out of his rucksack. He got the tripod up and worked out his angles and then he lay down on the tarmac like a slab of roadkill. The security light went off and he waited. He had cleared the table for her this morning. Clean for once. The papers put away, the ashtrays emptied. He had placed the laptop in the middle of the table, facing the door for her when she came in. He unlocked his phone for the last time. Now he hit Live Video, now he hit Go Live. He would leave this for her. He would let her watch. He did not know how long he had been down there when he heard the purr of the motor. From the corner blur of his vision he felt the car slow but he still didn't move as the engine cut the night back to silence. Clive stepped out of the car and the door shut with the softest click. Gravel crunch as Clive came closer.

You alright there, young man?

A step closer and Clive went into a half-crouch, inquisitive, his hands on his knees as he bent down, a sea of stars behind him.

This is private property, you know that yeah?

He readied himself, hands on the ground, as Clive peered down.

He crouched and sprung up until they were face to face – for a celebrity, Clive was tall enough.

Listen if I give you a fifty, will you clear off? Spend it on a night out, few beers, try get the ride. You look like you could use it.

They were both sweating in the moonlight.

Say your mother has to crack your sheets.

Shuttup!

I'm tight with the guards, yeah? I've had creeps and freaks before.

You're not the first, son. Listen –

Clive copped it then but it changed nothing. At the end of the day a Stanley knife is a Stanley knife and it slid zero fuss into Clive's torso and his eyes narrowed, like he was trying to bring it into sense or focus. The awful truth of the wound grew between them. The puncture sucked the knife as it slid out but with vicious force he hiked the blade up through Clive's stomach, finished the gash. The man's hot rich guts fell out of him, the confidences of his anatomy exposed. Clive's knees swung into each other and he had to grab him by the shoulders. He held him up with one hand and with the other reached inside his mouth. It was hard to keep a hold of Clive's tongue but once he freed the tongue web with a nick the muscle thrashed about until he steadied him against the wall and now he shushed him face to face and then clasped him and forced the blade up into Clive's long wild tongue. He yanked and yanked then pulled the whole thing out like a bloody mollusc. Now The Axeman watched him suffer and gurgle and he turned to the camera. He stretched out his arm and held out the grisly trophy for her. This was his chance and he took it and he did not sleep or listen or speak in the cells he was shuffled through as all things narrowed.

THE ART OF THE STREET

Conversations with COOL C and ESTR by Shane Curtin

As an early disciple of hip hop in 1980s Ireland I appreciated that there were four core elements. In essence, the DJ worked with the MC and the breakdancer responded from the crowd. Versions of these three elements slowly attained their own Irish identity but the fourth, the graffiti writer, remained elusive, a mystery. It was easy to spot the vibrant colours and intricate calligraphy of a graffiti piece in our drab cities but the writers operated anonymously. Their progress in turning obscure nooks and crannies of Ireland's cities into informal art spaces was slow. Their names would occasionally appear in the court reports. Still those early pioneers continued to walk the cities by night, seeking out new surfaces and braving the often-difficult Irish weather.

In the last decade, that journey has changed, with local authorities, festivals and multinationals rushing to harness this street-generated energy. The forms and styles on our walls are now varied, and ambitious, and the practitioners are safely able to move from cover of darkness to daylight. They are finally seen as artists; creators not destroyers.

Cool C (Cormac Cullinan) from Kilkenny, has been involved in the Irish hip hop scene for over thirty years. A graffiti writer and DJ, he worked for close to a decade in Ireland's premier hip hop shop, All City in Dublin, and was ideally placed to observe the changing nature of the grafitti and street art world. He now lives and paints in County Sligo.

SHANE CURTIN: *How did you become involved in graffiti?*
COOL C: I would have been twelve in 1984 when hip hop and breakdancing arrived in Ireland and to me, the music and artwork seemed to be all connected. So I would have copied graffiti pieces, from breakdance instruction books and street sounds compilations – they all had graffiti covers. Then, at sixteen, I would have gone up to Croke Park and passed a famous skate shop on Hill Street which had a full mural … it just like those hip hop sleeves and I was blown away. So I decided, okay, just find a wall … and the obvious choice in Kilkenny would have been handball alleys because they were big hang-out spots. So I did a piece and the next day a message came from the GAA along the lines of, 'Down with this sort of thing!'

I moved to Dublin at eighteen and met two guys from Drogheda, Rask and Artz. Rask was a historian of the movement and he was running the Bridge of Peace event in Drogheda. We were having cups of tea, there was always a sit-down aspect, you always had a sketchbook, sketching constantly and handing the books back and forth, sharing information, like, how you could spray so much more for campaigns in a short time with a wider cap. If you were going somewhere to do an illegal piece, in our naivety we'd bring a lot more paint and the sketchbooks in the bag.

While those Bridge of Peace jams were important, it was still a relatively small scene?
At that point, the hip hop scene in general was so small. I only knew of maybe seven or eight people in the whole country who did graffiti. If you saw a tag

on the wall, you'd spend half the day looking at it. I remember standing in Clive's Skate City shop, which stocked spray paint, and we were scratching our heads going, but where can we paint? And we just went to Windmill Lane because painting and graffiti on the wall there was totally tolerated in Dublin. So a bunch of guys went down and painted over probably two decades of U2 history with these big, colourful, New York-style graffiti pieces without any consequences. Windmill Lane became the place to go and try your stuff out and it kind of exploded from there. Then the People In Need Telethon in 1996 brought a load of us together to do a mural and that was a real connection.

There were two guys at that point who decided to walk the whole city in Dublin, and just start doing tags ... They kept them to the hoardings, the temporary surfaces all over the city, just to tag, like maybe a thousand times. Suddenly, there was a new attraction to this kind of infamy. But I just never had the nerves to get really crazy into that kind of tagging or bombing. I was very into the murals, that side of it.

That infamy brought into sharp focus the loathing official Ireland had for the graffiti scene. Newspapers and politicians regularly railed against it. I remember one minister in 2008 saying graffiti reduction was 'very important in the fight against crime'. How did that impact the scene?
By 2008, it had really exploded. We had a graffiti PlayStation game called Getting Up, there were chain stores pushing the clothes, all graffiti style. There were kids coming into All City top to bottom in these clothes. There was a glut of tags and the city had become so clean that when a tag got done, it stood out as messy ... In the '90s, if you coloured it, it nearly added to the whole area! There was a lot more aggression from the authorities, the council and the gardaí and we'd meet them in the shop and we had to have these debates with them.

There were hundreds of kids buying markers. I mean, we often had people walk outside All City with stuff they'd just bought and then tag the shop! Our first job opening on a Monday morning was to clean Crow Street and go three or four streets over and make sure none of the businesses that regularly came in to give out to us were tagged and if they were, we cleaned them. One thing that was to our benefit at the time is that the judicial system couldn't deal with it.

But things changed and began to calm down. When property prices went up in Brick Lane in London because of Banksy, even the judges and gardaí became a lot more understanding. The councillors also got younger and got very interested in it. For example, the Lucan skatepark caused a dramatic drop in tagging around the area when they put up walls where it was tolerated. Suddenly all the graffiti was getting absorbed. Workshops were showing a lot of success, too – lads who were just into tagging, suddenly they got a chance within their own community to do something more positive. I did some of those workshops and the kids were hungry to learn more about graffiti. We'd bring them to a wall and facilitate the whole thing. I regularly used to get inspired as these guys would have read every book ... But in the last decade, kids don't really care about graffiti at all, they're just happy to be doing a mural and they don't care whether it's got names or letters or any connection with hip hop.

This change over the last decade or so – how do you feel about what has emerged?
Street art exploded, which also kind of increased the amount of people on the ground discussing the possibility of doing walls with businesses. The Bernard Shaw [pub, in Dublin] was a very good example.

Has it all become too safe?
We needed a huge amount of safe stuff – there's a lot of people who just want to paint murals. But there was a slew of graduates who all painted similarly and took a lot of edge out of the scene. I lament the missed opportunities sometimes, because walls are scarce. I see so many walls I just won't remember the next day. But skills still rock across both street art and graf ... If you see a full colour trackside mural, whether it be letters or not, it blows your mind in a way that it simply can't when it's done on a regular permission spot. The layers of appreciation of graf are many compared to street art.

The guys who are really into doing the traditional New York style are few and far between now. Those guys are becoming more like a military operation, because security has increased. They are used to observing the city and its potential surface areas And I still love that and respect that. It's just two different worlds completely.

Your own practice at the moment is studio-based. How has your background in graffiti influenced that?
You don't see much reference to graffiti in my studio work – I'd see that as a cynical move to gain traction with a market. But my inner graffiti artist has in the last few years been honing the skills and sharpening up, not for anything illegal, but planning some large-scale graffiti style stuff. The best graffiti has actually the same principles going on as any good art.

I'm extremely excited about what can be done and all the possibilities. I'm also very inspired by people who were graffiti artists in the past who are doing fine art masterpieces now, like Conor Harrington, who was Mr Who when he tagged. The graduation from the scene has been very impressive. When I used to be in All City, I was at pains telling the gardaí about the positive sides to it all but as time goes on, I can really vouch for that.

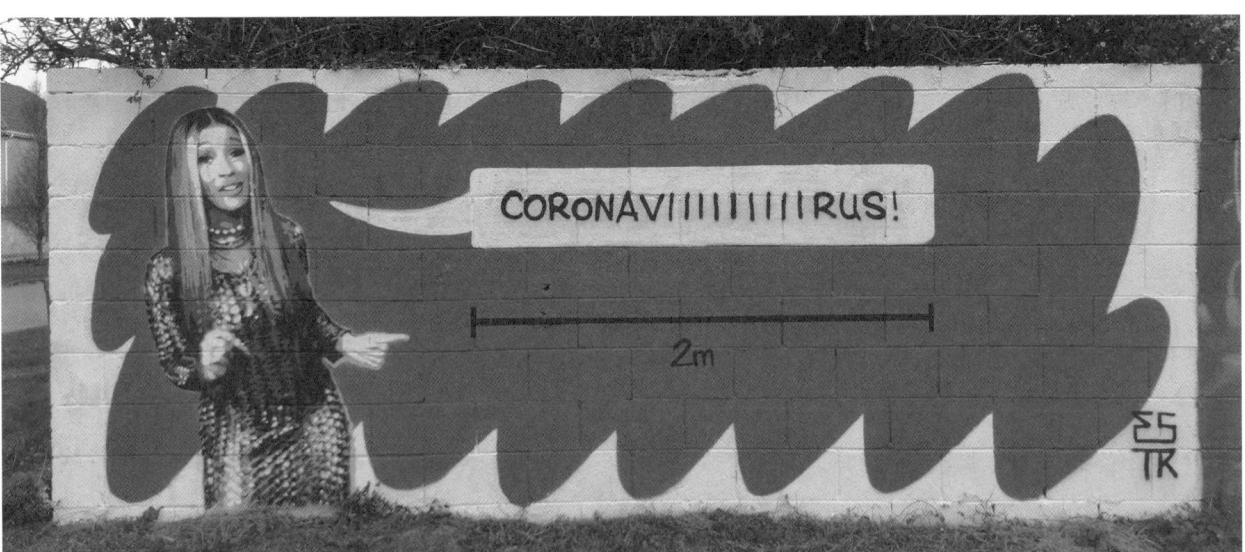

ESTR (Emmalene Blake) is a street artist and teacher from Dublin. Her work started appearing on walls around 2012 and it has often vividly captured the social mood of the time, with pieces focused on marriage equality, the repeal movement, Black Lives Matter, and much else. Many of her images have had a resonance far beyond the specific site, becoming viral hits on social media.

SHANE CURTIN *You're just after finishing the Kingswood Stay At Home project which shows that place plays an important role in your work. Can you explain how that came about?*

ESTR: I grew up in Kingswood in Tallaght. I've lived in Kingswood my whole life but I've never actually painted here. Back in March, I'd come up with ideas and designed a few pieces, and I had a couple of spaces in the city centre that I was going to go and paint in. But then the announcement was made that we couldn't go more than two kilometres, so that was out the window. I had a feeling shops were going to close so I flew out to the paint shop down the road and I got a load of different colour emulsion. So then I was just, like, well, will I just do it on my back wall? Because the back wall of my house is public facing. There was space for two, so I was gonna just leave it at that. But then loads of my neighbours started offering up their walls. I had a never-ending amount of canvases! And the community all love the pieces. They took it upon themselves to do a fundraiser to buy more materials and that raised over a thousand euro.

All the kids in the area love them and their parents told me it gave them something to do, trying to figure out where a new piece was and going for a walk around Kingswood to find it.

I had loads of people on Instagram constantly asking me, 'Where is this?', but I just ignored them all because I was, like, I don't want to have people coming into Kingswood when it's not within their two kilometres. Because the restrictions have been lifted since, I did a map. So now everyone can find them.

Going back to the start, what inspired you to be a street artist? Were there particular artistic influences?

I studied Fine Art in DIT. I've always been into graffiti and street art. I used to go around Dublin city trying to find and take photographs of all the different street art and graffiti that was appearing when I was in my late teens. I also started discovering online the work of artists like Keith Haring and Jean-Michel Basquiat. I love Haring's work – he's my favourite artist. Towards the end of my degree, I started going along to events in the White Lady Gallery, which was a street art gallery and I started going to the graffiti jams in the Bernard Shaw. I just started asking if I could paint at them. I started painting at these events regularly and met more people and then got asked to join the Minaw Collective.

The Minaw Collective is an all-female street art collective. When that was formed, Irish street art was still a very male-dominated scene. I can remember being at paint jams where less than ten per cent of the painters were women. How do you work as a collective and are there still barriers to participation today?

When I started out it would have been mostly male painters at jams but it's not really something that I would have noticed or that would have intimidated me. But I know for others it would do. Kathrina (Kin Mx) set up Minaw Collective. They formed so that they could go and just have chilled jams where there was no judgement, where they're showing each other different techniques and just being able to practice and have the chats and the craic. We also give each other advice and send each other any opportunities or commissions that we hear are coming up. I do think the younger generation should be seeing more female street artists – like, if you can't see it, you can't be it.

One of the other main barriers today is the lack of walls, especially now because the old Bernard Shaw is gone and the Tivoli, where the All City jam took place, that's gone as well. So there's actually nowhere left in the city centre. The other day I painted Sinead O'Connor but that's just on a temporary hoarding, that hoarding is going to be gone. There's a lack of actual walls that young street artists or people wanting to get into the form can go out and practise on. And if you have a lack of walls, you're going to have more tagging of people's property. We need legal walls for young artists starting out and also we should be progressing as a city, the way the majority of other cities in the world are, with large walls given over to street art by prominent artists. Most major cities in the world now have annual street art festivals where they fly international artists in and paint multi-storey buildings. If you look at people's photos of city breaks, apart from the main landmarks, the thing that people take most photos of is the street art.

The commercial world has certainly gotten on board – street art is being used by major corporations to give their brands an edge. What challenge does that throw up for someone like you, whose work is about making bold political statements?
I do use my work as social commentary for issues I feel strongly about but I also take on commercial projects. I painted Lizzo for Warner Music and I absolutely love Lizzo, so I was delighted to paint her. It has to be work I'm happy to stand behind. I have turned down jobs where I've been asked to paint people who I wouldn't be happy to be associated with.

There is a positive result of the commercial world embracing street art – it means artists don't have to solely rely on selling their art or on individuals commissioning work. Corporations tend to have more money than individuals to commission pieces. These commissions can help artists earn a living, and then be able to continue with their passion projects.

But you have a problem with brands using street art in adverts where they haven't got the artists' permission or compensated the artists. They seem to think because it's on the street, they don't need to, which isn't true. You wouldn't get these companies going into a gallery and shooting an ad in front of an artist's work without permission.

Take me through the artistic process for one of your pieces, from the initial idea to its appearance on the wall ....

Ideas for new pieces come to me all the time. I write them down, and then try make my way through the list. When I'm starting a design, I'll do a quick sketch of it. Then I'll decide if it's going to be a stencilled piece or freehand. This depends on the size and design. If it's a huge wall, I'll do it freehand. If it's a smaller wall but there's no portrait in the piece, I'll do it freehand. If it's a smaller wall and it's a portrait, I'll stencil it. If it's a stencil piece, I'll design it small and then I'll use a projector to project it onto card and I'll cut it out. Then I'll arrive at the wall, paint the background, paint the stencils, usually about five layers of stencils per piece, and then I freehand whatever other elements are going along with it. A smaller wall, with no portrait, I'll just go at it totally freehand. The other method, though, for a bigger wall with a portrait – say for the marriage equality piece that I painted at Hit The North – with this method, you paint the background, then doodle all over it, take a photo, open the photo in ProCreate on an iPad, drop the design onto the photo and turn the opacity down, so that you can see the photo under the design. Now you can see where each part of the design should go on the wall in relation to the doodles. It's a gridding system without the time and effort it takes of doing a grid.

Sticking with Hit The North, how did the Lyra McKee piece come about, and tell me about where it is situated?

I was already booked to paint at Hit The North, the month after she was killed. I didn't know her but we have friends in common, we're a similar age, and we seem to have a lot of similar beliefs and opinions. Her death really distressed and upset me and I just wouldn't have felt right going up and painting something unrelated. So through a mutual friend I reached out to her partner, and through the family solicitor I reached out to her family, and they said they would love for it to go ahead. I then took the words from Letter to my 14-Year-Old-Self and painted the words on the background of the piece, and then a portrait of Lyra and a main quote over the background. The wall that Adam from Hit The North sourced was on a little skinny street and directly facing the wall was a spot where some photos of her had been taken in front of a piece by Emic. Those were shared a lot online. It was also just outside The Sunflower pub, which would have been one of her regulars.

LET ME GO MAD IN MY OWN WAY

Elaine Feeney

I like driving alone. I wear shoes that are not suitable for driving, but that's okay, having no one in the car means there's no one to speak to you or speak at you. No *slow down*. Or *stop*. Or *bicycle! You sure you can drive in flip-flops?* I don't know exactly the physics of driving in flip-flops. I know that having people with me unnerves me. In the car. In the supermarket. In a swimming pool. In bed.

Love

I have never fallen in love. You may think this is a great tragedy. But so is falling in love – falling in love might be the greatest tragedy. Anything that requires imbalance or a giving of something personal or knocking yourself out is tragic. Like falling. Like time.

You see, I've always had an insatiable desire to shove someone from a moving car. Or to throw my dinner at the kitchen wall. Especially a roast dinner, to throw a roast beef dinner at the magnolia walls. Yorkshire puddings. Gravy. The warm rump of a cow. The back leg of a lamb. A baby chicken. The ceramic plate. Roast potatoes, sprigs of plants sprinkle dried from jars. Oh and to scream out *this is cold!* Or *there is stringy fat in this.*

Losing

When I lose my temper I can't quite remember it in detail. Except that it feels ferocious. And makes me confident. Even now after all that has happened.

I had bought a house with X but eventually we broke each other, and he took the Indian sheets, the duck-down duvet, a few CDs, a heavy ashtray, and a box of groceries, and left me with his dog and the girl. Our girl. Later I would come to consider belongings as chattels. Or as things that could choke me. After which it was generally agreed that I owned the kitchen, the small hallway, the child's bedroom, the hot-press and the outhouse where the laundry was done. Every woman owns the laundry room. He owned the living room, the inside toilet, the other bedrooms, the crystal whiskey tumblers and the outside – the driveway and the gardens.

I needed to purchase these rooms to complete a full house for the girl to live in. And I needed to get myself something to get around in, for he had driven off in the family car, swiftly changing its status. I bought myself a car off two hefty brothers one afternoon on the forecourt of a petrol station in Athlone. It was a green Renault.

X told me I had smothered him, he needed to roam, or be, and he didn't like the nonsense. What nonsense? The crying. Like a wet mat pulled from a burning house. Every time I deep drag on a cigarette, I think of him and his mother smoking in their kitchen and giving him big gulps of advice.

I was Bad. Bad girl holding my breath. Bad girl lighting one cigarette off the other. Bad. Bad lungs. Bad girl. Much of my pain seemed lodged in my lungs. So I ignored them. Much like I do with my breasts and between my legs.

Art

It's an art to ignore a major organ of the body like the way I can with my lungs and yet we all do it. Art. Ignoring things, focusing on small things, other things. We make lots of art that we don't even notice; we would never call ourselves artists, there's a confidence to that, to calling yourself something. But falling in love, walking down a street in love, walking down a street in fear, kissing beside water, eating a sandwich outside a café, lipstick, screaming at your child in the supermarket, crying at a staff meeting or leaving blood on a toilet bowl – it's art, right? We are always artists, often when we least expect it.

Giving birth to the girl in the still moments of light and blue, the TV on, Wimbledon, then the Simpsons, and sadness, the slices of you. Re: stitching. Re: sectioning parts back together.

I soak myself in pain like lying in a sitz bath. It's an addictive habit I inherited from my grandmother, who had the dozen children and went into and out of the bathtub three times a day after the birthings. Her life was art. Murals of self-pity, oils of self-loathing. Her walls in the kitchen were oiled. The condensation ran down them like on her forehead. I stick pain all over me, like she did in her house. This is intergenerational. All my colleagues' talk about intergenerational pain and trauma and disadvantage – they speak about it as though they landed here, existential beings, things that came from nothing. A thing from a rib. I'm almost done papering myself in it like how the wasps are settling in the little lanterns they make themselves in the fascia of the house, and in the crevices where we never look, how rarely we look up, its traversing my ribcage, stitching splinters of memory onto the intercostal muscles, same bit of pig we slather with spicy sauces and bar-b-que, though the supply chain of pork is in real trouble, or so I heard yesterday. I think about giving up eating meat when I speak to the heifers in the fields, or watch the lambs arrive as though they came from nowhere. I'm sure I can smell their wool when I roast their hind leg in the fan oven. But I can't be sure if I will give it up. Something about it is innate in me. I watched a pig once, upside down and draining from the neck. Just before death they reattached him and left the blood in the bucket and I leaned over it and looked in. The pig had closed his eyes.

Soon

After the money went into his single account, that now shared the double barrel of his secretary, with the prefix of *Miss*, then *Mrs* (same surname as our girl) for the rooms, X called to the front door, perhaps I should say my door, or our door, but there's a courage to this also. X was relieved we had finally sorted it, like we had an abacus, or the washing, and he seemed happy, like he'd just been laid. X was grinning, in that way men grin after they've fucked something, and said that we could share her, the girl, like a *share bag* of sweets in the cinema. I could have her for the weekdays and the sick days, and he would Sunday her if he was well, the girl, or in fact, he corrected, if they were both well, and perhaps Saturday her too, every second week, but he'd let me know about that one, give me *advanced warning*. He would Christmas her also, though this never materialized as he liked to sun himself at Christmas. When she grew, he liked to have her around a little more, girls who drive are useful to their fathers, collecting them down the pub, similarly boys who drink beer become useful to their estranged fathers.

The girl had on a green jacket with a fur collar and incredibly long fingers twisting back and over, pulling at us both, in an effort to get us to lie down, like we once had.

I Lost It

Lost. I lost myself outside the house with the rooms that day.

Lost the plot, they say, as if we wake up one day and have a plan to go entirely fucking ballistic. A beginning middle and end like the seasons. Utterly reliable and subconscious. And I lost it and told him with my teeth bared like a mad wolf that if he ever threatened me or the girl again that I'd eat his skin off and I'd start on his perfectly chiselled cheekbones. I think back and imagine this is what I must have said, I can't rightly remember, I have done things in rage and drink that I can't remember. I wish I could, because I feel in those moments so utterly in control and the face on him was white like dog shit and he left in the car he'd stolen from me. *Who's the cunt now?* I shouted out, but only the neighbour in the tractor opposite could hear me. And even he cleverly pretended not to hear me. The big dog and the toddler looked up at me, as if I had any clue what to do with them, so we stuck magnets to the fridge and I spelled out *fucktard* and *bowl* and *wine*, and the toddler spelled out her four-lettered name, and just as I was about to cry, the dog whimpered and hunched over and then shat on the lino bulging with water bubbles underneath. Not long after he drove away the entire house would flood.

And, I thought, how correct he was about me being this *cunt* figure that needed a doctor. I would always need a doctor. And I was glad he finally noticed.

Bathrooms

I walked back and locked myself into the bathroom and I sat on the edge of the bath and ran my shaking hands over black bottles of caffeine shampoos, Regaine, razors, face masks. There are not many ways to hide from a little girl. Why did Daddy leave, she would ask on a cycle one time. And I'd be cycling into a wind and scream out. Because.

Because?

Because someone had told me that he had once fucked a woman in a castle and fucked another in Paris driving around in a soft top Porsche that belonged to the woman he fucked in the castle, that he had fucked his secretary, and he had now fucked the babysitters, two of them, Latvians.

I'm not sure there's a difference between fucking in your head and on a bed, aside from the inconvenience of the latter, although my friend, my only friend, George, thinks there's a sea of difference, as though she is very educated in the subject. I'm not very educated in anything. My boss says I'm either incredibly naive or incredibly genius. I know which one of these is true.

Truth

I've watched that documentary about the free solo climber, Alex, with the big teeth and big hands and the gorgeous ribs that free solos Mount Cap, and Alex knows the difference between naivety and bravery. The difference is in the amygdala. That's the difference. That's what makes me like driving. I trick it into thinking I'm driving away, somewhere exciting, that I didn't even have time to change my shoes. And I'll pull in at a drive-through somewhere, talk to a machine, and eat in the car, fall asleep, cry.

My amygdala can be tricked over and over especially when I'm driving, going, moving on, when it's all a rush, a new start, or the end, sometimes it's the end, a drive, heading west, going nowhere. That's the thing with the inner machine of the brain – you can trick it, over and over. Like roads you can coast down, to get lost, just for a while, just a little while.

Photograph by Hugh O'Conor

THE LIVES OF THE SONGS

An interview with RADIE PEAT by Jim Carroll

Radie Peat is a Dublin-born musician and singer who performs with Lankum, the band who won the RTÉ Choice Music Prize Album of the Year for their 2019 release The Livelong Day. Peat has also won an RTÉ Radio 1 Folk Award for Best Folk Singer and the band have won multiple BBC Radio 2 Folk Awards. This conversation with Peat about her life in music is taken from the transcript of a Skype conversation conducted earlier this year.

JIM CARROLL: *Let's start with five-year-old Radie Peat in Artane watching her sisters heading off every Tuesday to a tin whistle class and wanting to go along. Was music part of the fabric in your home?*
RADIE PEAT: Well, that's my earliest memory. I suppose they must have been playing around the house as well. I never really questioned it, to be honest, because my mam plays banjo and mandolin and my dad plays concertina. I have three sisters and one of them is younger than me but the two older ones were already playing by the time I was five. I remember it just being something that I did for a while and then, when I was about nine or ten, I realised that I actually liked it and that I was really getting a lot of enjoyment out of it. A lot of that came from getting to play with other people. Trad music is so inter-generational that you can go and play with someone in their seventies or someone who is seven and, if they're a nice player, it doesn't matter.

What about singing?
The first singing I did was when I went to Scoil Neasáin primary school. It's an Irish school and we had this music teacher called Bean Uí Áinle and her philosophy was that everybody had to sing. There must have been at least 120 kids in the school so I loved singing with these massive groups of children.

I liked the philosophy of it as well. It wasn't really about whether you were a good singer or not. It was could you contribute to making this really big noise, this really full-sounding mass of children's voices.

In terms of traditional singing, I only really came across that for the first time when I was about twelve. When I was in school, they sent me over to Coláiste Íosagáin because they knew the music was good over there. I ended up in the same class as two really excellent sean-nós singers, Róisín Chambers and Saileog Ní Cheannabháin. It was great because they'd take us out of school and we used to tour around other schools playing trad music. We'd play tunes, and they'd sing songs.

I was really fascinated by how they sounded because I'd never really heard anything like that technique before. I was like 'wow, that's wild. What's going on there?' A lot of people sometimes mistakenly call me a sean-nós singer, which I'm not. I was fascinated by it because it's so different to what you usually hear people singing.

But I didn't consider myself a singer then. I did sing a bit when I was a teenager, but I hadn't really found songs that I connected with at that point. They felt like old songs and I didn't feel engaged with the subject matter.

At a certain point, probably between the age of about fifteen and twenty, I just wanted to be really good on the concertina. That became my entire ambition. I remember seeing Kitty Hayes playing in Milltown Malbay and that was really exciting.

Then there was Noel Hill who taught me concertina. He's a phenomenal player and still is. I still find some of the recordings he's made really exciting. He was an excellent teacher, really, really good, but really stern. He took it very seriously and he expected us to as well, even when we were very small. I was definitely a child when I went there first, I wasn't a teenager.

Can you remember your introduction to trad sessions in places like The Cobblestone?
I think I was about fifteen when my dad first took me to The Cobblestone. He just thought the style of music, the sessions, that it was really good, so he was bringing me in and getting me a half pint of Guinness. I think it was mostly to listen in those days, because I was a bit young to be playing. I remember it felt really far from Artane, a big trek.

The Cobblestone was just one place that my dad brought me, but me and my group of friends were all players and we'd go and make our own sessions. We'd try somewhere that would serve us drink when we were far too young to drink! We'd play a lot of tunes and yeah, we had a lot of fun. I suppose it's not the worst thing you could be doing as a teenager. We were doing a lot of underage drinking and being really bold, but we were also playing some pretty good music.

Mostly it was people who were doing it for the love of the music. You wouldn't believe the amount of amazing trad players that never release a record. They never do it as a job. They literally just do it as an outlet, a hobby, a pastime, a passion. They basically don't ever even think of recording a CD because they're like 'well, why would I do that? I just want to play the tunes.'

I started teaching tin whistle and concertina when I was sixteen and that's how I earned money when I was in college. I would have done sessions as well, where you get paid to go to a pub and man the session and keep the tunes going.

I took a year out and I went to live in Italy, but I couldn't play sessions when I was there and it's the longest I've ever gone without playing. The live music scene in Italy is terrible. There's no live music so I was really starved of music for over a year and definitely wanted to get back into it.

When I got back, I was living a few streets away from Cormac [MacDiarmada, fiddle player with Lankum]. We actually knew each other from secondary school so I started going down to some of the sessions that he was doing in places like Shebeen Chic and having a really good time, and that was how I met the Lynch brothers [Ian and Daragh from Lankum].

You've used a great expression to describe the rise of Lankum: 'it's a weird train we accidentally got on.'
I always think of the analogy of the train when it comes to the band. I actually have used that a few times when we talk about it amongst ourselves. You can't predict what's next, you have no idea what the next stage is going to be.

I remember when we signed the contract at Rough Trade Records feeling like we were taking an actual step and being like, 'Okay, now you're choosing this.' This is the point where you're putting your cards on the table and saying

'I am going to do this.' That was a moment that sticks in my mind as making a decision to do it.

We felt so lucky very early on from the response we got and we were just surprised at every step, 'Jesus Christ, people actually like this.' I suppose around the time we signed, we had to be like 'Okay, you need to stop being so surprised by this and take yourself a bit seriously.' If you're going to sign this contract with this label that you really admire, you need to feel this isn't happening by accident. You need to start feeling a sense of ownership and confidence in what you're doing.

But there was a long time when we were genuinely bewildered by what was happening. When we got offered the Later With Jools show the first time, we didn't know what to do because it was the first telly we had ever done. It just felt really bizarre, and there was definitely a feeling of imposter syndrome. Occasionally there still is, but at some point we just had to go, 'This is what we do, just do it.'

You have to have trust. Geoff [Travis] and Jeanette [Lee] from Rough Trade are putting their confidence in you so you'd want to have a bit of confidence in yourself as well, and trust that you can pull it off.

Lankum have recorded a few albums together now – what's been the hardest thing around that process?
The more albums you do, the more you become accustomed to the spectrum of emotions you're going to feel while you're producing anything. The first time you do it, it's a bit of a shock because you don't realize how low and how high it can get.

You'll have days where you go, 'This is the worst thing I've ever heard in my life. What were we thinking? I'm so bad at music.' Other days, you're like, 'Oh my God, I really love this.'

I'd say the same goes for writers, visual artists, all creative people. There's this weird cyclical thing that happens when you're trying to put something together. There will be a low point where you're really questioning what you're doing, but there will hopefully be the bit where you feel proud of it, too.

That emotional flux goes on constantly if you create things. You become more used to the range of your own emotions when you're doing it. You need to remember the overall picture – 'Yeah, yeah, you did feel like this before, but remember how you felt just afterwards?'

Sometimes we joke and say that if we don't lose our minds when we're doing an album, then we probably haven't put in enough effort. Unless you have some degree of an existential crisis while you're doing it then maybe you're just not giving it your all.

You talked earlier about finding and researching songs that resonated with you.
When you read about situations in the past, it's very hard to get a sense of the emotion at the time. If you read novels or accounts written by historians, they're often by people in positions of power and in the upper sections of society.

But the songs are coming from the viewpoint of everyday people that you might not otherwise consider or even get to hear, like women for example. There are really old songs where it's all about women basically ending up in desperate situations because of falling pregnant. You don't necessarily get to hear about that experience unless it's through the songs, because it's not stuff that gets written down in history books. There is a very strong protest vein running through folk songs. The more you research them, the more you find really strong human elements.

I think I was already researching songs before I met the Lynchs. I remember finding Willow Garden and thinking it was amazing. We're just four people out of a load of people who were around at the time playing tunes and singing traditional songs. There's this whole community of traditional singers, so you'd hear people singing songs and you'd be like, 'That's a great song. I've never heard that before.' You'd get to know all the older traditional singers and you'd be hearing all these songs and I just wanted to be more informed about it basically.

Once you start researching the songs, it's just endless. You'd never be done, you could never know every song. You could never know every version and that's really interesting, so you start to become really interested in the lives of the songs themselves. Why did they survive?

What's fascinating about Lankum's The Livelong Day album is the variety of sounds behind and around the words. It's not just folk and trad.
I feel like I've given you a very skewed version of my teenage years because you've been asking me specifically about trad music, right? So to actually paint the full picture, yeah, I was doing all of those things, going to sessions and drinking pints and all that stuff. I always thought trad music was a community and an outlet, and all that. But in my musical world, I wasn't a trad purist. What I listening to was anything but trad. There were little musical worlds I could go into on my own. I got really obsessed with Radiohead when I was about eleven. I got into old jazz stuff, like Fats Domino and Fats Waller. I was mad into Elvis, mad into the Beach Boys. When I was a teenager, I started listening to Portishead. It's not worlds away, but it wasn't trad.

I think Neu! were the first band that you'd call Krautrock that I came across. Obviously, I also listened to David Bowie, who borrowed so much from Krautrock, and Brian Eno, but I watched a documentary on Krautrock and I heard Neu! and I thought they were amazing.

Did that have an influence on your choice of instruments?
I basically wanted to be able to do uninterrupted drones. When we started to arrange songs, my main instrument was concertina, which is great for playing tunes on, but there's only some notes you can actually drone endlessly on – it's different on the push and pull, so it was inhibiting what I wanted to do. I've also always been really drawn to bass, anything really bassy and rumbly.

I started looking into reed instruments that were able to get that sound. The first one I came across is that Russian accordion that we call the bayan. There's this shop in Phibsboro and they sold a strange array of things like old furniture, mounted pigs heads, trouts' heads and old paintings. I found the accordion in there but it was broken and Daragh managed to figure out how to unbreak it. We were like, 'This sounds great.' It's really old and I've had to get a second one because that one died. It was getting more towards what I wanted, to get these really ominous rumbly bass notes.

It's the same thing with the harmonium. It was just to get more options, in terms of bassy reeds, low reeds, drone, full reed sounds.

Can you talk a little about how the opening track on the album, The Wild Rover, came about? That's one people are fascinated by.

I think myself and Ian were at a singing session where there were just traditional songs all night long. We heard Dónal Maguire singing that version and we were just like, 'Oh, that's beautiful, it's so moving.' He gave us a CD of recordings of Pat Usher and his sisters singing.

I think Ian sang it for the lads and they were like, 'Yeah, gorgeous, let's do it.' We just started chipping away at it in the same way as we approach everything, which is there are no definites, it's open, it's always up for grabs who might sing the main part, or if there's going to be harmony or not. It's always, 'Let's dismantle the whole thing, and then put it back together.'

Then there's the John 'Spud' Murphy [soundman, producer and engineer] effect. This was the first album where he was on-board from the beginning. When we first came across him, we did a track with that old Russian accordion and he was the first person who'd ever really gotten the best out of that sound. We've worked with him since then because we felt that what he was hearing and what we were hearing was the same thing. We loved so many of the albums that he has produced for the likes of The Jimmy Cake and Katie Kim and his own band, Percolator. It was really great to have that extra brain there, to have five brains from the start.

We went through a few permutations. I think the mad outro at the end came together down in the basement of Liberty Hall. We'd been in the basement for a good few hours and just went a bit mad and did the big outro. We also decided it might be more interesting for a woman to sing the song. Then we went into Spud and we got to use the studio as another instrument. That's the great thing about recording albums, the way you can layer things, so we got to add all these textures at the end. And Spud is so good at just keeping us on track. We call it metaphysical counselling. He'll just keep you on track.

A QUICKENING IN THE STILLNESS

Susan Cahill

Uncertainty has settled on me like snow, quiet and intractable, its secrets buried like seeds in the cold earth. I know about snow. I lived in Canada for eight years. I know its brute implacability, its resistance to a desire for change, until, when the time is right, it melts and reveals the stunted grass beneath.

We are all ploughing through uncertainty now, as I write this, in the midst of the coronavirus lockdown. Indefinite times, waiting for the end of the restrictions, the return to a normal life. But no one knows what normal means anymore and I can't hear the phrase 'the new normal' without gritting my teeth. It seems foolish, falsely soothing. Something else is growing under this disruption. What dazed foliage lies beneath the uncertainty?

To me, the uncertainty seems even more present, more pressing, more personal. The pandemic coincides with my first pregnancy. I am expecting, unexpectedly, at the age of forty. The date when this experience will end is unpredictable, too, though less so than the pandemic. I hope they coincide, even knowing that my return to life afterwards will be anything but normal. There will be a new person, whose face I cannot even imagine, with new demands and his own desires and needs. I'm not ready.

Pregnancy makes me think about opacity, the things that happen out of sight, alive to no one but themselves. Baking and gardening have been the obsessions of the lockdown so far. Batter blooming into banana bread, seeds splitting and sprouting, the alchemy of dark places, of ovens and earth. And my own unknown growing, bones and sinews forming inside me. One of my scans appears to show a face staring directly outwards, an amniotic ghost, surrounded by the grainy moonscape of my insides.

I come home to Ireland to tell Mum about the pregnancy at the beginning of March. One case is reported the day I arrive. The idea of a lockdown does not even occur to me. Now I am stuck in Ireland, in my mother's house. My brother is here, too. My partner is in London.

Days pass. I visit a friend. I visit my Nanna, who has grown frail. We sit in the warm familiarity of her kitchen, next to the heat of the Aga as I tell her about this new generation, her fourth great-grandchild. She tells me stories of her own pregnancies, when there was no certainty of blue lines on a test, no language to speak of the changes in her body, no manuals to ward against the screams of a brand-new human. I promise to visit her again.

The uncertainty heightens, falters, alters, intensifies. My flight is cancelled. I wait.

I turn forty-one, my birthday muted but lovely, a homemade cake in my mother's garden. It's a summer garden, she says. It will be beautiful in a few weeks. But it's beautiful now, in the April dusk, the flowers still retaining their revelations, and the view down over the valley where Clonakilty coalesces, a small band of sea visible through a hazy dip in the hills. From here, you can see the way the town dissolves into the rural, a puzzle of fields in various states of sowing and fertilisation, and the bang of slurry that assaults your nose as you drive out west.

It is not really my childhood home. We moved here, to the house and to the town, when I was eleven, and this is the point around which my childhood pivots, ends, and fades back into the past. This house was where my body transmuted out of the smoothness of the child into the distress of adolescence, where the adult world pressed on me like a mysterious smog. There is something strangely fitting to return here as my body makes another transition, pushing outwards, unravelling boundaries.

I do not know whether I will stay here until I give birth or try to return to London. I do not know how to make this decision.

It's numbing to oscillate between fear and acceptance, although it is not quite acceptance that I feel. That word is too positive, too mired in the language of wellness. What I feel is more passive than that, an acquiescence perhaps, a lack of energy to scramble. The word has a watery quietness, acquiescence, and it feels appropriate for the way I sink into the situation, the way I am submerged, all action delayed.

People talk about slowing down, about a breath for the earth, a time of recovery. Rest now, while you can, my mother says. You will need it when the baby comes. But you can't store rest. You can't pack it neatly in a dark cupboard, ready for winter. I feel it pulling at me, nevertheless, a dragging exhaustion, an insistence on slowness. Pregnancy is making me slow, my body rebelling against sudden movements, sharp shooting pains in my ligaments if I get up too quickly. I acquiesce to the slow advance of the unknown.

I am growing a baby, here in the stillness. Each day, I expand. April shifts from sharp winds to cool breezes. May blooms all around me, its greenness overwhelming. June brings the sudden tallness of foxgloves. My belly globes. Ferns uncurl on the daily walk I take with my mother. The birds are nesting. Everything seems overdetermined. One day, two horses suddenly have foals beside them, gangly and slick with new life. We see a heron twice (which I mistake for a stork), its awkward elegance cutting the air in front of us as it lands in a cool dim stream.

I am curious about what pregnancy is doing to my body, my mind, my self, though I have other feelings too. I am a compost heap of emotions. Apprehension, disbelief, excitement, terror. Things are happening in the darkness. The baby moves in his watery world inside me. I feel a foot or an elbow press against an inside place I was not aware of until now. I have learned exactly where my bladder's boundaries are inside me. It's reassuring, this small connection. I wait for it and relax a little when I feel it moving, over the weeks, from a flickering to a pulse, a knot of muscle tightening inside me, a reminder that I am not alone, though I feel so disconnected from the world.

Pregnancy is a loneliness. The first twelve weeks felt like sitting in a solitary waiting room, all bilious walls and scratchy carpet. Not a comfortable place. Very few people know I am in this room. No one can see or feel the loneliness of a body that has become a stranger, the flattening knowledge that everything has reoriented now, around this tiny flicker, deep in the darkness. It's not written on your body or your face. You hold it alone.

There are two doors out of this room. One, which may open after your twelve-week wait, allows you to join all the properly pregnant women, the ones with the bumps and that certain potential. Their future spelled out on their bodies. The other door sends you back into the world of the non-pregnant, though changed now and empty. I have walked through that door before, by choice. This time I would like to keep going. This time I hope to swing out of the suspension between my former life and an as-yet-unimaginable future with an as-yet-unimaginable little person. And so I spent my time in the waiting room and, eventually, I opened the first door.

But just as I dared to walk out into the world to declare my new expectant state, the world shut down.

Paradoxes abound. I am distanced but connected. Lonely but not alone. Longing to touch people but nervous of their proximity. Stuck but transforming. A quickening in the stillness.

I do not feel like two people yet, two subjectivities. I feel like myself, mostly. I have turned inward a little, I think. There is a new centre around which I orbit. There are different forces pulling me towards something I cannot grasp yet, or even fathom. I am hurtling towards a wall and I need to believe that I can pass through it unscathed, like Harry Potter on his way to Platform 9¾. I am making magic in unseen places. But the magic is not always benign. I fear for the loss of self that motherhood must surely bring. I worry that I will not have the love that I need, the endless capacity to care.

I am pregnant now in all of my dreams. Even my subconscious is pregnant. Sometimes I will forget this new absolute in the dream. But the realisation will always dawn on me, like being soaked in cold water. I have given birth, once, in my dreams. The baby looked like a stranger.

My sister drops off a bag of baby grows. I hold each one up, astonished that they will house a little body.

I search for memoirs on pregnancy. I do not care for facts right now. I am hungry for someone's experience, what it felt like for them. I want to compare. I want some reassurance that what I'm feeling is relatively normal. I find a few, though not as many as I thought. There seem to be endless accounts of early motherhood instead, of post-natal depression. But I want to know what it feels like right now, for someone else. I want to not feel so alone and inarticulate.

Hollie McNish's memoir is filled with a fiery rage and love. Anne Enright is precise and witty, her humour like a knife. Chitra Ramaswamy lyrically stretches toward metaphor: electricity, mountains, islands. Rachel Cusk registers an immersive shock. They spin their bodies into words, soothing and terrifying me in equal measure.

I find some of what I'm looking for in these memoirs but not everything. I sigh with appreciation, and not a little envy, when one of these writers crystallises a half-formed feeling I share into words, solidies emerging from the haziness – Cusk's description of the baby's movements as a 'live fish' is perfect for that wild flip of muscle.

I realise that pregnancy may have its commonalities, but the experience is individual and subjective. There are lines that connect us but me, my body, and the body of this baby, are their own universe, with their own physics, their own laws and stories. One thing I cannot relate to in these memoirs is the fact of their pregnant bodies out in the world, colliding with the rest of humanity, touching and being touched, out there amid the now forbidden closeness of other people's skin.

Several years ago, I found myself growing plants from seeds obsessively, checking the unmoving earth each day for signs of life. I have the same urge now but gardening is one of the many random acts that the pregnant are advised against. This is almost more infuriating than being told only to lie on your left side. I want my fingertips to press into the crumbling dampness of earth, want to see those half-moons of darkness under my nails. But instead, I have to live vicariously through my brother's efforts.

I find myself watching Gardeners' World, Monty Don's reassuring gentleness, his pristine and organised potting shed. I ache for his order, his control over the earth and its mysteries. The baby will be a Virgo, an earth sign. Can you catch your baby's energies? Do they seep back to you as nutrients funnel to him through my blood?

Outside, my brother pours worms into a compost bin. The worms arrived in the post, a plastic bag full of soil and shining, writhing energy. I marvel at the fact that living creatures can arrive in an envelope. Did the postman know what he was carrying? We watch as they burrow into the soil, blind in the sunlight, their bodies squirming for darkness.

Growing requires patience, an appreciation of the still and the quiet and the dark, until, suddenly, one day, the theatrical green shoots break the surface of the soil. I am fascinated by the fact that their growth is both visible and invisible. I cannot catch them in the act of growing, but can see the results, nonetheless.

Baking too, asks for trust in the invisible, the surrender of the mixture to the dark heat of the oven. Baking always brings back childhood memories of making scones with Nanna, standing importantly on a chair beside her as she parcels out a portion of the dough to my sticky, eager fingers. I am allowed to make my own shapes to accompany her regular moons of scones on their journey towards firmness. I tend to shape mine into people, my imagination turned by gingerbread men. I roll the dough into legs and arms, a belly rising hopefully in the middle. They are placed on their own baking tray, my creations. Nanna slides them into the expectant mouth of the Aga. This is my favourite piece of furniture in her house, a monster of heat and comfort. A saucepan of porridge turns creamy when left overnight on the warm surface at the back, where the socks also dry. It is the heart of the house, Nanna says, and I am pleased that something I made is transforming inside it.

My creations are a disappointment. I always forget this. They lack the springy softness of Nanna's scones; they are flat and hard and overworked. Legs and arms have often detached. The belly has sunken somewhat. Still, they are mine and I will honour them by eating them or at least feeding a body part to a grateful dog. But it is the baking that is important, that magic time when they are invisibly changing, locked behind the heavy door of the Aga, when all their potential is still to hope for. That is what I am here for. Darkness and its mysteries.

I write from this place, slowly, piece by small piece growing out of my fingers. It is not a sudden spurt of inspiration, but a gradual unfolding of words, ideas kicking at me like the throb in my womb. They sit somewhere in the murk of my mind, fermenting, connecting, and re-forming. They have their own life there, one I am not always partial to, and they often surprise me as they take shape on the page. I wonder what else is growing out of the pandemic, what new forms are wriggling in the uncertainty, when these will be revealed.

At night, insomnia pushes me naked from my bed. I stand at the window, my belly held out to the night and the stars. I want to move out into the garden, cool grass and earth under my feet. The air is too still inside, too confining. The only place for my pregnant body is outside, a piece of flesh in the dark, pulsing against the skin of the sky. Inside, muscles that are not mine move to their own rhythm. I do not go to the garden. Instead, I return to bed and lie still – in the stillness, waiting – and still tethered to the unknown.

HONG KONG DIARY

Oliver Farry

JANUARY 27

It's the third day of Chinese New Year and our turn to host the annual barbecue for my wife's extended family. All 28 of them. It is the first time more than one or two people have visited our new home so the logistics are a headache. All the more so since the outbreak, which started in Hong Kong five days ago. We remove all towels from the bathroom since damp flannel, which never dries out in Hong Kong winters, is a perfect incubator for the virus. Paper hand towels instead, alcohol wipes, plastic gloves for the barbecue on the rooftop, everybody's plates and cups are clearly labelled, with spares if there are mix-ups. I take care of the cooking, and I have a cough, so, even though I am wearing a face mask, I am mostly worried about infecting others. The memory of an earlier Irish cook in foreign parts, Mary Mallon – better known to history as Typhoid Mary – looms in my mind.

JANUARY 28

Hongkongers are taking the outbreak seriously, because of the memory of SARS, which crossed the border from Guangdong province in 2003, killing 299 people in the city – 38 per cent of deaths worldwide. While some people in the West say the virus is just like the flu, its symptoms are far too similar to SARS for that to be the case.

Schools will remain closed after the Chinese New Year holidays, people who can are working from home, and all large gatherings are cancelled.

JANUARY 29

Hong Kong is already out of face masks. Like most Westerners living here, I prefer not to wear one when I have a cold but, in the current situation, I don't fancy standing out, least of all in our neighbourhood, where I am one of the few white faces. I'm not going to be flashing my potentially pox-ridden *gweilo* gob to all and sundry. We have a few masks hanging around at home and I manage to find more online.

The World Health Organization does not recommend wearing face masks and says they are ineffective at stopping the spread of the virus. Health authorities in Hong Kong think differently and, just four months after the government banned masks at the height of the protests, advise people to wear them. After SARS, people here don't need prompting.

Frequent hand washing is also important. Hongkongers who grew up during SARS were taught at school to wash their hands for as long as it takes to sing Happy Birthday twice. A Donegal man I know who has been living here for two decades cheerfully told me that it was only during SARS that he started to regularly wash his hands. 'Typical Irishman I was, until it put the fright on me,' he said.

FEBRUARY 4

The first death in Hong Kong from the virus. A 39-year-old man who suffered heart failure after contracting pneumonia. He spent Chinese New Year in Wuhan, travelling there on January 21. Rather uncharitably, I think how foolish he was to do so when the risks were already well known.

FEBRUARY 6

Taiwan joins the list of countries, including Italy and the Philippines, to put a travel ban on people coming from Hong Kong. Hip, laid-back, arty Taipei, which to many Hongkongers is what Lisbon, Madrid or Berlin are to Northern Europeans, is off the table for the immediate future.

FEBRUARY 7

Healthcare workers are in the fifth day of a strike, calling for the government to close the border with the mainland. They say there is a serious danger of the hospitals being overwhelmed if there is a local epidemic.

The latest bout of panic-buying is in its third day: toilet paper, tissues, rice and other imperishables.

FEBRUARY 8

The Hong Kong government finally imposes mandatory self-quarantine on people arriving from mainland China or who have visited it in the previous 14 days. It stops short of the border closure that many have been calling for. People arriving must stay isolated at home, in their hotel or in a government-run quarantine centre for 14 days.

FEBRUARY 9

Nine members of the same family were infected after sharing a hot pot dinner in Kwun Tong on January 26. My wife and I had hot pot the other evening. I think we might give communal dinners a wide berth for a while.

FEBRUARY 12

Six weeks after it was first reported, the novel coronavirus finally has a name. The WHO has decided to call it COVID-19. It might be too late for it to stick though.

FEBRUARY 16

We are down to our final roll of toilet paper. On Twitter, I learn there is plenty of it in supermarkets in Tsim Sha Tsui. I head there and, sure enough, there is no shortage. I buy two 12-packs; everyone else in the place seems to be doing the same. We are second-wave panic buyers, belatedly as committed to creating the very shortages we fear as those people we ridiculed ten days ago were. I feel shame at the non-collegial individualism of the act, and at the indignity of hawking two large slabs of bog roll home on the MTR. In less than

Sheung Wan, photograph by Oliver Farry

two weeks, toilet paper has been transformed from mundane household item to a commodity of quasi-libidinal valency. You find yourself getting attuned to its lack with alarming rapidity. Every time I see someone carrying it on the street I wonder why, how, where. The other day, I saw a woman with two packs in my neighbourhood and the situation had the potential to be like the episode of Seinfeld where Jerry mugs an elderly woman for the last marble rye in the bakery.

FEBRUARY 19

A second death in Hong Kong. A 70-year-old man passed away this morning; like the first one who died, he was diabetic. The death toll on the mainland has now surpassed 2,000.

FEBRUARY 20

Luo Huining, the newly appointed head of the Beijing Liaison Office – China's top official in Hong Kong – says the medical workers who went on strike earlier this month are a 'political form of the coronavirus', which, as metaphors go, is a bit on the nose.

FEBRUARY 23

The virus continues to gain ground outside China. Japan has 751 cases and three deaths, South Korea has 556 cases, largely spurred by a religious cult, and four deaths. Italy has the largest outbreak outside Asia, with 152 cases and three deaths. This is the one I find most worrying. Westerners have little experience of serious epidemics and I have low confidence people will be quick enough to adopt the personal and social measures necessary to stop the spread, or take the virus seriously at all. Even in Hong Kong, Westerners often snigger at the wearing of face masks and, if successive surveys are to be believed, many

Europeans, men in particular, don't place much of an importance on washing their hands after using the toilet. Neither can I see Westerners putting up with the sort of restrictions we've lived with for the last month.

FEBRUARY 27

The virus has made steady but not particularly alarming progress through Hong Kong; we now have 92 cases. It is being fast outstripped in this respect by other countries. A month ago, people back home were anxious for my safety; now I am worried about them, my parents in particular.

FEBRUARY 28

Ireland's first case was confirmed yesterday, a woman from Belfast who travelled back from the north of Italy via Dublin. It is, of course, the responsibility of the North's HSC rather than the Republic's HSE but viruses tend not to respect political jurisdiction.

MARCH 3

Hong Kong hits 100 cases but has now been overtaken by Spain. The spread of the disease has been slowed by a number of things, mainly the vigilance of the public, who were paying attention to Wuhan long before anyone outside China.

But there are other factors too. The government has, after a faltering start, been stringent about quarantining arrivals from affected regions. And people here have signed up to a massive disruption over the past five weeks. The economy, already suffering because of the protests, is taking a big hit.

MARCH 5

Six more cases in Ireland – four south of the border, and two north. The government says it has no plans to cancel the Saint Patrick's Day celebrations. The parades themselves will be less critical than the heaving pubs, with punters from all over the world. If it were up to me, I'd close the pubs for three days, and only open them again on the 18th, when everyone is back at work. How have I, no slouch when it comes to the drink (though rarely in a jam-packed pub on Paddy's Day), turned into such a draconian killjoy?

MARCH 8

The Italian government orders the regions of Lombardy, Veneto and Emilia-Romagna, or one-quarter of the population, to be locked down, after they reported more than 1,000 cases in one day. It's the right thing to do but should have been done a week ago or more. Likewise, flights to and from the regions should have been grounded. Western governments are, to varying degrees, asleep at the wheel. The mistakes of the worst-hit Asian countries – China, Japan, South Korea – are being repeated in the West, while the actions of countries and territories that escaped the worst – Hong Kong, Macau, Taiwan, Singapore, Vietnam – are ignored. The outbreak in Europe will be far worse than in most of Asia; the United States, with a health care system that is dysfunctional by design, labour laws that discourage sick days, and an administration happy to declare it doesn't care about the crisis, will be worse still.

MARCH 9

A third death in Hong Kong yesterday, a 76-year-old woman who was hospitalised last week along with her husband. They lived five minutes from us. The first person to die, last month, lived on the housing estate where we used to live. Even in a city like Hong Kong that has been spared the worst, the virus can get very close.

Professor Yuen Kwok-yung of the Centre for Infectious Diseases at the University of Hong Kong yesterday asked Hongkongers to avoid foreign travel till the end of the year. I had resigned myself to being stuck here till summer at least but a longer spell is looking increasingly likely.

MARCH 10

The Irish government finally cancels Saint Patrick's Day parades across the country. No word on closing the pubs.

MARCH 11

The Hong Kong government yesterday placed mandatory quarantine orders on arrivals from Italy and from selected regions of Spain, France and Germany. In Europe, no government is doing this, despite having quarantined every one of their citizens that were airlifted out of Wuhan and elsewhere in China last month. Do European countries now think there are just so many potential carriers there is no point in quarantining arrivals? Or do they not want to admit the virus is now a European problem?

MARCH 12

Ireland's first COVID-19 death yesterday. An elderly lady in the east of the country.

MARCH 13

The Taoiseach announced yesterday that schools, universities and public buildings across Ireland would be closed until March 29. Large social gatherings are also being discouraged. Irish people, to their credit, have been far quicker to take things seriously than many others in the West have been.

A fourth person dies of the virus in Hong Kong.

MARCH 15

Things are happening at a dizzying rate worldwide. The shared experience of this pandemic is so total, it is rivalled only by mass sporting events such as the World Cup and the Olympics. Since the outbreak started here, people in Hong Kong – even those, like me, who have lived here only a short time – have become experts of a sort in the matter. Not medical or policy experts but experts by experience. At the risk of sounding glib, the nonchalance of Westerners looks to us like casual bystanders getting picked off in the opening scenes of a monster movie. If things continue the way they are going it will be Westerners who become the experts and who will have the hardened, traumatising experience. Our forewarned, forearmed knowledge will pale next to the bitter lessons learned by people in Italy, Spain, France, the UK, the US and possibly Ireland. Many of those countries are facing lockdowns, which we have never had. Hong Kong's success has turned it into a coronavirus backwater.

MARCH 16

Ireland finally shuts the pubs after outrage on social media on Saturday night. They will be officially closed till March 29 but in reality, it will be a lot longer than that.

MARCH 17

It's St Patrick's Day and I am theoretically more at liberty than my countrymen and women back home to go out and celebrate. But I won't.

MARCH 18

Every day brings a new record number of confirmed cases in Hong Kong – today it's 26, bringing the city's total to 192. It's a piddling number compared to most other countries now but, given the outbreak had largely stabilised over the past month, it is frustrating. The cases are now being driven by people, particularly Westerners, returning from abroad. Foreigners are the least likely in the city to wear face masks and they presumably felt they were bulletproof as they travelled the world despite being on alert in Hong Kong since January.

MARCH 19

I feel guilty making predictions, because when you do so, you have the expectation you will be right. You certainly don't hope things turn out bad but people don't like to be wrong either. Many of my predictions over the past month or so have been right in some way or other, if sometimes more conservative than what transpired – I didn't expect most European countries to go into full lockdown, for instance. I don't want to be continue to be right. I don't want the opportunity to blithely note how suicidal the approaches of the UK government continued to be, long after other governments belatedly started taking the outbreak seriously, not least because my sister lives in London.

MARCH 20

After its disastrous handling of the outbreak, going six to seven weeks without substantially addressing the problem, China is now going on the offensive to sell to a largely unsuspecting world its own narrative of how it handled it. China 'bought us time' or 'showed us the way', say apologists in the West – never mind the fact that people in Wuhan were in some cases sealed into their own homes to die and it was other Asian countries that dealt with COVID-19 more efficiently and with more transparency. Many in the West, let down by their own governments, are happy to buy this line, having not paid much attention

Photograph by Oliver Farry

to the virus until it came to be a problem on their own shores. Chinese diplomats and state media are even advancing the baseless conspiracy theory that the virus was implanted in Wuhan by the US military.

MARCH 21

Yesterday's death toll in Italy was 629, shattering the previous record. It is appalling but, in a few weeks' time, I fear we will look back at this number and think it small.

The other day I started reading Jean Giono's The Horseman on the Roof, an adventure novel set during the cholera outbreak in Provence in 1830. Like most works of plague literature, it reads in parts like science fiction, particularly in the sequences where the hero, an Italian hussar, chances upon deserted villages that have been decimated by the cholera epidemic. Outbreaks of disease are disconcertingly ancient and pre-modern phenomena, much like the altered scenarios of apocalyptic fiction. A few simple rules or parameters have rendered life as usual impossible. The current pandemic has emptied streets across the world. Familiar locations look very different. The social has been abolished, or suspended at the very least. We are finding new and different ways of circumventing that abolition but it has deprived us of doing what comes natural to most humans – socialising.

APRIL 2

Hong Kong this evening finally decided to close all bars, which have remained open during the outbreak, from tomorrow at 6 P.M. In the end they bowed to the inevitable, after closing karaoke lounges and mah jong parlours in recent days. There'll be a few disgruntled mask-eschewing Western expats but they can console themselves that they'd have it far worse back home. The city today reached 802 cases, with the addition of 37 new ones.

OLIVER FARRY   125

APRIL 9

Yesterday I interviewed a SARS survivor, who spent six weeks in hospital with the disease in March and April 2003. Now 37, he still lives in the same flat in Amoy Gardens in Kowloon Bay, where 300 residents of his block fell ill from SARS due to faulty plumbing. He told me people in Amoy Gardens have been hyper-vigilant during the current outbreak, even by Hong Kong standards. As a result, there hasn't been a single case in the entire complex, where 11,000 people live. He is the first person I have met who had SARS; by contrast, I already know half a dozen people who have had COVID-19, all of them thankfully recovered, including one, with cystic fibrosis, who was high risk.

SARS had a higher fatality rate than COVID-19, though was not nearly as infectious, and, other than in Toronto, where 44 people died, it barely caused a ripple outside East Asia. I wonder sometimes how a SARS epidemic would have played out if had gone global. There's a notion that, because of its regional nature, SARS simply died out but in reality, it was suppressed, thanks to a concerted effort by scientists, governments and the peoples that suffered it. That is why governments in Asia moved quickly to stamp out this new coronavirus, rather than sitting around waiting to learn more about its nature, which ought to be of interest to epidemiologists and virologists, not the general public.

APRIL 17

A plumber calls to fix our toilet. To our surprise, he arrives unmasked and, the five flights of stairs having taken a lot out of him, coughs and splutters in an alarming fashion. Neither did he remove his shoes, which everyone, residents and visitors alike, does before entering a home in Hong Kong. It is a bizarre sight, as if someone from one of those careless countries that now have tens of thousands of cases has been transplanted into the body of a Cantonese-speaking local. My wife tells him off and gives him a mask to wear. Fingers crossed we haven't picked anything up.

APRIL 18

In non-virus-related news, 15 high-profile pro-democracy figures are arrested by police on trumped-up charges relating to the banned marches on August 18 and October 1 last. The government is gearing up for another round of punitive arrests and prosecutions to stifle the pro-democracy camp, just as it did after the Occupy protests in 2014. I expect a lot of candidates for September's Legislative Council elections to be disqualified on spurious grounds.

APRIL 27

European countries are planning on lifting lockdowns over the coming weeks and some have already begun to relax restrictions. My two nieces in Seville, aged five and nine, were able to leave the flat yesterday for the first time in six weeks, which was like a second Christmas for them.

I'm not entirely convinced that governments really know what they are doing. More than a month on from locking things down, they are still improvising. While lockdowns are unsustainable, ending them without proper preparation is foolish. That includes centralised quarantine, which, as Asia has shown, is the way the virus is eradicated within a region. If mild or asymptomatic cases and their contacts are not isolated from the wider population, the chain of transmission will continue. The time to implement centralised quarantine, in hotels and college halls of residence, was during the lockdown, when those facilities were empty and there would be no more disruption than what was happening. I am beginning to think that Western countries have given up on trying to stamp out COVID-19; it is, rather, something that must now be lived with until a vaccine comes along, if it ever does.

Viewed from Asia, this is insane. When history affords Westerners the same perspective on their pandemics that geography gives people in Asia, they're going to find it strange how swiftly their governments decided there was nothing for it but to just shut everything down and hope for the best. Authorities in the West haven't even tried to seriously suppress the disease; countries such as Germany, which still has 200 deaths a day, are somehow lauded as having done a good job.

Within a few months of lockdowns being lifted there will in certain countries be second waves, some worse than the first. Governments presumably know this but have decided that, rather than stamp the virus out, people will have to muddle through. There will be further lockdowns, possibly shorter, later in the year. Some countries will have a rethink on centralised quarantine, and, just as they did with face masks, realise that this sorcery from the Orient does have something going for it after all.

APRIL 30

For the fifth day running, Hong Kong has no new cases. We're well on the way to eradicating the disease but that may all be for nothing, thanks to the incompetence and indifference of governments elsewhere. If all of Europe decides that COVID-19 cannot be stamped out and is something that people must learn to live with, travelling there, for the foreseeable future, will not be possible for me and my wife without submitting to quarantine for 14 days upon our return. That is something that will be hard to get employers to agree to. I am already resigned to not seeing my family this year; the way things are going it might well be difficult to get to Europe to see them for much longer than that.

MAY 3

I go for a haircut. Partly because I need one but mainly to taunt the half of humanity that can't get one and never stop going on about it.

MAY 9

The bars reopened here last night and, as expected, many of the spots favoured by Western expats were thronged, or at least the streets outside them were. Videos posted online show people gathered in groups far bigger than the newly raised maximum of eight. Police did nothing, in contrast to the small pro-democracy protests elsewhere in the city which they broke up, handing out €200 fines for violating social distancing guidelines. There's one rule for partying expats, another for troublesome locals. Social distancing rules are likely to be wielded for months to come as a pretext for banning and suppressing protests.

MAY 23

China's National People's Conference has decided to override Hong Kong's Legislative Council and draft a National Security Law for the city. On the mainland, China regularly uses national security legislation to lock up dissidents and critics of the government, such as the late Nobel peace laureate Liu Xiaobo and the human rights lawyer Wang Quanzhang. You'd expect it to do the same to punish anyone involved in anti-government protests. China and the Hong Kong government are playing up the threat of sedition, terrorism and secessionism, all of which are wildly exaggerated, even imaginary. Hongkongers just want the rights they were promised prior to 1997 to be respected.

I'm unlikely to be personally affected; the climate for a free press will deteriorate further in Hong Kong but the worst that might happen to me is my next visa renewal, in two years' time, gets rejected. My wife, who is president of PEN Hong Kong, is at greater risk, as the legislation intends to tackle 'foreign interference', which Beijing could use to shut down and outlaw international NGOs. Things are likely to get very bad indeed. My social media is full of people infuriated about the Dominic Cummings affair. I'm not saying they're wrong to be angry but, from the perspective of Hong Kong, it all seems trifling.

MAY 24

I go out to report on my first protest since January. The protests never really stopped during the pandemic but they were less frequent and very small, certainly too small to interest the international media outlets I usually work for. My gas mask and goggles are covered in a layer of plaster dust, having been in the meantime pressed into service for a spot of painting and decorating. I have to make do with the same yellow construction hard hat as before, which sits uncomfortably on my head. I tried to replace it with a heavy-duty climbing or cycling helmet, which are more tight-fitting, but they have been impossible to find for months since the government blocked imports of them.

The protest is an illegal one and is shut down promptly by police. There are thousands on the streets, though it's small compared to last year, and, apart from a few barricades and fires, the protest is mild enough. I get my first whiff of tear gas in four months. I attempt to charge into it to take some photos but I get pushed back and wind up kettled, along with other journalists and dozens of protesters. The Chinese-made tear gas the Hong Kong police switched to last October after the UK and US stopped selling it to them is exceptionally acrid and if you're standing in the wrong place, the gas mask doesn't make a huge difference. Police swoop and arrest 180 people, few of them acting in any way threateningly.

MAY 27

Another protest, at lunchtime. It's even more innocuous than the one three days ago but police still arrest 360 people, about 70 of them schoolkids.

JUNE 1

After 16 days without a locally transmitted case, there were two yesterday, a husband and wife, neither of whom had a recent history of travel. This is the

Photograph by Oliver Farry

second time in a month there have been cases after the perceived incubation period has elapsed.

JUNE 4

Police have banned the annual June 4 vigil to commemorate the Tiananmen massacre, citing social distancing restrictions. The vigil is the only memorial for the crackdown held on Chinese soil. Even so, thousands still flock to Victoria Park to light candles. Despite outlawing the event, police sensibly step aside and keep a low profile. There's a good chance that under the National Security Law, the vigil will never again be allowed to take place.

JUNE 6

The World Health Organization changes its position on face masks and now advises people to wear them, over 7 million cases and 400,000 deaths later. Lordy Lord.

JUNE 9

It's one year today since an estimated one million people marched against the Hong Kong government's extradition bill, sparking six months of protests. Now they are facing a law that will do everything the extradition bill threatened to do, and a whole lot more.

JUNE 11

After letting the Tiananmen vigil go ahead last week, the police charge four of the organisers today with inciting illegal assembly. World champions for petty vindictiveness.

OLIVER FARRY

JUNE 14

Hong Kong's Secretary for Security John Lee says that a new police unit he is creating to implement the National Security Law will have to keep its operations secret because they pertain to national security. Well at least they're not keeping the existence of a secret police a secret.

JUNE 25

Having gone more than three months without a single COVID-19 death, Hong Kong has had three in the last five days, which is almost as many as the four in the five months before that. Two of the deaths are related to the latest community cluster though the number of local cases remains very low.

JUNE 27

The EU is barring travellers from the US when borders reopen next month. It's not terribly surprising, given the latest rise in cases in the States, but there is also something seriously delusional about European countries resuming cross-border travel. France and the UK each reported about 1,500 cases yesterday. We are effectively back where we were in February and there is no sign of any country eradicating the virus. Under the EU's reciprocity demands, travellers from Hong Kong are unlikely to be admitted, which is absurd, given no European country is anywhere near its level of containment of the disease.

JUNE 30

As expected, the National People's Congress Standing Committee in Beijing passes the National Security Law. Hardly anybody in Hong Kong, not even chief executive Carrie Lam, had seen the text of the law before it passed. Not knowing the details of the law hasn't stopped members of the government and the assorted mediocrities and lickspittles that make up Hong Kong's business elite from rushing to support it in recent weeks. It reminds me of the way the Irish parliament voted itself out of existence back in 1800. The law gives the state a free hand for repression – ridiculing the government may now be sedition, calling for Hong Kong independence is secessionism and smashing up an MTR turnstile is terrorism, which carries a life sentence.

JULY 1

My first day reporting under the new law. I must have broken it at least a dozen times, as did many thousands of others on the streets. About 400 of them are arrested. I am briefly immobilised by some ancillary pepper spray during a media scrum when the police pull veteran pro-democracy politician Lam Cheuk-ting off a stepladder as he gives a speech. The police are enjoying themselves with their new sweeping powers. On several occasions they target by-standing journalists with the water cannon, sending them flying to the ground. It won't be too long before they start arresting us along with the protesters themselves.

Sham Shui Po, Kowloon

THE EYE OF A STORM

Oonagh Montague

The sun was an angry thing, prickling hard at the edges of the shade. Under the wisteria, Sarah sat with her book. A storm was coming. The grown-ups in the village had been saying so for days. In front of her, beyond the wilting grass where the cicadas were screaming, Kiki played in a blue paddling pool. Being in the sun was Kiki's choice, in as much as he had choices. He had not wanted his pool to be pulled into the shade, screeching at every hand that tried. Now, this far into the summer, his seven-year-old skin was a burnished hide, supple, dark, beautiful. Sarah envied him that.

'You're a bitch.'
'I'm a bitch.'

Kiki's real name was Philip. His mother had German measles while she carried him, and Kiki had arrived into the world blind and deaf, with a face turned ever upwards. Every summer, Kiki's father would come to visit Sarah's parents, bringing Kiki with him. Sarah liked it when they were there, not because of Kiki, who ignored Sarah, but because his father's presence changed things. A small, sandy-haired man with strong arms, he liked to play cards and drink wine and tease Sarah's parents late into the night, leaving them too distracted to fight with each other. Sarah enjoyed the peace of those evenings, lying in bed in the room she shared with Kiki, getting drowsy to the sound of laughter and the clink of wine glasses. Except last night, when Kiki's father had unexpectedly gone to bed early with a headache and Sarah's parents had started again.

'You're a nasty piece of work.'
'I'm a nasty piece of work.'

Kiki shrieked. Sarah breathed in deeply, trying to ignore the sound. Kiki liked to shriek when he was in the paddling pool. The sound echoed back from the walls of the garden, though he couldn't hear it. The only thing Kiki could hear was the grinding of his teeth, so when he wasn't shrieking, he ground. The noises he made flicked at Sarah's skin like the elastic bands boys in school sometimes aimed at her bare arms. He smiled as he screeched, lifting his arms high so that he looked like a ballet dancer in his paddling pool. Kiki was beautiful. Sarah wondered a lot about the point of his being beautiful when he couldn't see himself. Sarah wasn't beautiful. Over the last year in school, the girls had grown taller, rounder, their hair and laughter spilling around them and Sarah had been left behind. She was all angles, sharp corners, bitten nails. They talked about boys they liked and complained about monthly cramps and Sarah pretended to find it all exciting. She had cramps, too. Some days she could barely sit still on the school bus so much her belly ached, but it wasn't the right pain, just the fact of going home. Sarah's village was the farthest away and she was the only person from the school who lived there. Hers was a village of grown-ups. And, in the summer, Kiki.

'You're nothing but a shit.'
'I'm nothing but a shit.'

Last night, when she had heard Kiki's father say he needed an early night, Sarah had climbed back out of bed to come to her usual spot, sitting cross-legged on the tiles beside the keyhole. Behind her, she could hear Kiki's steady breathing. She had wondered again if Kiki knew she was there, that they shared a room, that Sarah even existed. He had never used his fingers to trace her features like blind people did in movies. Sarah always hoped he might. She sometimes thought Kiki deliberately tried to avoid her, that he skirted her presence in a room. He was like the grown-ups that way. She had decided to be okay with that. It was easier to be left alone. It was quieter than being needed.

'You've destroyed me.'
'I've destroyed you.'

When their voices grew too loud, Sarah had gotten up and opened the door. Her mother was on the sofa, holding a book, her father at the table with a newspaper, their mouths darkened with wine, the room stifling with heat. Neither had turned to look at her. Neither of them was reading. Sarah took her position between them. It was her job to stave off the next stage, when one of them would reach out to strike or break or throw or slap. Words were her father's usual weapon of choice, but he wasn't adverse to a sudden punch. Her mother was usually the one who shrieked and made the ragged ungainliness of the first move. But not this summer. This summer, while the village waited for the storm, her mother was trying something different. She had told Sarah that her psychotherapist had suggested she repeat everything her father said in a fight. She was to 'reflect him back at himself'. Sarah had said nothing, but she had wondered if this was the only bit of advice the psychotherapist had given. It didn't seem very clever. Sarah's mother had told her about her new plan in the car, the one place she would sometimes unexpectedly focus on Sarah, their eyes meeting in the rear-view mirror till Sarah itched to look away. Of her parents, Sarah's mother made her the more nervous. Maybe the psychotherapist wasn't stupid, because last night had not taken as long, the insults slowing, dwindling, till Sarah's father had stood abruptly and left the room and her mother had followed after. Sarah knew they would not fight any more. Her limbs were heavy as she climbed back into bed across from Kiki, still sleeping. As her eyes closed, Sarah thought how easy things must be when a person can't hear.

'You're not even worth hating.'
'I'm not even worth hating.'

Her mother's voice came down the darkened hall towards the garden – 'Sarah! Come set the table.' Sarah stiffened. 'I'm watching Kiki!' she shouted back.

No answer. She toyed with staying put and letting her mother come find her but she was afraid to try that for real. Her mother's anger frightened her in a way that made everything in her brain stop working until the anger had rolled on to someone or something else. Sarah reopened her book and carefully tore one page. The first one. The one with the contents. It barely counted. She wanted to tear out the next one, too, but she stopped herself. Just in case her mother saw. But she didn't get up. She pretended she hadn't heard. That could have been what happened.

Kiki shrieked again. The cicadas were getting louder. Sarah watched his hands crawling across the base of the pool, until his fingers found his yellow plastic cup. He began one of his rituals, filling the cup and holding it high, letting the water trickle inches from his face. He began to grind his teeth, so loudly she could hear it clearly over the cicadas. Sarah hated it more than the shrieking. She stood up. The time between her mother's call and her inaction was too long. The heat was around her, pushing at her face and hands, curling its weight to her back, setting itself to her legs. She made for the old iron water pump that stood at the place where the wisteria stopped, the sun began. Drawing the heavy iron arm upwards she began to pump. It took six or seven hard pushes for the water to be pulled up from the ground and she could feel it before it arrived – a slight cooling before it splashed out in a shock of delicious coldness on her bare feet. She couldn't put herself right under the icy water, it would stop as soon as she let go of the pump, but at least she couldn't hear the cicadas, or Kiki anymore. The screaming heat of the day was pushed back by the rush of water and the effort of pumping. Sarah felt something lightly brush her shoulder. Kiki's fingers appeared in the water. He had followed the breeze and was smiling as he let it spill over his hands and arms. He didn't acknowledge Sarah's presence. Sarah closed her eyes and let go into the weight of her own self drawing the curved arm upwards, forcing the cold water from the earth on the downward push, leaning into the sound of it, pulling and pushing and listening to the water until she remembered her mother, and stopped abruptly. This was wasting water. You don't waste water when you're waiting for the storm.

Kiki was silent, hands outstretched, waiting. Even the cicadas seemed to have stopped. Sarah watched as he waved his hands into the emptiness and his face grew angry, and she braced herself for the grinding of his teeth. But instead he made a new sound, a high wail, a keening that grew as his mouth opened wider and wider. Her mother would hear and come running to this sound. Sarah would be in trouble, more trouble than she was in already for not coming when she was called. She watched his open mouth, the ground-down baby teeth, the sound of fury and anguish, beside her but not at her – he didn't even know she was there and that was the worst of all.

'You make me sick.'
'I make you sick.'

Stop that noise. Stop it. Stop. Anger curled Sarah's hands into fists, and her mouth opened to scream as the hot air vibrated with something nasty, something small that could grow and grow and eat the village whole, swallow down the church and the steeple and all of the people, eat the butcher, the baker, the candlestick maker, pour them all in and swish them inside and then eat them both, head first, him, then her, snap off their necks and tear off their arms and toes and throw them back with water from the pump and let them find each other in the dark and stay safe in a quiet so complete they lose their voices.

'Sarah! Why are you screaming?'

That night her parents were calm. They agreed with each other, nodding as they told her how disappointed they were. She had been sent to her room, her supper left outside on a tray. Kiki's father was disappointed, too. She had frightened his boy. Their disappointment faded by evening. That night, when Kiki had been put to bed, the grown-ups played cards and laughed for hours in the dead heat. Sarah lay awake in the darkness for a long time, long after the house had fallen silent, listening to the sound of Kiki's breathing.

She woke in absolute blackness and in the black she felt the thing that had roused her. Small fingers, hands tracing across her face. Kiki was beside her bed. Sarah stayed still under his touch, allowing his fingers to stipple across her cheeks. He had never touched her before. She realised that the heat had gone. Eddies of cool air were moving through the room. She reached out and slid her hand down the length of his arm to find him. He was trembling, grasping at her hand, not letting go.

'I'm frightened.'
'You're frightened.'

Sarah threw back her sheet and gently pulled him towards her, wrapping herself around his slight limbs.

'I am alone.'
'You are not alone.'

Kiki burrowed backwards into her as if he could meld his back into her belly and Sarah wondered why he was afraid when there was no shouting in the house.

Then she felt it. A low rumble.

'Don't leave me.'
'I won't leave you.'

Sarah held Kiki and counted the spaces between the rumbles. Seven, six, five; the numbers decreasing as the thunder came closer and closer. Suddenly, a loud crack just above filled the room with a blue-white light, followed by a boom so powerful the bed vibrated and Kiki jumped, turning to throw his arms around her neck and burrow his face into her shoulder.

'Can you keep me safe?'
'I can keep you safe.'

Sarah wrapped herself around him, and her arms felt strong. Outside the storm screamed and roared into the sky and as the rain began to fall, Sarah began to speak out loud, whispering reassurances over and over into ears that could not hear.

'You see me?'
'I see you.'

And when the silence finally came, Sarah slept.

WORKS ON PAPER

Dónal Geheran

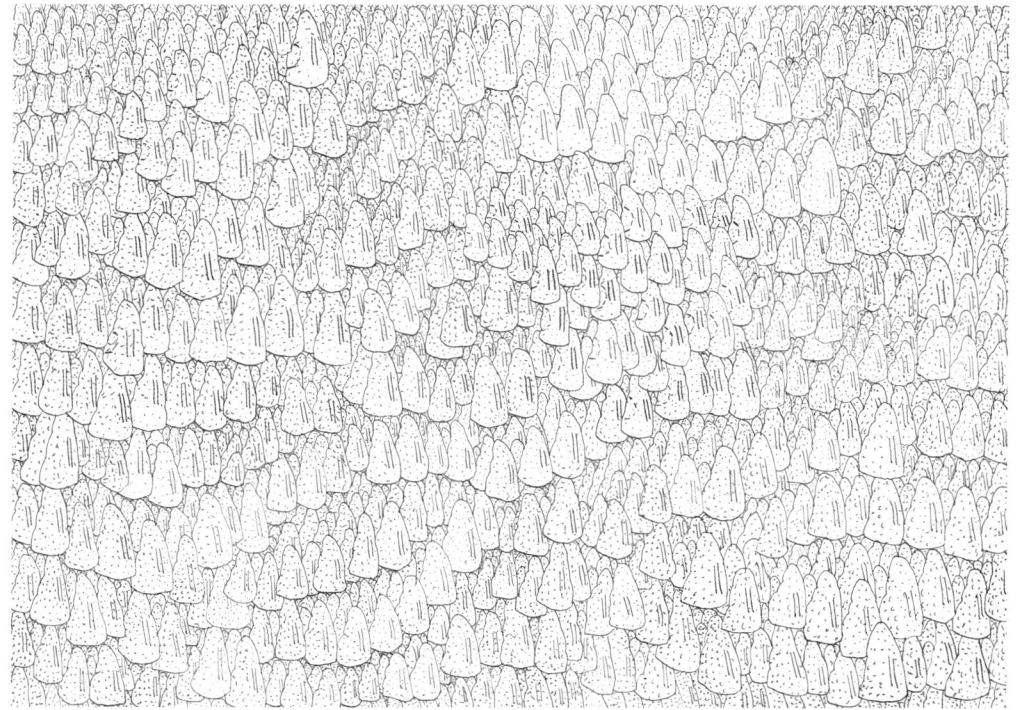

Guston rearranged, 30 × 42cm. Ink on paper. 2019

Sick of the office. 30 × 42cm. Ink on paper. 2020

Face paint. 30 × 42cm. Ink on paper. 2020

Death of an office worker. 30 × 42cm. Ink on paper. 2020

He had very long legs. 42 × 30cm. Ink on paper. 2020

Reality check. 30 × 42cm.
Ink on paper. 2020

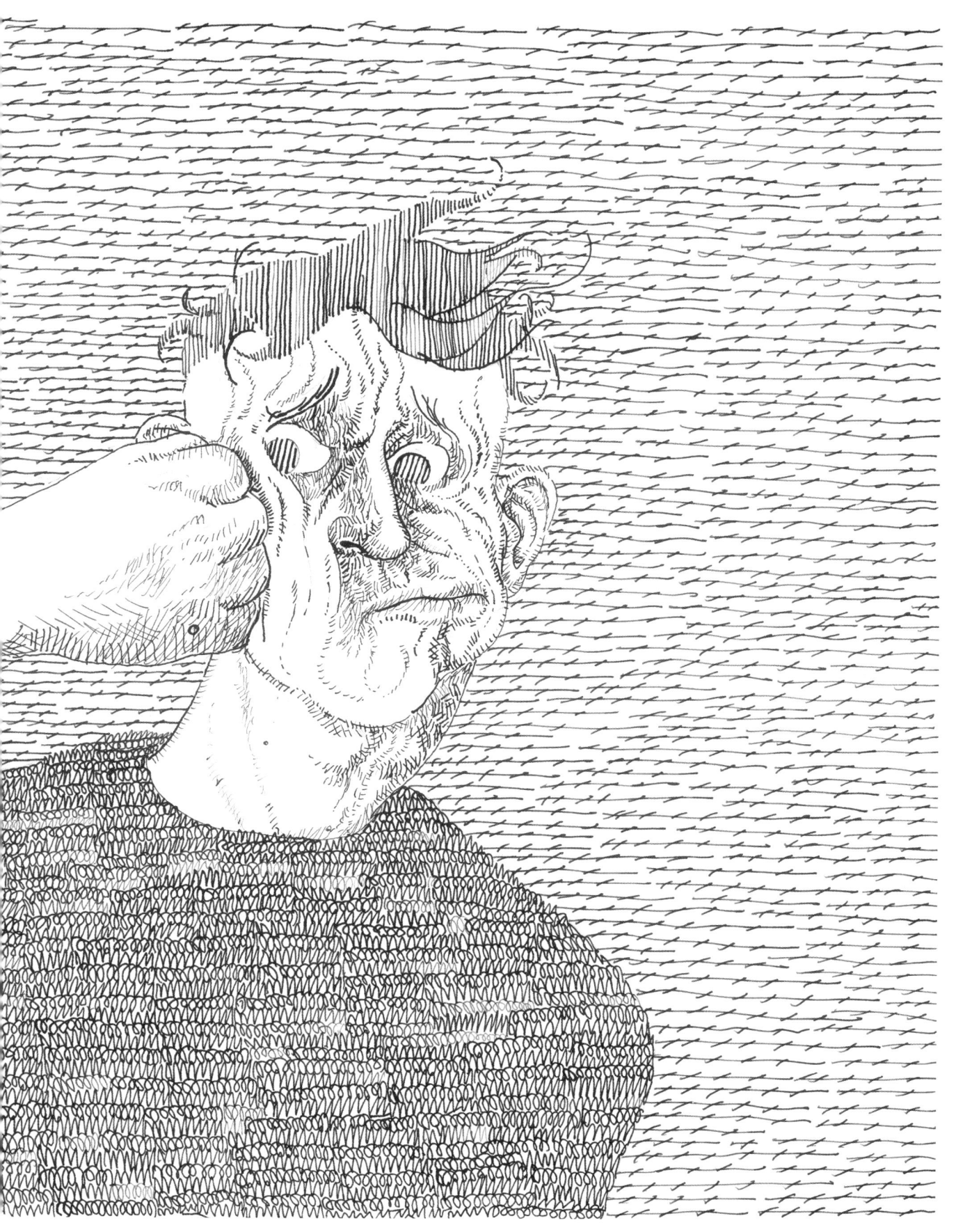

DÓNAL GEHERAN

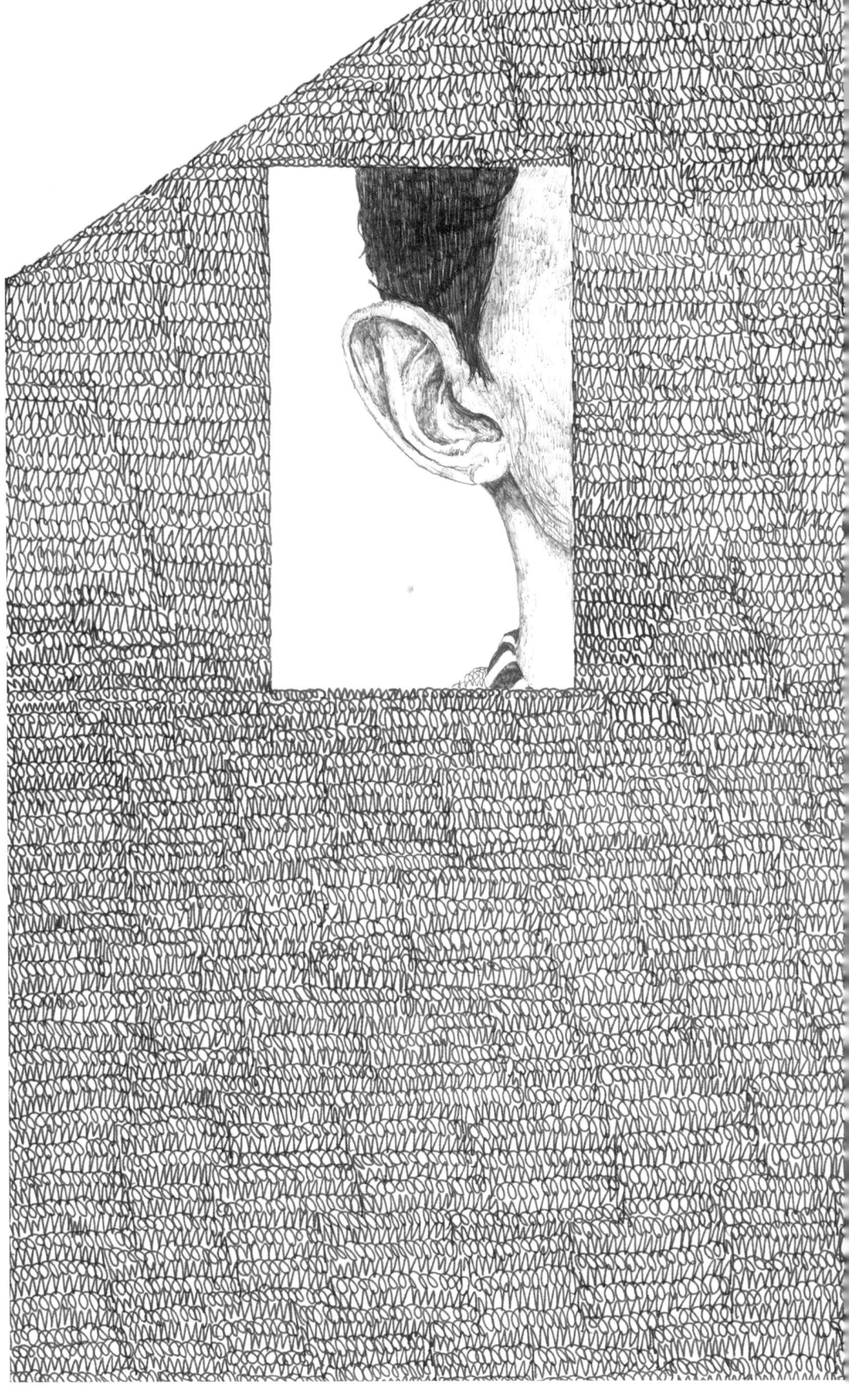

Listen. 30 × 42cm.
Ink on paper. 2020

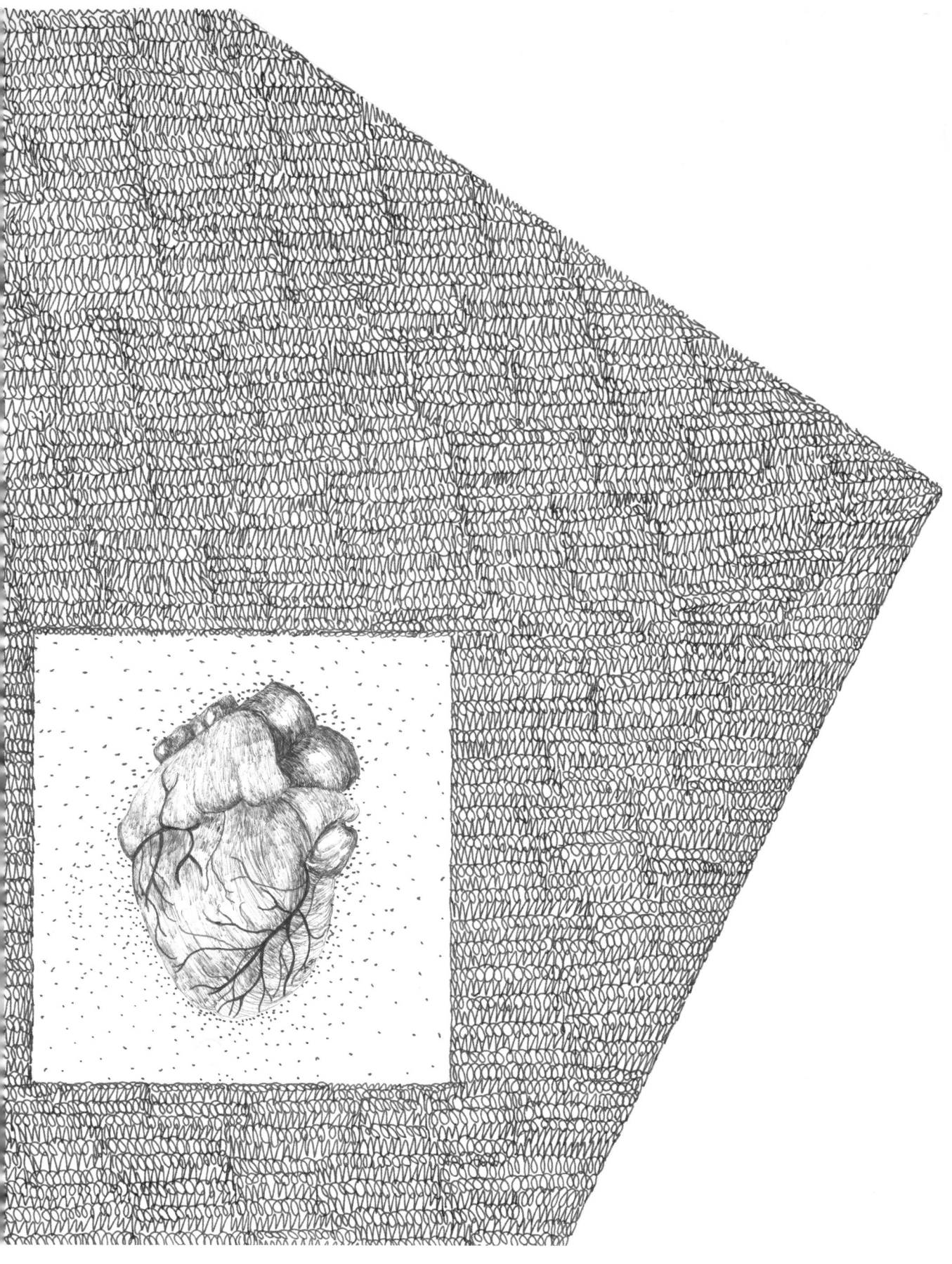

DÓNAL GEHERAN

DREAM OF A LOST FRIEND

Dominic Stevens

Anger. I know all about anger. I have grown up with it all around me, rarely in its fully expressed form, more often in its repressed, bound-up, knotted varieties, in dissatisfaction, in disappointment.

It hovered and was present in every small occurrence, action or comment. The floor not brushed, the hens fed late, things not 'in their place'. These things got remarked on. And they were right; she was right; how can you argue? A floor is either brushed or not, things are either left lying around or put away. The clutter of life, the living of a life is full of things done and not yet done, at any moment the world is full of things, some washed and some unwashed. I DON'T CARE. I really don't and that's not because I'm only just out of my teens, it's just that in this life we live in, we wallow in, we are up to our necks in imperfection. How can we be otherwise? I may be young but I'm a fucking expert philosopher on the subject of things left undone.

Mam. Was she remembering a perfect time? When she was small the world was easier. She was the daughter of wholesale food. A cash-and-carry. Her grandfather set it up; her father took it over. In a community of small farmers she never had to get her hands dirty. She grew up respected in town and things were done for her. She says that they had standards and I've seen the photos of gold taps and scalloped toilets. She was never expected to go to college, though her friends, her poorer friends, all did so in a desperate rush to escape this small town life.

Fuck. It wasn't her new husband's fault that the world went to shit, that Ireland's crazy lack of self-reliance got found out, that suddenly to have land to grow food became the most precious resource once more, that all of us outside Dublin got left to our own devices as budgets were slashed and the everyday things we expected like water and electricity became patchy. Expected? Well, she expected them but really this town, founded by a monk in A.D. 500, had electricity from 1937 until 2027, only ninety years out of a possible 1,500. Perhaps her generation was the exception, had lived through a blessed time of plenty. I look at them now and they seem like a generation of pure greed. And now, well, of gnawing disappointment. And anger. She takes it out on him, on my father. On me, on us. Nothing is right.

Anger of the purist form – I only saw that in her once. She grabbed, hit, punched. And then she sobbed. It was never mentioned again but it's all in there, behind her thin dry skin. I love my mam. No, I really do. I can't help it.

Do we ever know those around us? I've moved away now, I've removed myself and I should be rid of all the feelings of not being good enough, of not living up to it all. I've made my own bed and I'm lying in it but really I don't want to tell you about her, I want to tell you what just happened.

I'm telling you stories but trust me, this is how it went off. Well, something like this, because who knows? We see it through our eyes; we understand it through our brains; it becomes ours.

This was last week. It's fresh. I feel it still and that's cleaner than hard fact. I close my eyes and there I am. Back there.

An anxious feeling emanated from my sternum as I sat down. A dreadful nausea of expectation. Just under my ribcage is a little ball, smaller than a tennis ball. It lodges there and blocks the passage of feelings and makes me clench my stomach as if I'm holding it all together. I don't want to expect because to expect is to be disappointed. The thing is I'm not a ladies' man. My brother told me this. He just announced it like fact. I never questioned it but I feel nervous and awkward around women. My stomach tells me this. It's clenched. I'm anxious.

Annika fills my mind as I try to eat lunch in the hospital canteen. Annika. I say her name quietly to myself and wish that I hadn't. My throat fills with her, I scream her name noiselessly and feel the pressure on my temples of this explosion in my mind. It's a big thing that wants to get out but nobody knows. I swallow the spuds and somehow my mam forces herself into my mind, my mam, again, now? The spuds, would you like more of the spuds, Sean? Sure you're a growing boy. Now Annika, she's nothing like my ma, nothing like any woman that I have ever met, I have nothing to judge her against and I tell no one of her. I feel very, very sick.

I was drifting off in class a few years ago, looking out the window at the cows and feeling for them. Fucking weirdo. Thinking we need them, cows that is, meat that is. Even more now that the world is in shit, there are no seasons and food is in short supply. The break-up of the EU didn't help. I'm fucking delighted we live on an island. 'The heathen mess of Dublin,' said Father McDermott, drowning out my daydreams. Now and again, he said something that excited me. That's where I want to be. Not on my family's farm.

Why am I in Dublin? Fuck knows.

Art. That was a girl's thing. Miss O'Reilly told me it was a way for me to express myself. She said to the class one day, 'Sean is a sensitive boy.' I hated her for that but really I fancied her. Floral dresses, high-heeled boots, her rich long hair, and when she was close, a very nice smell, clean. She wore perfume. Studied in Dublin she had. Fishnet stockings, or tights – were they stockings or tights? I started to think a lot about her thighs. I hoped they were stockings, with suspenders, I thought, as my brain transported myself to a room, a soft warm room, and with Miss O'Reilly, suspenders and all, not crouched over a notebook, but standing before me. 'Sean?' she said waking me from my dozing fantasy. Your CAO form, have you filled it out? I had and my mam said she had sent it in. I had seen it later in the bin. The one for the burning. 'That Margaret O'Reilly? Sure it's up the garden path she'd lead you.'

Yes, Miss?

Job opportunities. Escape opportunities. Leaflets in school. I stepped out of line. I got on a bus. I had an interview. Bang. Underpaid health sector.

Now I'm lost in this place. I have no bearings. I have nothing to grab at. In a moment of panic I realise that if I disappeared one day no one would care or even notice really. I would be replaced by another country boy at work. My flat-mates would assume I had moved on and found a better place. Was this what city life was about? I was so far from the place I still called home. Back there, all was familiar, a pattern existed that I could understand and my position in the pattern was somehow integral, or it felt like that to me. Back there I knew who lived where, who they were a cousin of, if they were good in school, were they from a 'good' family or minor criminals or just fucking feckless.

But in the city anonymity means freedom. Freedom is a huge daunting place. I'm small you see but I do find pleasure in the anonymity, in the little pleasures of experiences not shared. Things I see that I tell no one about; conversations with strangers.

I work in a hospital. I'm nothing, a technician really, no more than the kitchen porter my mate Patrick is. We live in the flat together. The usual, shared rooms, mattresses on floors, night shifters, day shifters. He pushes food around, plates around, pots around and me? I push people around and they are cleaned. It's a psych hospital, an experimental one. Drug Assisted Dream Therapy is the official name for it but they clean their brains here is what it is. I chat to them as we glide down the corridor but I'm not sure if they remember later. I hate it all, I hate each day, the blank eyes, the absence and then the easy smiles and happy faces. DADT – the doctors said it worked. It worked because of the new dream drug. Fuck me, I wouldn't take one myself. But people did and they did it for fun. Fucked up.

Which brings us back to Annika.

Slipping. That was what it was. I was slipping. I knew it at the time and I know it now looking back but I'm a sucker for it. For what? For steep slopes to slip down, slip along.

A little while back I went home. I rarely do that these days. I don't really want to talk about it now. All fucked up. My mam didn't like what the 'city smoke' had done to me. I felt like I was neither here nor there. Dublin is not home, I sleep in a room in a flat with too many fellas snoring around me, maybe they are a comfort, some are from around me, in Ballymoylough. I feel that I don't belong at all in Leitrim but my mind hasn't told me that yet. Sometimes I almost say 'where I grew up' but I catch myself.

Way off-point. Focus! There is a story to tell and not long to tell it. Less time than you fucking think.

This trip home was fucked up. We argued. First it was with my mam and then my brother weighed in and that hurt more, actually. I couldn't stand it. It was summer, warm, and I fled, I went out, off to walk the little lanes.

I left the village. I walked down those country lanes, aimlessly, and I found myself somewhere I hadn't been for many years. It was where I used to walk with my mam when I was a small child but it had become unkempt and over-grown. She used to point out the houses of different relatives and often we would visit her elderly uncle. His house is so overgrown that I missed it entirely and had to double back to find it. Down a small lane. It was a mud wall cottage, a tin roof with the original thatch peaking out, as if from under a hat. Nobody mentioned this but it struck me back then. Something old hiding underneath something shoddy. He must be dead, I did my arithmetic, probably fifteen years dead? An old suit and a tired smell.

Now it had no roof and collapsing walls, a stone chimney survived as did the cast iron pot that sat in the fire. Built by his parents and their neighbours, one of a collection of houses on this lane, built together, neighbours, family, earth, stone, thatch. It sounds romantic when really it was probably crap but it binds you, it holds you, it makes you feel like you have roots. I feel torn when I'm here.

These houses, they did make me feel at home, connected to something. It's all a bit fucking grand to say to the soil and to the hedges. But maybe I will say that to someone given the chance, the right opportunity. You see it is a sense of earth, of picking it up, moving it 'round, building with it, growing in it, getting it under your nails. There I go again. Deep. I walked on and I passed more ruined houses that once were a-buzz, had fires, are so cold now in the falling seep of twilight dark.

I heard it before I saw it, a party. A fucked-up party in a field, no one from around here that I recognised but fun and scary. I knew no one. I trotted around. I hardly spoke to anyone. I looked. Torches, masks, symbols and a burning man, a wickerman for the summer solstice, the one fella I spoke to said. Dark. Flames. Mental music.

Which brings us to Annika.

She was the one playing the mental music on a laptop and I gravitated towards her. I was struck. Actually I was horny. Night time sunglasses, cheek-boned, she knew what she was doing, absorbed. Not of my world. But I could look, couldn't I? But maybe I shouldn't stare. Ha! If you put Miss O'Reilly in a field? Yes.

There were people dancing and I stepped from foot to foot to fit in. Not a dancer, I never was. I didn't see her approach. You're a long way from home, young man, and I turned. Annika, though I didn't yet know her name. I felt the heat of my face. I felt nervous and jittery. I wasn't a long way from home. I wanted to say, 'I'm close to home and I'm lost and I look at you and you can help me find the way back.' But that would seem weird. So I said I'm from down the road. She laughed, smiled, and said, well, enjoy, and she was gone. I rarely say what I feel. Poker face. Stupid fucking face.

Then she's fucking sitting on the bus to Dublin beside me. The rest is history. Which sounds dramatic but it's not, it happened, so it's history.

We meet now and again. Very casual. Well, pretty regularly, really, the same time, the same place; she laughs. In a café. I bring her the metahipnosivaxia, the dream drug, which she calls Sigs, after Sigmund, she says, but what the fuck. I get a bit of extra cash from her for the drugs. I have a system in work and no one will know. I think? What do I feel?

I'm slipping.

Actually we meet because I want to see her. I like it. I use the drugs as an 'in' with her. I tell no one. I know nobody else like her. She opens doors to brave new worlds, she says. I'm telling you stories, trust me, she says. Annika knows stuff and she tells me. And I listen. There's a young guy I meet, she must tell her friends, a country guy, he is quiet but sweet. Her world is wide but she lives in a small caravan. Our life together exists just in the café, never outside. Never elsewhere. Until ...

This is why I'm sitting choking on my canteen dinner with a baggy of stolen drugs stuffed in the bottom of my fucking shoe. We're having a dream party, she says, you should come. I'm fucking stammering, I'm staggered, and she laughs and says but you don't have to. She knows I want to. Annika likes me. Not like that, I don't think so, but it's relaxed. She says it's not a scene.

And that is why I'm in an abandoned building at midnight with a bunch of fucking strangers. Weird strangers, actually. Annika doesn't seem to want to talk to me with her cool friends around. Paranoia.

Her friends? Murphy's a laugh, he's a Yank of some kind. They all say, 'Why are you here?' Just with their eyes. Paranoia? From weird to weirder, Denis walks over, all darkweb podcasts and pills: Sigs, Carls and Electric Sheep. Try one? Put it away for later? It excites me, this group, this party, with its strange politics, this intense sense of newness, of opening. A brave new world, she says. There's a weird girl from Russia who says she can read dreams without drugs and she sits with strangers and absorbs their torments and desires. She actually says that. I sit down, blush, and she says she would rather not. Excuses. Dances and drinks, drinks that loosen the limbs. I must imagine myself a part of this intense dark otherworld.

Which brings me to Annika.

She walks over to me and I'm looking extra fucking awkward. Chill. Share a dream? Sig? I can't fucking share a dream with her where the fuck is that going to go? 'Uh, yes,' comes out my mouth and she pops a tablet into it and smiles and my feet are rooted to the ground and I'm sweating and I hold her close and I realise that the dream is shared. Between us. It is together we go as the mists lift, we are who knows where and we are off. An us that now exists. We move into each other, her breathing matches mine and as I feel her small frame, her angular boney shoulder blades, I forget to be uncomfortable. I squeeze her tight. My heartbeat matches hers. If I died now I'd die fucking happy.

Our hearts beating in unison, that feels like the first and most describable thing so let's start with that –

The dreams of another, the forgotten dreams of ourselves. She dreamt in pictures, I saw city streets, demonstrations, and I experienced her loss. An ache and a screaming void of wholesale pain, the end of her place, the death of her family, and the cold hard reality of never again, of that's it, of is that it? Of wanting it all to end.

Our hearts beating in unison, every thing speeding up, we are running across a crowded street laughing, dodging speeding cars, through a crowded market, grabbing food from vendors and eating as we run, I grab a blanket and throw it over her and she falls laughing and we are on a mountain side, sun on our skin, grass, daisies stuck to our clothes, millions of them and we are rolling down as children do, dizziness increases and we stagger into a bar full of old men – 'Becherovka,' she shouts, 'Nastrovia,' she shouts, 'LET'S BE FRIENDS FOREVER,' she screams and I know what she means. Down the hatch and out the back door and she tells me that keeping an old apple in a pouch of tobacco keeps the tobacco moist as we sit in front of the fire drinking instant Turkish apple tea and it's off to a gig in a basement, a band, a joint, and chips on the way home. Smoking Superkings because we are royalty we draw the smoke in together and feel clever together as we traverse the country getting dodgy lifts in sports cars and arrive wet soaked on a Sunday evening in a campsite for holy fools. We work together, the dishes, make food. The old lady we live with is an alcoholic. Quiet times too as we gently mature together. Decorating the house, yellow is the colour, it makes you think. Shopping, cooking, gigot chops, cheap. So everything is yellow, can you paint ceramic tiles? Not in Germany you can't. I'm feeling fat, she's feeling thin, as we jump over the bonfire and walk on gilded splinters. We are on bikes with a multitude, hedgerows flashing past us, we are flying, clouds and ancient mountain tops. These are the times and they flash past, how many frames a second? What is that even?

A ship at sea, a clipper ship, a great big clipper ship, but that's just a song. As things slow down and time stretches.

I feel her fading, we are in the wilderness, hunkered down under a scratchy tree beside a raging river. She is weak but fighting. She doesn't know whether to hold on tight or escape. I feel her desire to save me from it and I feel her pulling, wrenching our entwined souls apart, pulling away and it's me that's clinging on now as she says, 'I must. I don't know where I'm going but I'm going to try for the kingdom.' 'I must go and join the others,' she says. I feel her memories again and abruptly realise that I'm not everything to her.

I'm clenched now as I hold her and she struggles, her blood is surging, pumping, and I feel her slipping from the end of my fingers as she plunges into the river. SEE YOU ON THE OTHER SIDE is the last thing I hear.

The party goers scattered as the police arrived. Annika was pronounced dead and I just sat there, slumped beside her. Dazed. Silent. No officer, no, I really don't know.

It ends with death, it always does, but in our dreams we carry with us always those who touched us.

The end. It really fucking was.

Faultline (2019),
Performer:
Nandi Bhebhe.
Photograph by
Pat Redmond

A TRUTH TOLD FROM THE BODY

LOUISE LOWE and OWEN BOSS in conversation with Jessica Traynor

It's 2010, and I'm suffering Fringe Festival burnout, having seen what feels like hundreds of shows across Dublin in my capacity as Literary Assistant at the Abbey Theatre. Like any festival, the Fringe is risky; a fifty-fifty toss-up between the chance to witness the emergence of genius, or to rubberneck at a car crash. At the end of two weeks of over-stimulation, I'm walking towards Foley Street to see a production by ANU Productions, who I'd worked with the previous year on a show called Basin. This new piece is called World's End Lane, and it's about the infamous Monto, Dublin's historic red light district. But the street I find myself on is no Joycean Night Town – September sunshine bounces off the plate glass windows of The Lab, Dublin City Council's modern gallery and studio space. The surrounding buildings are identikit Celtic Tiger apartment blocks and only the cobblestones suggest the history beneath. I wait, in the reception of The Lab, for something to happen.

An actor I know comes and splits the waiting audience members into smaller groups. It's immediately apparent we'll have to interact with the actors, and a panicky static rises from the group. We look at each other for help, before we're picked off and begin our separate journeys.

How to sum up the hour that follows? A slow peeling-back of reality. A painful rebirthing of empathy. A trip without chemicals. At one point, I'm hiding a plastic bottle in the shape of the Virgin Mary under my coat. It's filled with lurid purple methylated spirits, and I've promised to give it back to an addict who had pleaded with me for help. Confronted by a pimp, I hand the bottle back, flooded with shame at my own cowardice. Moments later I'm in a small, black box where a naked man is dragging a woman to the ground by her hair. I know this man – I know he is an actor – but my body won't believe it. And then I'm in a brightly lit gallery space where an omniscient brothel Madam turns – slowly, achingly slowly – until I'm caught in the beam of her gaze. None of this is history. None of it is safe. It is all happening now. When I'm finally spat back out onto the familiar territory of Amiens Street, and start to make my way home, the hallucinatory feeling remains. The day has been kinked off its axis, and every passer-by could be another actor in a play that's spilled onto the streets. It takes a long time to feel normal again.

This is the work of ANU Productions, one of the most ground-breaking theatre companies working in Ireland today, continually pushing boundaries with their site-specific, immersive productions. Since their foundation in 2009, they have been a compelling presence on the Irish theatre scene, making work that challenges the notion that history can ever be safely consigned to the past. A trip to see an ANU show takes a special toll on the body. There's danger and adrenaline but, above all, a sparking of empathy.

For this conversation, I meet ANU's co-artistic directors, visual artist and designer Owen Boss and director Louise Lowe, via Zoom to look back over the company's first decade. It feels like a reunion of sorts, despite the distance of the screen, and it's hard to believe that more than ten years have passed since ANU's beginnings.

JESSICA TRAYNOR: So I'd like to jump straight in and ask you, how did ANU come about? What was it brought the two of you together?

LOUISE LOWE: You know what, Jess, I always answer this question, so I'm going to pass it over to Owen …

OWEN BOSS: But you always answer it so well!

LL: *(laughs).*

OB: Ahhh, Louise of all the times to … *(laughs).* We met on a postgraduate certificate in Youth Arts in Maynooth University in association with the National Youth Council of Ireland in 2004. We fell out spectacularly on the first day, because we were in this circle discussing 'What is Art?' and we had this huge argument shouting across at each other, which resulted in Louise throwing her notebook into the circle, saying 'Is this art?,' and me saying 'Well it could be if it's framed a certain way'… and we both went back to our respective best friends saying, 'There's this idiot in my class and it's gonna be a very long year' … and Louise's best friend was Debbie, and I went on to marry her. At the end of the year there was a project where you could team up with a classmate. I was from a visual arts background and Louise was artistic director of Roundabout Youth Theatre at that time and it turned out we had a very similar ethos around young people. Louise approached me and we ended up working for a summer with twenty-five young people in an abandoned flat in Ballymun, in the context of Ballymun being the largest regeneration project in Europe at that stage, and applying for funding through Breaking Ground/Per Cent for Art …

LL: What was interesting about the Breaking Ground scheme is that the show we made, Tumbledowntown, was the first Per Cent for Art grant that had been given to performance. Before it would have been public art, sculptures. It was interesting to change the thinking to an idea with young people at its centre … Despite the ephemerality of performance, it still had meaning to the public in terms of capturing the zeitgeist of that regeneration. Tumbledowntown won a Fringe Festival Award – which came with money, and space, which led to us coming back the next year and making something else. I don't know if we would have come back and made something else otherwise? In between, Owen went back to do his MA in Fine Art in NCAD, and I went to Central in London to do an MA in Directing and Applied Theatre. It gave us space to develop our practice, but we were sill working together.

JT: What do you think your youth theatre background brings to your process?

LL: I had spent, at that stage, twenty years working with community groups. I'd still say now that we would be socially engaged artists.

OB: Yeah.

LL: We don't make a project now for the sake of making a project. If the 'why' of it isn't there, as we've discovered …

OB: *(laughs)* Yeah, Jesus …

LL: ... it fails spectacularly. And sometimes that 'why' changes, or is generated by the place itself, by the people. But ultimately it was those twenty years ... I was working in juvenile detention centres, in prisons, with women in Ballymun Resource Centre ... I suppose most of it has come from my sense of: who gets to make art? Who gets to tell their stories? Our work is about those voices who are on the periphery – including my own, I'm not standing away from that. In fact, that's probably what propels it, more than anything else ... Anyway, I think those experiences are central to what we're doing. Creating communities of space, place or interest. Community is often seen as an appendage to art, but to us it's central. It's about class, participation, access ...

OB: And equality.

LL: And equality of access ... I was talking to the Arts Council recently about this. The UN Convention of Human Rights says we're entitled to culture. But if you don't *know* you're entitled to that right then you don't know you've never had it. And then the arts experiences you're offered – the ones that were offered to me as a young person – are curated with a very particular ideology. One of the first things that I was told was that I was disenfranchised, and disadvantaged. So all the art you experience in schools is about giving back that access. And I suppose for me, I became obsessed with going to the Hugh Lane with Debbie. I became obsessed with Renoir, and I remember the doorman saying, 'You shouldn't be here.' Every time I would see myself represented, particularly on the Abbey stage, was as a trope or a joke. It's fundamental to our work that we give voice to the parts of Ireland we don't see represented.

OB: I agree that we're socially engaged. But we also invite experts in to collaborate with us. Sometimes those experts are fifteen-year-olds from Ballymun. Sometimes they're a GP from the north inner city. Sometimes they're architects. It's about recognising that you, as the leader of a research project, are not the expert in the room – you're there to facilitate a process that brings a particular artistic outcome.

JT: That brings me to my next question, around collaboration with multi-disciplinary theatre artists, but also those experts you mentioned. Louise, I remember with Basin (2010), all the people from Dublin City Council whose arms you had to twist to make the show in the gate lodge in the Blessington Street Basin that you grew up in – can you talk to me a little about this process?

LL: Every show demands a different process.

OB: It's problem-solving.

LL: Eighty per cent of our work is not in the rehearsal room. It's talking to building owners about health and safety ...

OB: It's stupid stuff, like ... how do you get thirty people across a road?

LL: Or it could be working with experts who come from the community you're working with, and they become your collaborators. It's the conversations that happen on the balcony of the block. It's about positioning yourself in that world so you're not a voyeur, wherever that place is – it could be the National Museum, or the flats on St Mary's Place. We've been very lucky with the historians we've worked with – Diarmaid Ferriter, Catriona Crowe, Lar Joye – because they're the people who throw things back at you. Like in the middle of Pals – The Irish at Gallipoli (2015) they're talking about the massacre on North King Street, which inspired These Rooms (2016).

OB: I think when those collaborations work, they tend to extend over time – six, seven years.

JT: I love the notion that the logistical challenges can sometimes provide the best content.

LL: They really do. The thing you think is going to be the headache and the heartache is the thing that works itself out. And the thing you think you're going to fly though, very often you have to lose it at the end, because it hasn't earned its place. One of the strongest collaborations is a project called Torch (2018), part of the Arts Council of England Ambition for Excellence Award. That was four years in the making, working with women in domestic violence centres across Merseyside and St Helen's. I worked with the Chief of Police, with the Head of Traveller Services, three midwives, the Chair of the Mental Health Association, with a librarian who was a drag artist. We decided it had to be an all-women show, everything from the carpentry to the performance. And that came about because the head of the Arts Council in England had seen Angel Meadow (Manchester, 2014). In the end of the show, watching those women come together ... Often, the play is not the thing, the show is not the thing.

OB: It's bringing communities together to see their own experiences reflected ...

LL: ... and asking the performers to leave the space for audiences to explore, saying to them, 'They might be more interested in rummaging through these drawers than looking at you, but that's okay.' We place the audience at the centre of the experience.

JT: To go a little deeper into notions of place – from Monto, to Manchester, to North King Street – how do places begin to speak to the two of you?

OB: Sometimes we find places ourselves, like Monto in The Monto Cycle (2010 – 2014), sometimes they're proposed as a commission and we need to find our way into them. The interest for me is oral histories, lost archives – why have they been lost? Why have histories been used in a particular way? My job is to design those worlds so that audiences feel that immersion you mentioned.

LL: You talk about the moments where things contradict.

OB: That's what I love about histories. Take These Rooms, which was built from the civilian inquiry into the North King Street Massacre. Then we looked at the military inquiry into the same incident. They're contradicting each

These Rooms (2016). Photograph by Pat Redmond

other, but they're both truthful to a degree. How do you, as an artist, take those contradictions and manifest them into a space?

LL: It's a terrible way of saying it, but it's a kind of Cubist dramaturgy. (*Laughs*) He hates me saying that …

OB: No, I don't! No, my issue around the term – Cubism, especially as associated with Picasso, is a very male-centred term, considering how we look at women's issues and stories …

JT: There's a powerful symbolism to the spaces you create, Owen. For example with Faultline (2019), to choose those three spaces to represent the cataclysmic events of 1982 and their impact on the Irish LGBTQ+ community – the office space, the toilets, the bar – all of which exist on the quotidian level, but are loaded with meaning and symbol. They sit on the knife-edge between realism and dream.

LL: Owen's not designing from text – sometimes the design elements form the provocation for the piece. For Faultline, huge elements of the show were provoked by talking to men who'd been involved with the struggle for gay rights in Ireland – this was after they visited the toilet space designed by Owen. Elements also come from the performers, from the bodies of the people who make the show – the Haka at the start of Faultline, for example. One of the performers wanted to explore the language of cruising through movement; the objectification of the male body and place memory of those involved – Owen pushed together all these moments in his design for us to play with.

JT: So you didn't even know the toilet space was going to be there at the beginning of the project?

OB: There were three rooms in Faultline, and we knew one was going to be the bar and one was going to be the office and then we had this other one. We thought about it maybe being a bedsit, or a cloakroom ... but how will an audience engage with that? So, say it's a bedsit, that creates a temporal shift. It doesn't feel right. I was working with set designer Maree Kearns, and we found this Martin Parr photograph, these lads in the jacks ... and we thought, that's interesting.

JT: You don't think about these things at all in the experience, but afterwards – it is that perfect transition space between the office and the bar.

LL: It makes the whole space subliminal. Something like The Lost O'Casey (2018) offers very different challenges. You're in the real world and you realise: those traffic lights are on a different timer depending on the time of day, and Sarah Morris's speech needs to be *twice* as long at five o'clock as it does at seven o'clock, or she's going to arrive in on the other actors mid-scene ... you have to build in all of these timing structures that are almost mathematical.

JT: Can you talk about the first of your shows where you had to navigate those logistical challenges?

LL: Probably World's End Lane (Monto Cycle, 2010), on Foley Street. I was thinking about the energy of the street, the safety of the audience. Things you don't necessarily expect to have at the forefront of your mind when making work became very important to us. We parachuted ourselves into the community for four years before we began. I remember talking to Amanda Coogan and she said, 'This is not one piece of work, it's your life's work.' And there's a degree of truth in that. And of course Belle [Owen's daughter] goes to school there now. And Owen, you're still on the board of the school.

OB: I am indeed.

LL: Never to leave the Monto! In terms of the energy and the mechanisms you were talking about, World's End Lane was the first time we did it. It was a simple fifteen minute rotation. Almost *simple*-simple. Audiences saw it in different orders. I suppose narratively, that's something we've continued. That there isn't a particular starting point or end point. You become the auteur. Brian Singleton [Samuel Beckett Professor of Drama and Theatre, TCD] talked about it being like a fully embodied memory. For me, the most critical thing is the work is not leading towards a crescendo. There's no traditional arc, no reveal. In terms of the body politic of that, you're asking your audience to think of all of the subjectivity that they're bringing to the work. Depending on who you are, you'll respond in different ways ...

OB: The work itself and the audience will often dictate the mechanics of the show. Three audience members, three sections. There's no text book.

LL: Laundry (2011) that followed the year after World's End Lane was a stagger rotation. The audiences of three came in every fifteen minutes. We're managing twenty-four audience members in different places at any given moment of an hour. It's really about the relationship between the performers and the audience members. Where power is shared.

OB: Yeah ...

LL: Often with immersive work the audience *or* the performer holds all the power. There's no invitation for the audience to really engage. That's why I've sometimes turned down bigger shows, because the power dynamic isn't shifting. The audience being there must really matter. After seeing Amanda Coogan's piece The Fall, in 2009, I think that changed everything for us. She was just climbing a ladder, stopping and falling ... I remember going to see it and thinking, this just changes everything. Because what if the audience being there matters? The way that I seem to matter to her, in this moment of liveness? Some shows we've been able to do that with real conviction, like The Lost O'Casey. For me, the best shows are where you find those moments of communion – the fizz of it! And the actors all say in that moment the energy is extraordinary. People often say to us, 'You must have a lot of improvisation in your work ...'

OB: Yeah, no ...

LL: There's no room for it! Because it's all timed. And if an audience member gives a longwinded answer to something, that becomes the scene. The actor doesn't take up where they left off. The clock is king.

JT: There's this phrase that gets bandied about, 'audience development', and in a way this is a sense of what you'd really love it to mean – building an audience, building a community, building a narrative, who aren't at a remove through the proscenium arch.

LL: Truthfully that is the thing I am most proud of, that our audience isn't the typical demographic. We give the shows different flavours. Some, like Pals and Hentown (2017) are more gentle. But then the audience will come back, and they might go and see a show in Dublin Theatre Festival like The Lost O'Casey. Having done the research with the University of Ulster and NUIG, we know they're members of the communities we're working in, and they've continued with us since Basin. During Living the Lock Out (2013) I came into 14 Henrietta Street, and there were two older women waiting outside, on deck chairs, with flasks. And they said, 'We're queuing for cancellations.' They'd been there all night!

OB: And what does Louise do?

LL: I went in and said, 'You have to let them in!' There's nothing in this world I'd queue all night for.

OB: There was a couple of people from Kerry came to see Angel Meadow in Manchester. All that way to see a one and a half hour show.

LL: And it's happening in reverse now. People who went to see Torch are coming here to see the work. And the kindness that people show. One woman came up to Dee [Deirdre Burke] and said, 'You've been wearing the same pair of pyjamas for three weeks. I've got you new ones.' Dee took them and wore them as her costume the next night. And then I think of Kunle [Animashaun] in Vardo (The Monto Cycle, 2014) sitting in Busáras telling his story over and over again and he was reported to the police every day, because they thought he was scamming people ... Sometimes these things show the damage in society as well.

JT: I'd love to talk about dance, movement and choreography. You've really been at the forefront of bringing dance and movement into contemporary theatre. Talk to me a little about where that process came from.

LL: I think it started off with Basin, Jessica, when we were all working together ... I was thinking about my mam and dad's relationship, and I remember talking to Emma O'Kane about how to tell the story. My mam and dad met because he was a ballroom dance teacher and I thought maybe that was the way to figure out the relationship between them. It kind of became that demented tango in the sitting room. And then realising that there's a truth that's told from the body that doesn't need to be articulated through narrative, through text.

OB: Basin was the start of the nuance, where it all became alive.

LL: I've never trusted my own choreography – having Emma O'Kane to work with was an inspiration. Her generosity of spirit as a performer, too. We've transitioned more into movement. Sue Mythen, who we work with, is not a choreographer, but her movement work around how the actor would re-engage with their body after a moment of trauma has been so important. The first step choreography we had in anything was in These Rooms, and it was terrifying. But it was brilliant to work with David Bolger, and I did some of the choreography myself, too – the widow sisters piece.

OB: That piece was made without any male gaze.

LL: I wanted to make something about the stripping and remaking of these widows in a way that wasn't sexual. It's hard to say something like that to David Bolger – 'Can you step away please?' – but he was brilliant about it. The feminism in our work is upheld and led by men. I think that's down to Owen in loads of ways.

OB: Ah now ... I think the choreography is almost a contradictory thing, it can hold two spaces at once.

JT: It intersects so much with your design though, Owen. There's always a symbiosis between the spaces you create and the movement. Does the choreography and movement respond to the design or does it develop in tandem?

Pals, The Irish at Gallipoli (2015), Performer: Liam Heslin. Photograph by Pat Redmond

OB: In tandem. There's a real precision to what Louise does that cuts through the abstraction of the movement in the space. There's a truthfulness behind those dance pieces – there's the abstraction of movement, but truthfulness based on archival material, on research.

LL: We've also worked with people who are not dancers. Stephen Quinn in Faultline is not a dancer.

OB: Or Tommo.

LL: Or Tommo [Thomas Reilly]. He's not a dancer, but he's in his body – he wants his art to be articulated and he does it really well. Or someone like Matthew Williamson who has no formal training, but can move his body like no one I've ever seen. I could give him a dry archival document, and he just somehow manages to push it back out to you. The performers joke with me that I'm making up wanky dance language ... (laughs) ... But probably Faultline was the first thing I ever choreographed. Turning up that first day in Dance Studio in Annaghmakerrig in my leggings and t-shirt. I can't tell you the fear that was in me! I think it was because I didn't feel like I had the right to tell this story, because I'm not gay, and I really struggled with that in Faultline in a way I haven't with other shows. And then Stephen Quinn turned around to me and said, 'But you weren't a Magdalen either, love,' and I thought, you know you're right. And I wasn't in World War One ... So why *now* do I feel like a fraud? But for the first time I knew the meaning behind every single piece of choreography. All of it is based on things the performers have experienced. I found the notebooks the other day …

OB: Don't throw those out!

JT: I want to bring you back to something you said earlier about representation on stage. You said that whenever you saw yourself on the Abbey stage it was as kind of a joke. Can you talk to me then about what it was like going back to the Abbey and reclaiming the lost O'Casey play, Nannie's Night Out, for your show The Lost O'Casey? Was it a sense of coming full circle?

LL: I was thinking all about the hinterland of the Abbey, the social hinterland. And walking over the real life of the hinterland to engage with the artifice of what that representation might be. I remember Sean O'Casey saying, 'The real drama's happening out there, not in here,' and then talking to Shivaun O'Casey [O'Casey's daughter] and discovering that Owen's grandad and O'Casey were pals. We'd been working with Street Medicine, with the SAOL Project, and with Soilse, but the articulation of the character of Nannie, one hundred years later … It was the hardest part we've ever cast. Finding Sarah Morris, who I knew from the Lir Academy, what she brought to that role was astonishing to me. She has that capacity to transcend herself. She went out for nine months to work with Street Medicine, herself and Leanna [Cuttle], who was playing the doctor. They trailed the team every Thursday. She came in with 190 pages of scribbles and went, 'Here. That's what I've discovered.' We took it down to essential moments. One of our first audiences at the Abbey were the women of the SAOL Project. I was sitting in the ambulance with Sarah as she started the show, and as she started to speak, a couple of the women from SAOL started to say the lines – the line that came next. And only me and Sarah knew the show. She'd ask the audience, 'What do you think it'd feel like to be drownded?', and the next line was, 'Peaceful, I'd say.' And if no one in the audience responded, she'd just say the line. But this woman, this time, said, 'Peaceful, I'd say.' The hairs went up on the back of me and Sarah's necks. And I realised in that moment, we'd come full circle. They were the audience that mattered most. And they said afterwards to Phil [Kingston – Community and Education Manager, Abbey Theatre], 'If we thought plays could do that, we'd come.'

OB: Lost O'Casey was made at the right time. I wonder if all the work we've done as ANU was leading up to that moment? When O'Casey wrote that work – what was it, '24? – it was a very particular time in Irish history. We'd made Pals, we'd made 1916 work. We knew exactly, historically, where it was placed. We knew the people. But then you think – if we know the people *now* who are the equivalent of the people *then* – why has nothing fucking changed?

LL: I think it was one of the most sophisticated things we've ever made. And the most dangerous. And O'Casey's play, asking, 'What has changed since the Free State?', allowed us to ask the same thing one hundred years later. For me, it was less about what has changed at the Abbey – I don't know what's changed for the Abbey.

JT: I was going to ask you about your residency at The Gate and whether that was a fruitful experience for you as a company?

The Lost O'Casey
(2018), Performer:
Sarah Morris.
Photograph by
Patricio Cassinoni

LL: It was. I think it's worked so well because, ironically, we had no designs on the stage. It's been a brilliant, fortuitous relationship. They came to us to do Shadow of a Gunman which was supposed to open ...

OB: Now!

LL: I think our opening night was supposed to be May 20th? That's really bittersweet as we put together a brilliant team. Owen designed a model box!

OB: *(laughs)* I designed a model box for the first time! See what happens Louise? When I do a model box?

LL: The Gate are hoping to do it again ... Selina has reached out during lockdown to say, 'What now?' She's had it rough, and has offered nothing but support and encouragement.

OB: It's one of those good relationships where you work together, but you also leave each other alone.

LL: I don't know any other organisation who would give you the keys to the building and 24-hour access.

JT: To finish up, I wouldn't dare ask anyone, at the moment, 'What's next' – because who knows? But I do want to end by asking, what's obsessing you at the moment?

LL: The Lir Academy is on my mind. We're going into term three, which is usually our devising term, with second year actors and MFA directors. We know whatever we make has to be digital, which is an entirely different form. I've no idea if it's possible to create theatre in a digital form. And we've started a new project called Goatsong which is looking at very rural middle Ireland. We've brought a film-maker in, Jason Branagan, who's been working on immersive stuff – things like Bandersnatch, to try and see how we can catch some of that liveness and disseminate it further.

OB: I've become obsessed with my great grandfather. His name was P. T. Daly and I kind of visited him in 2013 for our commemoration of the Lock Out …

LL: Oh, for a moment I was like, 'You met him?'

OB: *(laughs)* And he was quite an extraordinary person. I didn't know much about him because my family were secretive about him. I'm working with Genevieve Hulme-Beaman on a piece called Secret Spaces. Her great-grandfather was a guy called Bat O'Connor and he built all these secret spaces, these hiding spaces, for Michael Collins. And I'm looking at P. T., who started the ITGWU, he started Sinn Féin, he started the Labour Party, he was on the Supreme Council of the IRB, and he misappropriated some money, he wrote a manifesto …

LL: With Sean O'Casey.

OB: … for the ICA. He did all these extraordinary things, but no one knows who the hell he was.

LL: He also set up a milk scheme for schools. And a sexually transmitted disease clinic in the Monto.

OB: He was on Dublin Corporation and set up all these things. When he was kicked out of the IRB, he was replaced by Tom Clarke. It's almost like he's out of focus, and I'm interested in placing him back in there somehow. His daughters set up a bonfire and burnt his memoirs. So there's a gap in the archive. It's about trying to fill that gap. It's very frustrating *(laughs)*.

JT: I just think it's amazing, as a state, how complicit we've been in our own erasure. I don't know any family who doesn't have a burned memoir or two.

OB: And that's what it's about, how that has affected the descendants of those people. It's about the secrecy of those double lives.

LL: And I'd like to finish by saying I really hope that we get to have an opportunity to reform and reframe ourselves during the current crisis. At the moment, we're talking about the value of the artist and not the art, to society – how art can heal, how art can provoke – and I think if we reframe those conversations, we might have more success. That's my wish for us all.

A FALSE CRAWL

Una Mannion

A vehicle vagrancy ticket arrives in the mail for our Toyota Corolla. It's from a parking lot in Dayton, Ohio. She still hasn't registered the car in her name. We've been receiving citations from the state which I keep hidden from my husband. He didn't want to give it to her in the first place. She's already a car wreck, he said. Why would we put her behind the wheel of ours? I call her number over and over. I send text messages. Emails. When she finally calls me, she's vague about the registration, thought she'd done it. She tells me not to worry, that if one were to sleep in a car, one would do it in truck stops or Walmart parking lots where there are always others sleeping in vehicles. Plus, and this has nothing to with her but it's important to know, in most states it's not against the law to live in your car. She knows a lot about sleeping in cars. I wonder does she even have a licence and if she has an accident will we get sued. REGISTER THE GODDAMN CAR GINA, I text her, all caps. I'd told my husband all the paperwork was finished. I look up living in cars and find nearly a million Americans are doing it. And, as it turns out, Walmart does allow people to sleep in their parking lots overnight. So do Cracker Barrel and Home Depot.

My youngest daughter is learning about the Vikings, Marco Polo, and Columbus. Her teacher says that explorers are people who venture into the unknown. My daughter puts her hand up and tells the class that her mother's best friend is an explorer called Gina. That's one word for it, says my husband. My daughter tells us that one of the boys shouted, There are no girl explorers! I tell her that's exactly what Gina is and consider my daughter's tilted angle on the world: an explorer, not drifting but discovering. Gina has never been able to settle or keep a job or open a savings account, but she knows things, has weather lore, can name scud cloud and cirrus, can read the night sky. She can name tectonic formations and fossils and knows how glaciers moved and rocks formed. She forages food, scrapes fungus off trees with a knife, but gently so that it will fruit again. She eats goldenrod and picks ferns she calls fiddle-heads and says they taste like asparagus. She brings back clumps of wild leek and a mushroom as big as a child's head and calls it chicken-of-the-forest. We grimace at her table offerings but bask in her adventure, like she's a hero in a story.

Gina's sister rings me from Tennessee. Have I seen her? Do I know where she is now? She was there a few months ago. She slept through days and spent nights online researching and buying things she couldn't afford. She used my credit card to buy rare orchid seeds, her sister says. Not just a few. Thousands and thousands. She said she was going to cultivate them. Her sister said send them back or she would report her for stealing the card.

I tell Gina's sister about Dayton and the car. I google growing orchids. Not only do they have the smallest seeds in the world, they require specialised conditions to germinate and you could wait years and years for the first flowers. Maybe this is her future planning, maybe she's waiting for the right place to plant them, a place where she might stay. My kids say she's on Snapchat and try to find her on their phones using Snap Map, but she hasn't shared her location.

When we were twelve, Gina and I ran away from home for a day. We followed the town river downstream for miles and miles across county borders. We pretended we were lost on a strange planet. Gina had taken her brother's walkie-talkie set. We communicated to ground control our struggle to survive, the hardships we'd endured, our last wishes and our dying words like in Space Oddity. We used English accents. I gave my last words, finishing *over and out.* I laid on the ground because I was supposed to be dead and looked up at the streaks of clouds above me and wondered what it would be like to be lost in space, to die there, to never be able to touch the earth again, to never go home again. Gina said we weren't really lost because the river would show us the way home. In the grass, I shut my eyes and listened to the steady cadence of water through the rocks. The earthy reek from the bank hung in the air. The river was there, something safe and deep close beside me.

When it seemed too much time had passed, I picked up my walkie-talkie and tried to make communication. *Ground control*, I said. *Can you hear me?* Nothing. I sat up and looked. It took me a minute to find her, a distant shape in the grasses the other side of the river, ducking the blows of imaginary enemies, running, somersaulting, stick-fighting the invisible inhabitants of the planet we were lost on.

Gina, can you hear me? I shouted into my transmitter.

I watched her stop, lift the walkie-talkie – *There's something ... Over* – and disappear into golden rod and meadow grass.

When night fell, I was the one who cried to go home. Gina wanted to keep going to get further away from where we'd been. I thought of my mother looking for me, calling people, driving the roads. Please Gina? I said.

In June, she is in southern Appalachia, posting videos of Blue Ghost Fireflies lighting up a forest edge, a glittering constellation suspended a few feet off the forest floor. She films them every night for a week, and my kids and I watch like it's a Netflix show. She works for free on an organic farm in North Carolina. She says she is learning about permaculture and soil. I wonder if it's for the orchids. She leaves with people she's met there to go to Missouri. She won't answer the phone, but late one night she posts pictures of skinned squirrels. I imagine her sitting around a campfire with Ozark hill-folk, the squirrels on spits. I wonder how they're killing the squirrels and if they're safe to eat. I look up how to hunt squirrels and diseases they might carry: rifles, you shoot them, and Creutzfeldt-Jakob's, the same as mad cow disease. I paste a link to a New York Times article on her Facebook page and write, *Don't eat the brains.*

We lose track of her those winter months. I keep checking Midwest weather; Missouri is in Tornado Alley and twisters are most common there in the spring. But by early summer she's back online and posting from Kodiak, Alaska. She's working in a wilderness lodge on one of the archipelago islands, bringing tourists on bear-sighting hikes where they camp in the open. She is so far north, she writes, it never gets dark. Kodiak bears aren't dangerous, and she sometimes sees up to ten a day. She has a boyfriend who travelled there with her. They set up the camp, cook food, help the guides manage the treks, carry packs. In her pictures, she's tanned and holding up a salmon on a fishing line. She is on the foreshore of a lake and a band of bears splash in the water less than a hundred yards away. Child bears, she captions. Kodiak bears have the same hair colour as hers, blonde with auburn undertones. Her boyfriend is in some of the pictures, too. I think he looks healthy, like a Canadian, or a fisherman, or a wilderness survival guide. He looks normal. But it turns out he's from Pennsylvania and has a meth problem and by August the relationship is in ruins.

Gina says she's going to winter at the lodge when all the tourists and other guides head back to the city. She's tired of people. She needs time. I make jokes about The Shining and send her clips from YouTube. Her sister calls me. She is worried about how the days will darken and all that solitude and a woman on her own in the middle of nowhere. Also because it's Gina. I google Kodiak winters. The sun rises close to ten and sets just after four. Average snowfall is sixty inches and for weeks at a stretch the sun never pushes through the grey sky. I try to talk her out of it, but she is staying. It will be a winter of self-improvement, she says. She has a stack of books, a camera, a freezer full of salmon and halibut and cords of seasoned cedar and birch. A neighbour a few miles away has a two-way radio and so does she, should phone signals go down. We send her a set of lights for Christmas, and she strings them around the branch of a birch with fishing lures and sardine tin lids as baubles. She sends pictures and my kids want the same decorations on our tree.

Now is the winter of my discontent, begins her last Kodiak post. One of the owner's nephews shows up in early January, a trust fund brat with a coke habit. He can't cook or split wood or even carry it, apparently. His chaos unhinges hers, and she needs to go. She leaves during a snowstorm in the Corolla. She never got snow tyres for the winter, but she did organise the registration.

She arrives at my house on a summer afternoon as if she's just walked up the road for a visit. She cooks a plant that grows through seaweed and tastes like arugula. She rambles miles along the foreshore every day and discovers the spine of a dolphin completely intact and sun dries it on my roof. She takes my kids for trips to McSquirrels, their code for McDonalds, thinking they have one over on me. Mornings they go crabbing and she makes up stories about a rabbit catcher who sets traps for children, and they can't go to sleep alone for days.

The summer after I finished college, I said I was going on a camping trip with Gina. I was pregnant and she was the only person in the world I had told. We'll go to a place out of state where we won't see anyone we know, she said. She organised everything. When it was over, she was there waiting for me. She helped me to the car, had a blanket and pillows and the passenger seat reclined. Your own little ambulance, she said. She drove us southeast towards the coast and we didn't talk. She boiled water on a camping stove and filled a hot water bottle. I curled up in a nest of sleeping bags and watched her pitch our tent, putting down stakes and adjusting guy lines. She plugged something into the car that sounded like a hair dryer: a blow-up mattress she had bought for me. You're not sleeping on the ground, she said.

That weekend we saw the loggerheads lay their eggs. June's first full moon is the perfect time, said Gina. We waited for the turtles, crouching downwind in the dark on the white dunes. She told me that the loggerheads come back to nest in the exact place they were born. After more than thirty or even fifty years, and thousands and thousands of miles, they return to that very first place. We stopped talking when we saw the first one struggling up the beach towards us. She came near, started to dig but stopped suddenly. She turned, abandoning the effort, and trudged her way back to the sea, all her eggs still inside her. It's called a false crawl, Gina whispered. They change their minds; nobody knows why. They can't nest and they return to the sea without laying anything.

We waited there in the dark and soon another loggerhead came and started digging a body pit right below us, shovelling with her four flippers, scooping out the sand. She burrowed down into her cavern and used her back flippers to dig out an even deeper chamber. The turtle slumped for a few minutes and lay there in the moonlit hollow she had dug. I thought she was done, too tired out.

But then she raised herself on her rear flippers and it began: the eggs popping out, one after the other, nearly a hundred in less than twenty minutes, soft shells like wet ping pong balls. All that glistening possibility in the dark. When she was finished, she covered it all up, scooping damp sand back to the chamber, filling it, covering the body pit, kicking dry sand, trying to keep her clutch safe. And she left, lumbered back to the sea, leaving her hundred babies behind her. She does that two or three times a season, Gina said. Leaves hundreds of turtle babies that she will never see again. Maybe one in a thousand will survive.

My husband says he's going on a fishing trip when Gina starts feeling unwell, spending more time in the house and in bed. I ask him not to leave, to please help me, to let me do this one thing for my friend who needs me. Make her go.

I don't know how to help Gina, but she says she just needs a few days and a dark room. We leave food outside her door that she barely touches. Gina's still in bed, my kids announce to my husband when he returns, tanned with a cooler full of catch. It's nice for some, he says, like Gina in bed is a choice she's made, a kind of selfish or indulgent one. When she re-emerges, she is pale and exhausted, her hair lank. She says very little. She is better, more herself again and after a storm finds a carrier pigeon blown off course. She feeds it and it follows her around the garden and shits all over our doorstep. She reads the foot band and tracks its owner who doesn't want it anymore because once a carrier pigeon goes off course, they can't race anymore, they're done. They can't find their way home. She writes a letter of complaint to the Homing Union.

One night, Gina takes my kids out on the boat. They motor back home across the black bay under a bright moon, and I watch them from the hill behind the house, all in silhouette – the small boat, my best friend Gina the skipper, my children her awed passengers – all that shimmering beauty she can bring, and I think there is nothing I wouldn't do for her.

My husband and I fight. Gina's been leaving food for the pigeon outside, and he's seen a rat. I'm at my wits end, he shouts. Stop investing yourself in a lost cause. Make her go. Gina is at the door. She walks through the kitchen past us and up to her room. I sleep in the bed with my daughters. One of them wakes me that night. Aunt Gina's crying. We listen to her muffled sobs on the other side of the wall and I think I can't breathe.

The following morning, she is gone. She leaves the pigeon and a note telling me how to feed it and its name. I make pancakes in the kitchen waiting for the kids to wake up. I think feeding everyone will fill the black holes inside us, inside the house. I think that if Gina came back I would put a stack in front of her with the blueberries she picked and everything from the night before could be forgotten.

I start sleeping in Gina's room. In the closet I find her winter fleece folded on a high shelf. I try it on. It is practical, made for a real winter, like in Missouri or Alaska. I slide my hands into the deep pockets and find something wadded. I pull out a packet of orchid seeds, so worn the instructions are no longer legible.

Gina is what is wrong between me and my husband. Not her, but what she is for each of us. He doesn't want anything messy in our lives, not a difficult conversation about our relationship, undone paperwork, dirty dishes, not complicated emotions or damaged people. Not Gina. He doesn't want to know other people's pain; he doesn't even want to know our own. I don't know how to explain that Gina is the part of me from before that's gone now. Not just my young self, but a version of me that was searching and most alive even when I was lost, along a river or lying in the dark watching the loggerheads lay their eggs.

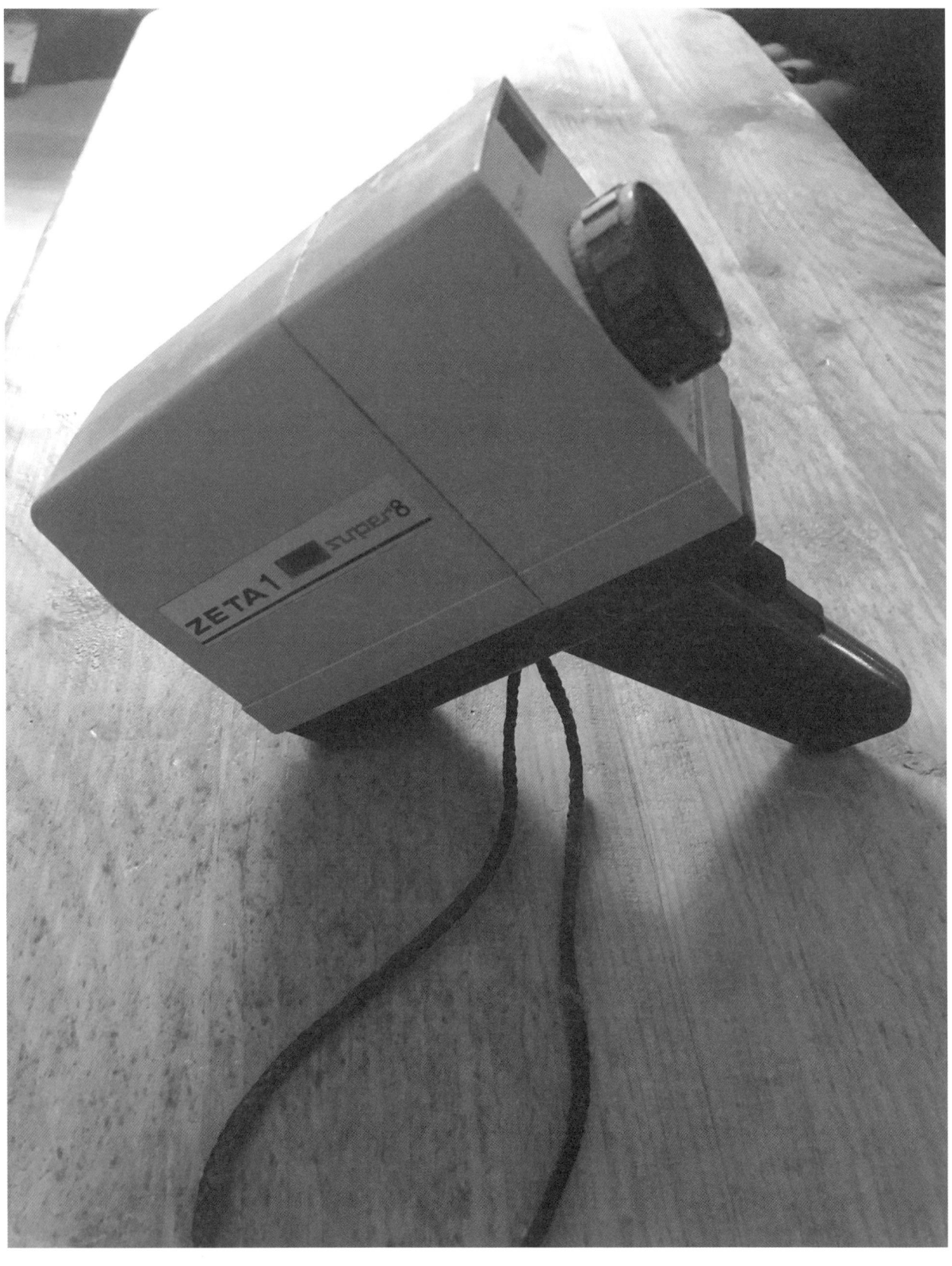

Photograph courtesy of Keith Walsh

THE UNSPOKEN LANGUAGE

An interview with JILL BEARDSWORTH and KEITH WALSH
by Peter Murphy

Twopair Films is the trading name of husband-and-wife documentarian team Keith Walsh and Jill Beardsworth. From Waterford and Sligo respectively, now based in the west of Ireland, the couple operate as a sort of mobile guerilla film unit, swapping roles as camera operators, editors, directors and producers, depending on the project. This fluidity of assigned roles and resulting ease of movement not only simplifies logistical matters, it also allows the film-makers to embed with their subjects for extended periods, be it their own neighbours in Gort, or natives of the Levant.

Each of Twopair's films to date is predicated upon a single image or idea. Apples of the Golan (2012) focuses on dwellers in the Golan Heights, the Arab-inhabited interzone administered by Israel since 1981, captured from Syria in the Six-Day War in 1967. Apples are the only produce allowed to be exported from inside the region to Syria, and even then it's with the assistance of the Red Cross.

The thirteen-minute short film Analogue People in a Digital Age (2013) features eight men drinking and talking in a Gort pub on the day RTÉ switched transmission from analogue to digital. The pair's most recent production, When All Is Ruin Once Again, released on Vimeo this spring, charts seven years of austerity in the west using the central metaphor of an unfinished road in south Galway and north Clare.

These films differ markedly in tone: When All Is Ruin feels almost millennial at times, influenced by the writings of WB Yeats and John Moriarty, haunted by Caoimhín Ó Raghallaigh's score; Analogue People is a wry fly-on-the-wall pub crawl; Apples of the Golan bears echoes of epic tragedy, stories of young brides forced to abandon their families for love, tensions between patriotic elders and apolitical youngsters who want to pursue their dreams and escape from the stranglehold of historical conflict.

I interviewed the two film-makers separately, four days apart, in late summer of this year, via Zoom, with a short follow-up email from Keith inserted into the text.

I. JILL BEARDSWORTH

PETER MURPHY: *When did you begin to think of film as something other than entertainment?*
JILL BEARDSWORTH: That goes back quite early for me. I grew up in a house where photography was quite a big thing. I guess our family was quite liberal as well, very open to their kids having a relationship with the arts. I grew up in a small town called Enniscrone in County Sligo. Just to give it some context, my father is from the north of England. My mother left rural Sligo, met him in Lancashire, got married, had us, and then we moved back.

Did that set you apart from the other children?
I was certainly the only person in my class that had a parent that wasn't from the area, so I guess there was a small bit of exoticism about us. We were baptised in the Church of England, and then when we moved to Ireland my mum was

like, 'We're sending them to the Catholic school.' The priest had to divest us of our Protestantism – it was this joke for years that he had to go down to Beardsworths' and say Mass in the kitchen to rid them of their Englishness. That was certainly exacerbated by the name. I grew up with McGabhanns and McSharrys and so on. There was no unusual name in the phone book at the time, let alone the classroom.

What was your entry into the film industry?
I decided to go and study film in DIT. There was something about cameras I really liked. When I finished college I had a couple of jobs as a runner on productions, but I found that wasn't getting me anywhere, so I ended up moving from Dublin to Galway and finding work there, mainly as an editor. I was lucky enough to start directing a documentary when I was quite young, in my early twenties, for TG4. Keith was also directing, and we decided to pool our resources and make stuff together.

Did you work together before you became a couple?
I needed someone to shoot the first film that I was directing, and I'd heard Keith was a cameraman – he'd just directed a film called I Was You, about homelessness. It was a subject you'd think would lend itself to a traditional narrative, but Keith made this unusual black and white film for RTÉ. I knew he would be a good person to get on board, so I hired him to film this documentary, and that's how we met. We pretty much fell in love over a camera. That sounds cheesy, but it was work first and the relationship came afterward.

It's interesting how you swap roles on different productions. You've been the editor, the sound recordist, the producer, the director; Keith operates the camera and edits and also directs. It's like you're the drummer on one album and the singer on the next.
It means you can film something really quickly, you don't have to adhere to a shooting schedule, like when you're hiring crew. We're lucky in that we can move at a second's notice, we don't necessarily have to plan. That's been good in the sense that you can be very reactive to something, bad in that you can end up taking years to make something and not being able to pay yourself properly, or it turning into a labour of love rather than something that you can make a living from.

The dreaded 'labour of love'.
Yeah, I've used those words in emails and I've stopped because it's disrespectful to one's art or one's practice, it just diminishes the meaning of it, takes away any monetary value one would attach to it.

What are the pros and cons of being married to your creative partner?
It's a curse and a blessing in equal measure. It can be very all-consuming. We were making films before we had kids, and we were working weekends, working long hours if the project was really important. Then when kids came into it that shifted a little bit because you can't work all the time, you need some structure in your day or your week so that you're available to other things.

We do also have separate work freelancing for other people, but I'll still want to know how Keith's day was, he'll ask me how my day was. I guess it can be a bit claustrophobic in one sense, but in another there's a great ease of communication. We sometimes know what the other is thinking while we're filming or editing without having to say it, there's almost an unspoken language, and that can be exhilarating when there's a flow and a synergy. When we were filming in the Golan Heights it was very easy for us to get close to certain people because we were a couple, not a film crew going in with three or four people, intimidating.

Trust seems integral to your practice. In Analogue People the subjects allowed you to film them yammering away in various states of inebriation in the pub in Gort.
Me being from Sligo and Keith being from Waterford, we're both perceived as outsiders. You're in this unusual position of being a glorified confidante. People will tell you stuff they'll never tell their close neighbours or friends of the family. There's something bestowed on you as an inside-outsider that lends itself to the kind of film-making we do. They don't know who our families are, what side of the Civil War we were on, or if my uncle scored a point in the GAA final in '64 or whatever. It's Keith and Jill calling around for a chat by the fire rather than the film crew coming for a documentary that they're making. We take a lot of time to make our films, we don't just parachute in. In a way, we're embedded in the community.

Your films tend to revolve around singular symbols or events that define the narrative: the exporting of apples, the building of a road, the switch from analogue to digital broadcasting. Do these images arise as you're shooting, or are they a guiding principle from the outset?
With Apples of the Golan we knew about the apples before we decided to make a film there. We knew we could tell a story through the apples. With Analogue People, the analogue/digital switchover was happening, we'd filmed in the pub for I think about ten days, and it was only during the editing process did we decide to cut it so that it was one day. With Ruin, the road was the catalyst for making the film, we knew that this thing of great change was coming to the area. We didn't know where the film was going to go, but what we'd been doing spoke back to us and told us how it should come together.

That sounds a bit hairy.
It can be quite unnerving because we don't have an idea at the beginning, we don't necessarily have a script that we're going to adhere to. We don't use narration typically, and we do use a multi-character device to tell the story. That adds a huge workload. You might have filmed fifty people, and you might use ten of them. But by casting the net quite wide, I think it allows things to happen according to their own rules rather than us imposing something on it from the beginning.

You tend to use a lot of wide shots and ensemble scenes. These films are very much about the collective and the community. The camera betrays no sense of ironic distance from the subject.
We found that when we were in the Golan Heights, at the beginning, there were people who came towards us who were spokespeople for the community, they had a well-trodden narrative that they would deliver in a very eloquent and newsworthy way, but that wasn't interesting to us. I find that I'm drawn to ordinary people – there can be a depth and a wealth of expression that's way worthier of exposition on film than the expert or the academic.

In Apples of the Golan we see diehard supporters of Bashar al-Assad speaking about flags and homelands and blood, juxtaposed with images of young rappers and rock musicians having fun. I was reminded of the role music played in defusing sectarianism in Northern Ireland, those legendary Horslips and Rory Gallagher gigs.

Those young people in that film really just wanted to play music, they had no problem going to Haifa in Israel and playing a gig. Art is one of the things that can be a balm to wounds that are old and deep. I don't think Apples of the Golan set out to do anything like that, but it is interesting that you mention the music. We end with a scene where there's a couple salsa dancing in the orchard – that was very much intended to represent all the different cultures that go into anyone's life in the modern world. I guess that scene is a set-piece or a crescendo to show all the sources that were at play.

I found it the most politically charged scene in the film. The vitality and beauty of a young couple dancing in stark contrast to footage of old men playing patriotic music through tinny speakers.

Absolutely. The religious elders had a certain hold over the village, there was this conservatism among the older people but then the young kids, particularly the girls, were very beautiful and showing flesh and not conservatively dressed or anything. There was always a bit of tension there, a schizophrenic force in some way. The kids were influenced by Israeli culture, by American culture, and the older people identified with Syria, they were part of the old country, that was what they wanted to bring forth toward their children. But the kids were into other stuff because it was way more sexy than the Syrian national anthem. That frisson was interesting, it helped us create conflict, or drama, within the film.

When All Is Ruin Once Again, by contrast, has a more end-times feeling, the sense of an age drawing to a close.

The mention of Yeats and civilisations at the beginning – he had a notion of gyres, of time being cyclical rather than linear, and we felt with climate change coming on, that was happening in a way.

An abandoned road provides the narrative spine of the film. Literally a road to nowhere ...

The road was described by some film festival programmer as a fossil of asphalt, and that resonated quite strongly when I heard it. We live quite close to the Burren and there are fossils everywhere, sea creatures going back millions of years. When we started the film, the fact that the road was coming to the area felt like some huge geographical shift, and by the end of the film-making process the road felt like this symbol of modernity. But for what, and at what cost? Once something is changed, it's never going back. There's a man in the film who stands on the bridge as the road opens, and he just turns around and says, 'It'll never be quiet again.' It's very telling, that simple line. It will never be quiet again, ever, because there will always be noise coming from that motorway and floating into people's homes nearby. There's something so definite and so permanent to that kind of a construction. What the film was trying to do was in some way [ask], 'What will be left of this time, this place, this culture, when nature takes it all again?'

But there's a sense of regeneration too. I'm thinking of that extraordinary scene I mistook for a line-dancing competition, until you enlightened me.

The scene is actually Brazilians doing what's called a quadrilha: a line of people and a DJ playing a Brazilian dance tune. Every year in Gort, which has a huge Brazilian population, they do this dance, it's almost like a dating ritual. It's interesting, because their culture is being brought into our culture. When I was doing research for the film, I was chatting to a group of Brazilian men that stand outside one of the shops in Gort every morning looking for work – they'll go and paint houses or do some farm labour or whatever needs to be done. And there's a concrete step on this particular shop, and that area became known in the Brazilian community as 'The Stone', as in, 'Yer man, did he get work from the Stone?' I found it really interesting that that step will probably forever be known as The Stone, in the same way that local fields have names or wells are given names. Or there'll always be this hurler named Leonardo Gomez who played on the team in 2008, that'll always be in the local lore, that culture will always leave its legacy.

II. Keith Walsh

Peter Murphy: *What was your initiation into film-making?*

Keith Walsh: I'm from a family of two, I've one brother, and he's fourteen years and a day older than me. When he was about twelve, before I was born, he got a Super-8 camera, a projector and a couple of reels – it was a deal that was in some newspaper, that would have been back in '77. My father bought it for him and he made a couple of movies with his mates. He got a VHS camera when he was twenty-seven, I was thirteen. My mother suggested he take me filming weddings as second camera. He just kind of left me at the church with the groom and went off to the bride's house. My job was to try to film all these people who were basically saying, 'Fuck off and stop filming me.' I very quickly had to learn ways to make people feel comfortable in front of the camera, because my brother was quite hard on me, he really wanted to get the best footage, he critiqued every single shot. So that was the genesis of it.

What's your first memory of being emotionally affected by a film?

I remember a video tape that was around the house that my brother had recorded. It was a documentary about war cameramen – I watched it over and over again. It featured Nicaragua, the North, Iran/Iraq, Lebanon, wars that were going on in the '70s and '80s. When the cameraman Mo Amin died in 1996 there was a documentary about his life and work in Ethiopia on the TV that really hit home to me, the potential of a camera. I think I realised subconsciously that not only could this camera be my voice and my tool for learning about the world, but it could also be a weapon. When I did my Leaving Cert oral exam we had to choose a photo to talk about, and I chose a photo by Giles Peres of Bloody Sunday. It was of Barney McGuigan lying dead, with a guy holding his head in disbelief. Thinking back now, I can't actually believe I did that, but it resonated greatly with my seventeen-year-old self.

When I went to college I saw La Haine, and that just blew my mind. It is an amazing film, but what really struck home to me was that the French Prime Minister convened a cabinet meeting in the cinema and made all his ministers watch the film. The potential of that is incredible.

It is strange how one's life's course changes on small moments. I don't think I would have ended up in the Golan Heights without those video tapes, and I wouldn't have ended up doing what I do without a small ad in the paper. Some part of me would still love to be running around a war zone, but maybe the boreens of south Galway and Clare are where I need to be for the next while.

How did you get into actually shooting documentaries?
I went to film school. I couldn't get into Dún Laoghaire so I went to Galway, GMIT, the first year of that course. Basically we had the run of the place. There was no demand on resources, they had equipment for the three years, but there was only one year, so we had a field day. That gave us the opportunity to experiment.

It sounds like a proper arts lab environment.
I think a lot of the time in film schools there's no experimentation, it's all fixated on the end of year project, the end of the semester, there's such a focus on, 'I need to get it right because I need to get my marks.' And there's also a lack of resources, so you can't take out a camera and just fuck around and make a film with you and your mates running around Galway city at night. That was a godsend.

There were an awful lot of film-makers around Galway Film Centre at the same time looking for people to work for cheap, and I got a lot of jobs. Before I left college I'd shot and edited two half-hour documentaries for RTÉ. The editing only came because a film-maker named Paddy O'Connor asked me to film a documentary about a Galway rowing club for RTÉ. I learned to be an editor just by being in the room with him. The one thing I've learned from Paddy, and from Pat Collins as well, is the importance of being able to work the material, and work the material, and the more you work it, the more it reveals itself to you, and that can only be done with time, without the pressure of a deadline coming down.

How did you navigate the shock of life after college?
I got a job in Concorde, which was Roger Corman's studio in Connemara. I was up there for a couple of years, three shoots a year. I was working in the camera department as a clapper-loader, second camera system and stuff, but I never found camera departments very nice places to be. The attitude … At that stage, the camera to me was somewhat sacred, and that was really making me feel negative to it all.

Then, in 2002, the Galway Film Centre ran a great scheme called the ID Projects. Different community groups were assigned a mentor, and the mentor would have forty contact hours or whatever, and go in and teach them to make a documentary that expressed their own identity. I got assigned to a group of homeless men in a shelter in Galway. I spent the summer hanging out with them, and we made a fifteen-minute observational documentary filmed by the guys themselves. When we finished, we had loads more footage so we went to RTÉ and RTÉ gave us some money to make a [full-length] documentary.

Was it always documentaries? Why not fictional drama?
There's something about the energy of a small crew – you are there in that place with these people. The flow of that suited me a lot more than the big crews and

the staggered nature of the drama. It just never appealed to me. Growing up, I was always an observer rather than an instigator.

How, then, did you end up making a film in the Golan Heights?
Someone in our distant family was married to a man from Gaza, and every Christmas we ended up spending nights chatting to him. A little while later, I walked into a room in the Galway Film Centre and came across a guy called Gearóid Ó Cuinn, from Waterford as well … He had been doing human rights research in the Golan Heights for three months and he said, 'I think there's a great documentary in it, but I can't make it.'

I suppose the main thing that gets you is the Syrian Bride phenomenon – basically a bride can come from one side and get married in an exclusion zone and she can never return – and the shouting: not only is the place cut off from its homeland and its people, but there's a hill where people shout across with megaphones. Those two things captured us straight away. As opposed to Gaza or the West Bank, it's not a place that people know, or are aware of the complexity of, [or don't know] that it is an occupied part of Syria. They're pretty much all apple farmers, and there was something quite beautiful about having the story about these people farming, the orchards. But everything there is political: the apples are political, the seeds inside the apples are political.

What was the timeline of the filming?
We started in 2006, I think, and we finished there in 2011. Trying to finish it was very difficult because the war in Syria at that time was gathering pace, and in retrospect it probably affected the life of the film afterwards. It was only subsequently that it seemed to be the playground of geopolitics, and prob-ably still is. We were told afterwards by a pretty high up guy in the European documentary world that he really liked the film, but he said it's very difficult to show people loving Bashar al-Assad now, that's why you're not getting as much traction.

There's a definite sense of democracy in all your films. Everyone gets a say.
My family wasn't very artistic but there was always a compassion in both my mother and father for people on the margins. I was never taught to be fearful, I was always taught to understand or to embrace. There was always someone on the outside of the family brought over for Christmas. I was taught not to be afraid, they were not bad people, life had just been tough to them. I find it much more interesting to film and be with people on the margins, or regular people, I suppose. I find the ordinary extraordinary.

But myself and Jill are not very big personalities, we don't dominate a room, Jill is quite gentle. I'm getting less and less gentle now – I have to watch that – but generally speaking, we naturally go to the edges. We're trying not to interfere when we have a camera in front of someone, we always try to get to that point where everyone forgets what we're doing, including ourselves.

CACOPHONY OF BONE

Kerri ní Dochartaigh

A handful of objects crossed my path this year; things I never once set out in search of, on a laneway, the like of which I had not imagined I would ever dwell. They came, at first, in that thin gap, between the winter and the spring, as the hag clears the path for the cailín, as the snow makes way for the May. And now the summer has come, as always it must, (scan your memory, and see it: winged things & green things, bone-fires & veins of light), and even still, they are coming.

I never meant to call these things, beckon them up or out, over or from, the places to which they must have first belonged. It was never my intention to steal them, or to borrow them; to haul them out of unseen, silent bellies. I never meant to gather things that were not mine to take – but I swear I did not call to them, I did not call these things; I did not even know they were there.

It began two days after the winter solstice, as all stories begin, with light that tinges the clouds with hues, the kind which you cannot fully trust, and with a flock of birds, signalling something, half-sentences scrawled by clawed feet, that you will never quite divine. And so it might go, a little like this, you see. The light on that raw, post-cusp morning was unreliable; it shifted and spat, coughed and spluttered like an old hound by the side of a rusted shipping container. The person the light was waiting for did not come, and we lay in their place instead; beneath its grief, its phlegmy, sea-green bane. In limp and ceaseless sleet, my lover drove our Transit, below a metallic dove-grey sky, flecked with starlings. Those oily-feathered, maundering ghosts tailed us, across an invisible border, from Derry to the bottom of an isolated, mucky laneway, in the back end of nowhere. Particular creatures, like particular places, have evolved in ways conducive to the act of being read. Others, either through choice or by the weight of an unknown hand, remain knotted, thorny as those overgrown dreamscapes of childhood, their slanted scripts indecipherable. There was no way, back then, to translate those pewter-polished, winter-boned birds; their tinny-throated song, their bitter-cold, fish-wife tidings.

Other creatures lingered, too, in the backcloths of that flitting, ashen, winter's day. Ones for which I'd pined and longed, hoped and begged; creatures that were not coming across the unmanned border, in that once-white, Northern reg'd van. Those other creatures were, it must be told, not coming at all, in fact – on either side of any border – and those creatures were the reason why we moved here; to this abandoned, stony railway line, in the musty heart of the winter. I came to grieve those unborn things, those creatures that I could not coax to land, in the sickly, pink dawn of any morning. This laneway seemed the place that I might mourn them, mark their echoey, empty absence, on a forgotten stretch of land. I came to change my life, which is, of course, the reason any of us go anywhere; we take to sea and sky and land so we might learn, once more, to breathe.

I would throw myself (I had decided) into words; into that thankless, aching feat of writing, of undoing all that once we said we knew, whilst being asked, then, silently, to thread it back together: differently, more brightly, more full of what is real, and of the whole. I would loosen, I would soften, I would cry, I would be quiet. I would walk the fields, I would get a dog. I would nourish, instead of creatures, the words. On that first winter's night I was lulled to sleep by a clattering, haunting lullaby; tin being thrown against wood, in unseen places. The moon, from its milking-barn roof, woke me up five times. I imagined, so it must have been, night-birds cradling me, in wildly soothing, fleshly darkness.

And so it went: the dog came on the first day, the field on the next, and by the third the first object had found all three of us, in one foul swoop. It was St Stephen's Day. Wrens, at the edges of the scene, were not being hunted; the place already had begun setting out its stall, one far removed from tradition or from folklore. Or maybe it was the case that the opposite was true: that this silent laneway – all the spaces pegged out, too, on the map of its surrounds – was so seeped in the past, its layers so embedded as to be like bog-oak, that no room was left for such stifling, archaic custom. Perhaps the place need pay no heed to blow-ins, our romanticised views; it could ignore every broken-boned scrap of what we wanted, hoped, or needed it to be. No wrens were to be hunted that day. Instead, those small brown birds played their own part – as large as their song – in the oddly calm unfolding of the place. (Already I have lied to you, I have given the heart over to its sentimental needs, unwittingly.) It was not silent. It is never silent, here; nor even close to it, it has always a felt sounding I cannot quite describe. It was, that day, noiseless, so to speak, but there were living things on the laneway, there was an ever-present hum; there were bodies, there was movement, there was life. No sound could be dragged out from where the hips and haws were held, no individual beat or drip, shuffle or screech could be identified for what it was, or for what a melancholic outsider might have longed for it to be. Rather it was still, and quiet, in a very specific way; in a way that I would really have to bring you here to prove. Silence is a thing that depends, for its existence, on the air being full of sound you cannot place; bleeding into the very soil, a bell being rung, over and over, spanning oceans & time & yearning. Silence asks for noise, for sounds so knotted to the outside world, both natural and its opposite – that you see that it, the silence, is only ever to be found inside. Birthed beneath our skin; we try to haul it out, to laneways and other places of our choosing, but when it meets the morning air we find it gone. We, like Orpheus, have looked back instead of forward, and the silence dissolves, like longing, at our feet. And so I moved, that St Stephen's Day, through a landscape full of unknown, quiet sounds, tracing the air like a haar, unshifting, unnerving. None of those, though, were the sounds of a wren, being hunted, from its place within the world.

When we reached the lane's end, a metal gate stood between the field and us, and she slipped right through – the dog that I had only just met – and so I followed, for it is what I always have been wont to do, but had never really before found the means. I followed the dog – my dog – into the field I had never once before set foot in, because it was winter, and I had come to change my life. I had come to walk through fields that were not mine to walk through, beneath skies that were not mine to lay beneath, in a place that I had no claim over at all. I had come here to do this because for long, so long, for too long to even admit, I had been left to find my own way through – and I was sick of it, I was sick to the back teeth of it; I had come here so I could finally go, instead, where I was led. And so it happened, that very first time I entered the field, that it stood there in front of me, the very first object: a wall made out of stone. An object made by man, keeping the sodden grass in its place, a skein of blinding winter light falling; it revealed numbers, carved into its surface long ago, a scar from when the wall had been wet, newly formed: *1921*. You understand, of course, that this first object did not come home with me, not in any way for which I could be indicted. We walked on, the dog first, and I followed her, always following in her shadow, until no more light was left by means of which we could go further still.

That night, as I made for sleep, my dead grandfather's hands came to me, crackled, cradling the living eggs of a goldfinch; at the part of the border from which we gathered dandelion heads, on a summer's day lit by light which memory had created with its own hands and had tended to every day since, long after the moment had its shortly lived unspooling. My grandfather, the border, and the field's stone wall, all on their way to being a hundred years old; three ghosts, not quite gone, not quite here; it had never really felt like winter before that night.

It becomes a little more muddied now, both the soaked earth, and my spare, murky memories of it all, of all that began, so suddenly, to happen. My birthday came, bringing wind and rain and damage, so much damage, to the lane. Next the New Year, the dog terrified by sounds she could not see but she could feel, beside her guts, the parts that keep things moving on the tracks of her insides; the dog refusing to stand with us at the door, as birds hid in bare trees, tiny dots of clamour and of colour, against a black sky, giving itself over to January. It howled and raged and pelted, with the winds and sleet and rain, for two months straight, every weekend a new name given to the same weather, in the same season, until even the field became too treacherous to traverse.

We took, us three, to keeping by the stove, tracking time not by the light, for there was none, you see, but by our animal needs: eating, drinking, emptying, warming, sleeping, mating (or not). As January became the shortest month, on its very last day, talk of a teenager from these parts filled the radio with a bloodied, angering history of loss. Over the years, in company of women I revered, I bit my tongue when I heard her name, too full of shame to admit that I did not know, that I had not read, that I had not ever taken time to really hear. Too full of shame, all of my own, to see the ones that long had stood before; shame that keeps us from those that we should honour, and so I ran – in rain that cut my hands – and stood beneath the sycamore, with one bar of signal, and read of her for the very first time. Ann Lovett and her wean, Ann Lovett and her pain; I saw it then, I felt it then; all our pain. I wept and as I did, I felt it kick, that thing inside the belly that wants to break, that wants to smash and howl and kick until they listen, until we, ourselves, do too, until we learn to lift our eyes up from the ground. That thing that makes us scream that we no longer are ashamed; by what we do not know, do not feel, do not want, do not carry – that we are women, and we want this all to change. There is a border cutting through this island; invisible, ancient, still more thought of than us, and we are no longer going to lie down and be silenced. I stood and thought, really thought, about shame. About how they made it feel so bound up in our bodies. About how we carried things that were never ours to bear. How our bodies are not able, any longer, to be quiet; I felt mine join this new cacophony of bones.[1]

January gave into the bowels of the winter, February slithered around my feet like an eel. I lifted a heavy grey stone, not really sure why, even and there, in that world beneath, as unknown to me as my own kith and kin, I found a creature I had no way to name. Returning to the barn with its roof that rattles at my sleep and teeth, I googled it. An Irish newt, rare as change – but as real, and as living, as the same.

There was, that year, an extra day to winter's count, a delicate, quite unreal gathering of hours, like small, clumped cells, and when it came it carried frost that reflected the light, a light too graceful to even try capture, on film or paper – on screen or memory – it felt like winter was loosening its jealous, devastating hold. That day, the dog and I explored, a little, the milking barn beside our home, and I sat on a broken trailer, below the first blue sky of the year; it was the only thing that I really could call my own, and I wept. I cried for reasons I felt no need to take apart, for reasons I likely know but just as likely know I need not name; I cried until the dog dragged me, with her wildness, towards the outhouse. Its roof had long caved in, all traces of its purpose had been swept or flooded away, but still a sense of value, of purpose, filtered, like light, through rotted slats. Three objects found me there, in that ivy-clad, ghost-ruined space, only two of which I lifted, from their hiding, and brought, without a thought, into my home. I carried those objects – fallen, abandoned, beautiful – away from the damp corner of the shed, one smaller than the other but no less fine, as gently as I could, the most exquisite pair of nests, and I wish that I could say that I regret it. I wish that I could say that I was wrong, that I felt shame; I wish I could pretend that I would have stopped this, if I could, but I will not lie, again, to you, or any others.

It took less than a week, after the nests, to sense that something was not right in the world outside the lane, a world we only glimpsed in scraps. If enough signal could be had to search the news, we read enough to realise that the winter had come back. That we would not now be emerging; not travelling out from our centre, in search of places beyond the island's boggy middle. That we all, in fact, would be remaining where we lay, in those parts of land we'd spent the long-drawn winter, for a spell it was too early, then, to forecast.

(I know that you have suffered; I see the salty lines still visible on your skin. I will not send this all back down upon you, for it is much too soon, to revisit it through words.)

All we must recall, you see, about that certain time, is that we all were held in place like stones, like objects carried through the wrack and tide, laid in places

---

1 'Cacophony of bone' is from the Paula Meehan poem 'The Statue of the Virgin at Granard Speaks' in Memories of the Home (2013) courtesy of Dedalus Press.

that either we belonged to or did not, and we were being asked, back then, to stay there, to resist the flow of seasons and of order; we were asked to keep away from one another, as a kindness. And so we knuckled even further down, us three, into this laneway, and nestled among its not quite silent, not quite empty limbs. You know, of course – what need have I to tell you? – that we kept within the radius allowed us all. Only just, you see – we still could make it through the field, into the bog, to where white cotton housed the waiting moths (so softly). To where the cuckoo, I'd been told, would soon be coming, to where the snipe outlived the curlew above the birch. We could not download the proper app, with its distance, and its sites of quirky interest, so I studied the paper map as best I could. I circled the end of my own line, I knew that anyway none would find me in that middling, barren place. I thought, of course, how quickly it all can change, how swiftly the circles we run in might fade away, how we all might find ourselves – achingly, humbly – held in a place outwith our choosing, a place we never thought that we might be, a place we cannot, in the morning fog, locate. A place where time might show its lurking ways, become the truest it can be: moth-winged, moon-lit, where time reveals itself – so unlike what we ever took it for; a veiled and formless thing – that only we ourselves can learn to live inside. Maybe it all really started with the nests. When I began to brood, not over a clutch but over time. When I began to try to sculpt it, day by day, alone, wandering, again and again, without scale or horizon, the same field, the same lane, the same stretch of wet, hungry land. When I stepped, in a way, outside & inside, above & below – the flow of it all, the flow of my own blood; enough to really let those objects come. To notice and to hold them, give my furry body over to their coming, to stop hurrying through life like a person shamed, by my female body and its traumas, by my past, by what that body could not have, what its parts could not produce; the objects, when they came, swept me with them in their flow. Their poetry lay in their familiarity; in the sheer, unrivalled intimacy of their being.

And you see, it really happened in this way, and I really can tell it no other way than this. At the bottom of this laneway, objects came from everywhere, ordinary and flawed, on days when time and place no longer knew the way, and I took them. I took every single thing into my arms and hands and home; I was compliant. I knew at every turn I could not go back to how I lived before the objects came, to how I'd breathed and ached and mourned: they were an invitation I could do nothing but accept.

Creamy white dove eggs, opened but unbroken; the skull of a badger, too sculpted to even seem real; on Mother's Day, (my heart cracked open like a dry seed-head), a perfect, otherworldly antler, from the field's exact middle; I took, I took, I took. Bone after bone, porcelain white and willowy: sheep and deer, horse and fox – the pelvic girdle of a delicately bird-like rat – objects so creaturely as to make the longing I had dragged here, slowly, quietly, ease. I struggled, at first, to talk of them. Their hold felt hex-like, fiercely personal, I only now see how terrified I was it all might stop. My lover continued through that unfamiliar spring as always he had before, as though he had been made for it all, as though something inside of him had kicked into action, (something chemical, biological, mechanical), spluttering like the tractors the boys here use but once a year – it was as though this part had started up in him, this year, no matter how surreal, without the need for oiling. The turf's still being cut out from the earth, he seemed to say; there are decent local lads, texting decent local girls as they drive. And though, he seemed to say, we don't approve, though we want to shoo them all away like butchering cats, it means the world it still is turning; look-it, it means the world still holds a hope for what yet might come.

As the weather brightened, we took our animal bodies outside, and I watched, each day, as he cleared the broken parts away. Rotted decking, thorns of white and black – their poison lying in wait a decade through; I watched him clear, from the unloved space, an opening. A garden, from the spoils of loss, and it really happened, although I find it hard to put across, that when he called me to the very first birds, it was on the spring equinox. He called me out to finches that were golden, on a feeder made from damaged things; to creatures we had never seen there, even once before that day. When they came it was the solstice, and we took them; we took them and we never gave them back. They came, from then, in vast, unruly droves. It never crossed our minds to try to stop them. We never talked of who might own them, all these birds, of who we might be leaving, now, to mourn. We took each creature, gratefully, as they came.

Time did the things it does when we aren't looking, and soon my love began, while walking on his own, to find things, too. Things, you understand, that never once had come his way before that year. His nests were, to my eye, more gorgeous than my own, but I felt no jealousy. It was such sweet relief, at last, to speak this truth. We sat, each night, as the names of those we'd lost were read aloud. A silence took up residence; it lay in circular objects, things we knew had once been crafted by the careful, repeated movements of the bodies of birds. We held them, and we mourned for those we did not know, behind the daily count; faces we had not seen but could not turn away from now. We thought, aloud, of those left behind; of the things, as well as people, that we knew would be no more; we thought of this as the nests, carried in from the world outside our door, filled our shaky, red-raw hands.

The grief, the one I came here first to bury, still came in waves, as we all have known it to; the water that none of us will ever fully swim through. It paled though, so incredibly, in the face of the sorrow of those days; I held it to the sky and watched it fade, I saw its steely greys and charcoals water down. I watched the ache for what I did not have turn chalky, I stood and let the fledglings drink its milk. It sounds formulaic, as though I forced it in some way, but this time came to me like a field of bleached white bones; these objects like the moment before drowning: I took them and I cannot give them back.

In Granard, as the spring began unravelling, in the fiercest light this place had ever shown, a swallow – singular, solitary – thrilled the sky above the graveyard hill with arrows of moving light. I sent the sighting off to distant strangers; on Instagram, we hailed this bird a messenger of hope. Bone-tired little bird. It was the sixth day, then, of April; the first swallow of this year (the year like none before) arrived in Granard on the birthday of Ann Lovett. Bone-tired little bird, alone: a scout. Asking us, in its little bird way: Am I safe – safe here? Is it safe here? Has this place learned how to give shelter to its young?

In April and May, in the light like none before it, in a turning, emptied world, we watched as our home, quietly, became theirs. My love cut, in the highest gold one noon, the straggled hairs of me and her, and watched them scatter, clumps of brown and fawny cream, beside the seedlings I still can't believe we grew. Cornflowers and lettuce, foxgloves and beans; hairs in every corner, we watched in disbelief as birds swooped down to claim them for their own. Great tits in the eaves, blue tits in the gap the rats had made above the dripping gutter; their fluttering, awkward movements above our heads, in bed, as we held each other close in stroking heat. The wrens played it safe, two nests in place of one, and how we worried when the sycamore tree grew hushed. The cat, in wont of butchering, revealed the second nest; we chased him from our fledglings like a crow. The farmer only believed the house martins when she saw them; they have, says she, not come this way in decades. The door had just been painted when they came; 'crushed lemon', now speckled brown, with dripping mud, like a song thrush.

And I know, it seems, that this could never happen, but I have learned, it seems, to forget about being believed. And so this is how it happened, then, at sunrise, on the first summer solstice that we've spent in this new world –

The door had been left open through the night. I awaken, as if called by my full name, as if called out to the living room, by the presence of another, called to the blood and bone, the heat and beat, the flutter and the fear. The dog, in the corner wakens too, and we are a three, now, in this room, and one of us wants out. Wants let back out, into that other world of newly-fading light, shone through feather & gathered hair, through stick & through leaf, through mud & moss. One of us is scared, and wants back out, to the world in which she has only just woken up, out to the world beyond this stone home; the world from which she has somehow, for a moment, slipped.

It is the solstice, and one of us – this speckled bird, newly-formed – lingers at the window, now opened, for long enough that I think, for the briefest moment, that she might settle, on the nest beside her, carried in from the lane just the night before. The dog, in her confusion, has gone out the door.

One of us, heart-caught and shaken, sees the speckled wing of the other, long after the window closes, after the fledgling's trace has left the empty room. She came, and when she did, I could not keep her, that little one. Her coming in, you see, was really all it took.

Some creatures come without you even calling. They arrive, while you are sleeping, through your door. It is the solstice, and the light out there is changing; stand and watch, now, as it bleeds out from the sky. Particular light, though, when it comes, it comes to change us. Some light, when it comes, it comes to stay.

It takes our grief and helps us sculpt it into bone. It nestles in, beside those bones, a porcelain silence; some creatures, through their absence, bring the light.

THE MOON IS A HEALING BEING

Chiamaka Enyi-Amadi

the moon is teaching me to heal the fear, of being and not being seen the scourge, of many eyes or worse none at all lone- ly is living without another being, next to me at all times breathing without, another body to match the rise and, fall of my chest some nights she surprises, me her face beaming with satisfaction, a day well spent caring for her own self, she tells me just because a person has, eyes doesn't mean they see you doesn't mean, they would hold your hand through all your phases, each night the sky is a firm silver chest, cradling her head basking in the blue, of her glow full of gratitude for her, having come at last to keep it company, bringing it laughter full to the belly, on some nights she's worse off joy cut in half, needing to cry and go to bed early, the moon is a healing being washing her, silver hair thankful time is on her side, longing to lie her weary head on the, warm cotton chest of her pillow not long, now till daybreak bringing a damp cloth to, her aching arms and chest black soap kissing, the soft dimples on her lower back shea, butter massaging her skin soothing each, pore from toe to chin cherry balm sweet on, her lips she cries she sings nothing is tru- ly fixed not anger not fear not even grief, she cools her sore eyes with fresh cucumber, slices her bedtime snack lavender, drops on trembling fingertips pressing, into the nape of her neck the base of, her temples have stopped ticking time is still, on her side as day breaks into a cold, sweat she settles into sleep dreaming of, the distant sky knowing it will soon light, up when it sees her rested smile beaming, over Dublin bay

THE HEALING BREATH: POETRY AND THE MAKING OF DOCTORS

Martin Dyar

We submit to the doctor by quoting to ourselves a state of childhood and simultaneously extending our sense of childhood to include him. We imagine him as an honorary member of the family.
John Berger

Over the past twenty years or so, in medical schools in Ireland, the UK and the US, as part of an academic movement commonly referred to as 'medical humanities', students have increasingly been studying literature and creative writing. Much to the satisfaction of medical educators, these tailored arts and humanities offerings have proved reliably popular, particularly in the first two years of a medicine degree, before the more intense phases of clinical placements have begun. For the new recruits there seems to be something natural as well as novel in the undertaking. The explorations and discussions involved tend to be genuinely stimulating, in addition to being a counterbalance to a curriculum that typically presents major challenges.

In Ireland, if you ask medical students their opinion about the value of reading and writing poetry as part of their training, one likely response is that the validation of such things within the medicine curriculum, along with the opportunity to develop an artistic interest, comes as a great relief. On entering medical school, many students begin to rally themselves for extreme exam preparation. A combined vision of endurance and success can come into play, as they tell themselves a limiting story; namely, that they must be prepared to block out all distractions, all temptations, and almost all extracurricular interests for the sake of the job at hand.

Being given an outlet that is arts-based, and being required to slow down and reflect, are not unwelcome, and neither are study requirements that are enjoyable for their novelty and sociability. But such things as enjoyment and artistic ambition are not often uppermost in the thoughts of the people responsible for curricular developments in medical schools. Certainly, behind the bulwarks, a concern for the wellbeing of medical students exists. The idea that medical training is at times unnecessarily demanding is not a contested one, and neither is the idea that something should be done to ameliorate the built-in stresses of the student experience. Some academic doctors write about their students in compassionately holistic terms. Since the advent of medical humanities, there have been calls to use literature in medical training as a counter-cultural force, as a way to tackle the forms of medical inhumanity that too often alienate the trainee. There has been some powerful writing this year questioning the presumption that medical students should volunteer themselves as frontline workers, and about the phenomenon of graduations being fast-tracked as a way of addressing personnel shortages. In an article emphasising the risks posed to students' mental health by pandemic unpreparedness, the risk of what has been termed 'moral trauma', and the untried altruism of the students themselves, one fiery commentator wrote, 'No more should be expected of medical students than of the general public.'

Viewpoints of this kind reflect a lesser known culture of advocacy, and an established sensitivity to the phased transformation of medical students from members of the public into medical professionals, things which tie in with arts and humanities initiatives in undergraduate medicine. But the main reason student doctors have been encouraged in recent years to read and write creatively is that a belief that it might make a difference to the patient's experience of healthcare has begun to take root in the pedagogical ground of medicine itself.

Such things as curiosity, and a willingness to try to relate to the patient, to listen to them, and to interpret their symptoms in the light of their experiences, together with an interest in the nuances of language and expression, have attained importance, and it is for the sake of these virtues that many medical schools have sought to make budding writers and critics out of their new recruits. In a recent New Yorker interview, Johanna Shapiro, the director of the University of California Irvine's medical humanities program, framed the link between literature and the doctor-patient relationship in striking terms:

> You think a patient is going to be like a well-organized essay, but what you really get is a poem ... You're not sure what they mean, and they don't tell you everything all at once, up front.

Embarking from this image of a doctor palpating a sonnet, I'm going to explore two recently published poems by Irish poets: Mary O'Malley's The Heart Man, from her 2019 collection Gaudent Angeli (Carcanet), and Stephen Sexton's #7 Larry's Castle, from the collection If All the World and Love Were Young (Penguin), also published in 2019. On their own terms, both poems are engrossing and impressive, and I will try to identify some of the technical secrets behind their respective powers. The fact that both have illness, healing and healthcare among their themes allows an additional approach. By looking at The Heart Man and #7 Larry's Castle in the light of the idea of a medical poetry audience, one that wishes to embrace literature as a means for doctors to become better attuned to the individuality of their patients, as well as a medium through which new insights into its institutional biases and hang-ups might be attained, I will be trusting an unusual critical angle, but one that I'm confident will help to reveal something of the true depth and substance of the poems. Ultimately, mindful of the shadow of the coronavirus pandemic, I want to attempt to illuminate something of poetry's value as an offering to the doctors of the future, those for whom that same shadow is likely to become a kind of professional habitat.

Possessed by an idiosyncratic counter-cultural spirit, Mary O'Malley's The Heart Man catches the medical humanities eye in the way that it excludes mainstream medicine and science from a story of illness and healing, almost to the point of casting imagination as the primary carer. Through a third person narrative mode, articulated from the perspective of a wry speaker, we meet a male patient, the eponymous heart man, who is remarkably self-possessed in the face of a serious condition. The poem begins with the pursuit of a diagnosis:

> ... When he is asked
> to picture it he sees a dark space

a metal wrapping locked tight
to protect it from the touch of ravens
and whatever else is there.

There's a valuable strangeness in this depiction of the patient's insides
as spacious, a place populated by ravens and other shadowy presences. The
opening lines of The Heart Man hold a metaphor for the ways that our sense
of ourselves and our relationship to our physical bodies are often inseparable.
Patently, if this was a real patient's response to a real doctor's question, the
doctor would have to try again in order to extract a more medically relevant
answer. As requested, the heart man has taken an inward view, but he has
failed to anatomise himself. His heart has clouded his tongue, and made it
over-figurative. Or to put it another way, his personal poetry is at odds with
the prose of science. It's as if he cannot speak without reflecting a dream
perspective. Importantly, that perspective is expressed in matter-of-fact terms.
O'Malley has given her readers no verbal cue that she wishes the poem to be
read as particularly high-pitched. This adds an appealing tension, and the sense
of an ironical leaning towards transcendence.

Quite sensationally, though again O'Malley's diction is without showiness,
the heart man puts himself in the care of a shaman, who in turn applies an
intense visionary treatment. This involves the ailing heart being flooded with
'the healing breath' of love, and a quasi-surgical attempt to expose 'all that raw
flesh' to the 'pulsing red light' of the shaman's 'inner eye'.

These efforts fall short. Instead of a manifest recovery there is a creaking
sound inside the heart man's chest. This might represent the fact that the
illness is persisting; or it might suggest a biological willingness to meet an
ancient therapeutic method halfway, a kind of murmuring identification.
Whatever its significance, the heart man now feels exhausted. The following
morning he wakes with a vision of self-healing. He feels that the shaman's
efforts have helped him to locate his heart more precisely, and he has a new set
of approaches. He resolves to relate to the embattled thing beating in his chest
as if it were a bird, and to breathe upon it. He also decides to try to banish the
'rust' from his circulatory system.

These memorable images of an improvised, questing, non-scientific
medicine are carried forward in the closing two stanzas of The Heart Man. Our
patient has had some success, he is out of the woods, and his next step is to
return to a way of life that is at once nourishing and celebratory. With a logic
that connects to a number of other O'Malley poems – most significantly the
Gaudent Angeli poem A Jig in Spacetime, and Uileann from her 2016 collection
Playing the Octopus – he goes to a traditional music hotspot, a pub where
he further revives himself by listening to a live performance which stands as
another alternative practice, a veritable tonic that 'lifts the heart and makes
time fly'. By the end of the poem, his condition temporarily forgotten, the heart
man has begun to dance.

There is something undeniably surreal in the shift from the shaman
encounter and the efforts of self-healing to the setting of the pub. But O'Malley
has tonal control. Ultimately, this odd segue allows a deeper version of the
shamanism theme, lending as it does a special form of credence to ritualistic
medical practice, before arriving at a more humane evocation of acceptance
and strength in the face of death. This is another selling point for The Heart
Man as a medical school poem: death is not a subject defined by fear or sorrow,

and it is not a matter of medical futility or failure. At the close, conventional thinking and assumptions have been side-lined. We've been transported to a secure place of wonder; and from that vantage point, mortality looks different.

In the following, the final verse of the poem, Madame Bonaparte is a reference to a hornpipe tune, often played on solo accordion –

He was dancing with Madame Bonaparte
when it cut out. He folded so quietly that
the music played on, nice and stately.

Nature has run its course. A man appeared to get a new lease of life, and he made the most of it. The poem almost seems to say to the reader: that is all you need to know. But the description of the musicians, oblivious as they are to the presence of a dead man in their midst, as their playing continues 'nice and stately,' seems to go further. An uncanny view of life's continuity is suggested, together with a community that accommodates death, and a consciousness that seems willing to confront the fact that a heart, like an engine, can 'cut out', on radically accepting and imaginative terms.

Confrontational in other ways, Stephen Sexton's If All the World and Love Were Young is a formally strict sequence of poems that explore the poet's memories of his mother's death from cancer. Innovatively, the turmoil, sorrow and grief, as well as the love and courage that belong to the experience, are presented as part of an exploration of Super Mario, the classic Nintendo platform video game. The Nintendo atmosphere of the sequence draws on a palate of nostalgic fandom and retrieved innocence. Throughout the book, Sexton plays with the visual aspects of the hierarchical worlds of the game and the mythic and heroic implications of its quirky and complex story lines. In the context of his mother's illness and decline, Super Mario is an escapist medium for the poet's younger self, a kind of self-anchoring through recreation, as well as an assertion of the stuff of boyhood and adolescence in the face of an oppressive reality. But the great poetic resonance of If All the World and Love Were Young depends on what cannot be escaped: the emotional demands and consequences of a core experience. A path of fear, longing and questioning must be walked; a trial of holding on and letting go must be endured.

A number of the poems dramatise time spent in hospitals, with particular attention drawn to the conflicted role of being a visiting relative in a clinical environment. In the following lines, from the poem Valley Fortress, the vending machine conveys the limitations of the setting, while the fact that commas have been exiled from the page represents a form of driven memory heightening the sense of a filial bond in extremis, one that is all the more compelling for the way the son's attempts to reassure his mother are blended with a primal argument against her suffering –

My head is heavier than stone. I read yesterday's newspapers
eat crisps from the vending machine I want to die is what she says
not either asleep or awake let me please die is what she says.
It's me I'm here is what I say but I am not since she is not.
Then she says I want to go home once more for one once more one night
and I say you can't go home now she says I know not now after.

The granulated syntax in this passage is representative of the book as a whole. In part, this style prevents a demarcation between the speaker's inner world and the unfolding action. But by communicating a sense of living thought, it also creates moments of contrast between the son's mind and the ambivalent order of the hospital.

This same contrast is an explicit theme in two poems which mention one of the great classical sources of medical ethics, Hippocrates II, the Greek physician and writer who produced the endlessly adapted principle, 'First, do no harm', and whose name endures in the Hippocratic Oath. Hippocrates is Sexton's nickname for an otherwise anonymous doctor who, if not quite aloof, appears reticent when he brings the protagonist news about his mother in the poem Chocolate Fortress. But the unflattering portrait contains no ordinary sense of grievance. What comes across instead is a graphic take on the function of medical communication skills –

> ... With his stethoscope slung around
> his broad shoulders like an athlete with a towel Hippocrates
> says for now the pain must stay here in the small room without flowers.

If these words evoke a tide of inconsolability beneath the surface of the exchange, the closing lines of the same poem carry forward the sense of an unsettling power dynamic, mixing them with a set of irrational hopes that draw on the pixelated beauty of Super Mario worlds –

> In the forbidden pharmacy he goes about the magic task
> of grinding down a rhino's horn to infuse with ground down rubies.

In #7 Larry's Castle, the inscrutable athletic doctor returns: 'Hippocrates arrives again and I ask him what will happen.' These words are more alive by virtue of the fact that they are preceded by a concentrated sense of a vigil.

> No clock ticks in her room but if one speaks light fluently one can
> tell the time by the shadow the fountain casts across the courtyard.

The uncanny directness with which the notion of speaking light fluently is expressed locates the reader squarely in the protagonist's thoughts. Because we are, in one moment, made to identify with that aesthetic peak, when the doctor answers the question in the next, he sounds all the more remote. The poet's mother is close to death; she might die that very day. The single additional piece of clinical information is provocatively concise: '... asleep he says but still aware ...' These words mark the end of a dialogue and the beginning of a passionate passage where the poet recounts his efforts to make sense of this update. He asks two questions of himself: 'what am I say to her ...' and 'what kind of story do I tell ...'

In response, the poem concludes with a dual intention: to narrate the mother's life beyond its natural limits, and to attempt to rejuvenate her through a boy's unshakable faith in the Super Mario apple, a symbol of restored health and delight. As such, where the doctor dryly accepts the futility of further treatment, the son cannot –

what kind of story do I tell apple is the longest story
I know let's see how does it go again apple apple apple.

There is great tenderness in these lines. At sea in a palliative care scenario, the son's instinct is to spend an eternity saying goodbye. When John Berger says 'we submit to the doctor by quoting to ourselves a state of childhood,' he captures the fact that we often have no choice but to trust that doctors contain within themselves a ready impression of who we truly are. We must trust that our vulnerability has a power over them, that they perhaps understand it with their own hearts. This trust, of course, is sometimes misplaced, and the systemic picture is always sobering. The coronavirus pandemic has introduced a terrible new logistical pressure that will result in fractured and impersonal healthcare. But the art of the face-to-face encounter and the deep literacy that pertains to true healing are not forgotten. The doctors of tomorrow, as they prepare to enter a troubled arena, are also, in their idealism, picturing themselves as warm communicators and as wordsmiths.

To be like the son at the bedside in #7 Larry's Castle, to find yourself in that isolated position, and then to hear words that let you know your predicament has been recognised and understood, is to benefit from an ecosystem of care and imagination that is always under threat, and always within the realm of the possible.

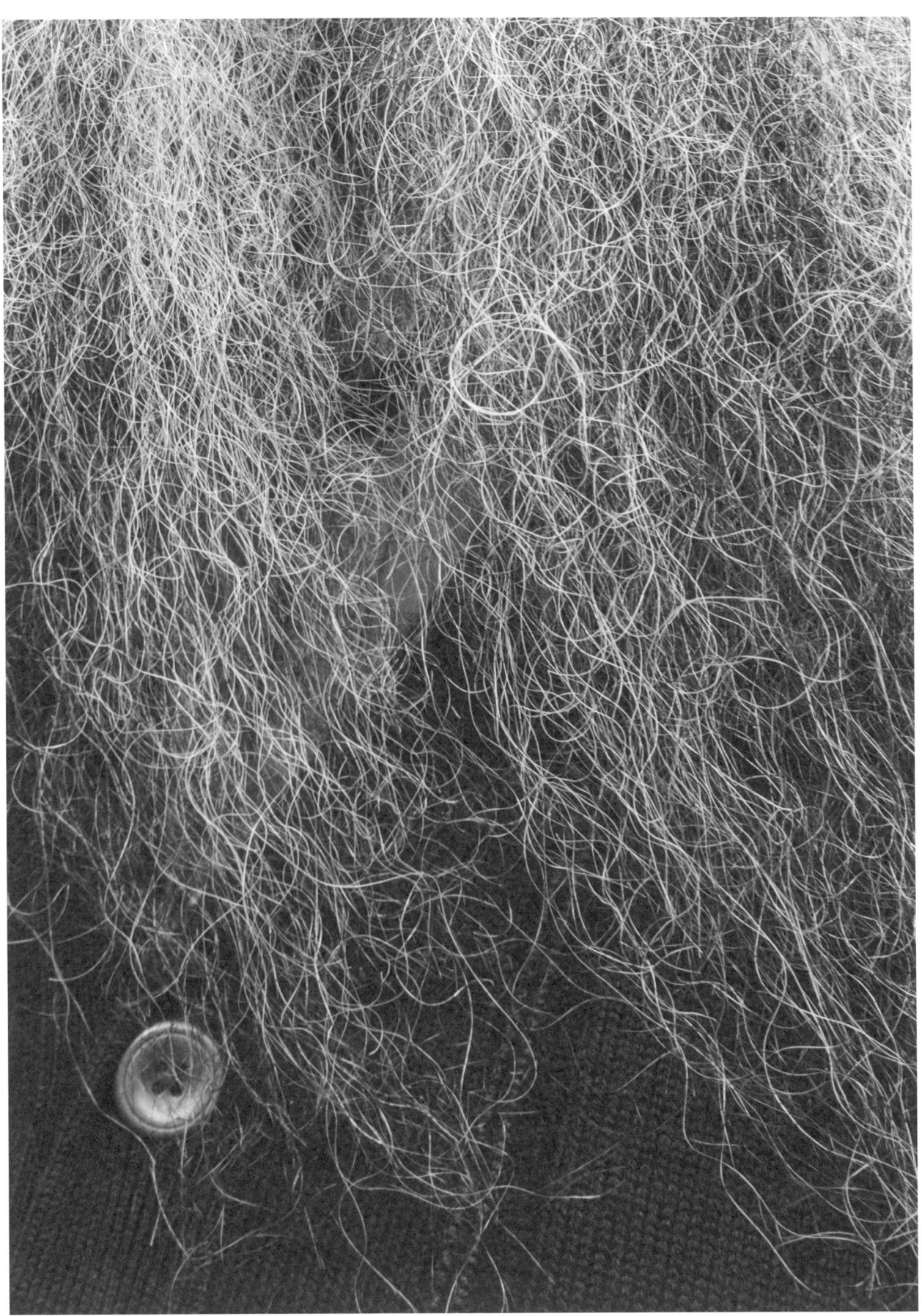

Photograph by Ruby Wallis